PIONEERS OF
ENGLISH EDUCATION

PIONEERS OF
ENGLISH EDUCATION

*A Course of Lectures
given at King's College, London*

*

Edited by
A. V. JUDGES

FABER AND FABER LTD
24 Russell Square
London

First published in mcmlii
by Faber and Faber Limited
24 Russell Square London W.C.1
Printed in Great Britain by
Western Printing Services Limited, Bristol

CONTENTS

7

CONTENTS

1

INTRODUCTION

*

BY

THE EDITOR

I

It might be well to give an explanation of the way in which
this book came into being. No doubt it has the defects of
all collections of the views of a number of people—defects
which the circumstances of a course of public lectures on set
pieces do nothing to mitigate. Still, even if it must be admitted
that we were giving joint service to no single theme, we did at
least try to fit the pieces together in advance and to keep a
common eye on the question: what elements of native[1] originality give interest to the notions and practices of the 'pioneers'
selected for treatment? The lectures were given to audiences at
King's College in the Lent Term of 1951; but already whilst they
were in preparation we were talking about their publication.

Nearly twenty-five years ago Professor John Dover Wilson,
my predecessor at one remove in the King's College Department of Education, was led to publish in book form[2] a course

[1] James Mill was from Angus, Robert Owen from Montgomeryshire. We
are here concerned with their effect upon England. When in this introductory chapter I speak of English institutions and English ways of thought
I mean English in the restricted and only proper sense.

[2] *The Schools of England, a Study in Renaissance.* Edited by J. Dover Wilson,
with a preface by Lord Eustace Percy (Sidgwick and Jackson, 1928). The
title is too narrow for the range of subject matter. One or two of the sections,
though written for the book, were not given as lectures.

of public lectures, to which a number of colleagues and friends made their specialist contributions, dealing with different aspects of English educational life.

There was a good deal of history, as well as of current discussion, in these chapters, most of which have worn very well and are still consulted as guides to the types of institutions covered by them. What impresses the reader is the attention given by nearly all the writers to the roots of things and to the colour and appearance which all these things acquire in relation to the soil in which they grew.

The editor argued with some vigour that there was more of continuity and native interest in the past life of our schools and universities than the 'journalists of education' generally gave us to suppose. Moreover the authors of change had not all been foreigners. Pestalozzi could be honoured without being hailed as the father of our system of primary education. 'We can reverence the august name of Froebel without supposing that he was the first to give thought to the teaching of infants.' Professor Dover Wilson took pride in saying that his own great-grandfather (who himself came under the influence of Samuel Wilderspin) launched a large infant school at Walthamstow in 1824, two years before Froebel's most famous work, the *Menschenerziehung*, reached the public. This indeed was in the same year in which Robert Dale Owen wrote about his father's experiments in the education of very young children in his *Outline of the System of Education at New Lanark*. However we may choose to evaluate the differences in outlook between the very practical leaders who took part in the promotion of new kinds of schooling in our island on the one hand and the prophet of Yverdun and the God-intoxicated reformer of Keilhau on the other, we are bound to admit that the stages of growth in this and other parts of our educational system owe much to the original thinking of the men on the spot.

That the English are prone to exaggerate the importance of foreign names in this field is of course contestable. Yet few would challenge the view that in actual reality the influence of the great continental reformers was in all cases exceedingly slow in showing any notable results here. More is the pity. England can take no credit from such a record of negligence.

Who then provided the impetus to experiment and change?

If this volume is in some sense a sequel to the earlier one, it is because we try once more, from standpoints mostly a little farther back in time, to examine the claim that the Englishman's own contribution in this most interesting sequence of events is really the greatest part of the story. And the method adopted is the biographical one—for the most part.

In estimating the worth of contributions from an arbitrarily selected group of pioneers there is perhaps some danger of our overlooking the familiar and commonplace argument that the pressure of circumstances and events deserves more consideration than glimpses of ideas offered to their contemporaries by individual thinkers and men of affairs; that we are repeating the blunder sometimes held to have been made by Matthew Arnold when he urged that a study of the lives of educators was the most useful part of pedagogy, or by R. H. Quick when he launched the study of the history of education for educationalists in the form of a flotilla of small biographies of the world's educational reformers who took highest place in his esteem. If this were so, I wonder if we should perhaps not be happy to err in their wise and stimulating company. But in fact my colleagues in this volume do not attempt to lift their subjects out of the heat and clamour of their times. We are entitled now and again to find some escape from the positivist fallacy, and to seek in the expression of past ideas the things which have moved events. To show that we take a broad view we have brought in some political personages and administrators as well as philosophers. The party of course is far from being complete. If we have omitted John Stuart Mill we have also excluded Robert Morant. Thomas Arnold has no place, nor has H. A. L. Fisher. The names of other notable absentees will occur to the reader, who will be convinced that he could have made a wiser choice, and some at least of them we should have wished to include had the list been a longer one. Where are the women? Where is the women's higher education movement, the claims of which to consideration surely always receive far less than their due in the history books? Why are the fundamental contributions to our way of life made by the public schools dealt with so slightly? If we have been as over-selective as these questions suggest, perhaps another opportunity will be offered later on.

II

In Chapter 2 Sir Philip Morris is endeavouring, without actually providing a narrative of the century and a half covered by the volume, to draw attention to certain salient characteristics of our educational development. One looks in vain for a planned system at any stage; and there are reasons, as he suggests, for believing that our apparently haphazard mode of advance has paid better dividends than our fathers (had they ever given themselves the chance) could have derived from the adoption of a uniformly patterned and all-embracing structure. The very lack of system of course inhibited stocktaking of even the most casual kind, so that no-one could at any time claim to speak for the national mind or really pretend to see the picture as a whole.

There is something of the amateur in all our pioneers. None had the assurance or the knowledge or the universality of mind to speak of a *general* policy of education. None—unless we except Newman—was willing to handle the most difficult questions of principle, or to get to grips with the innermost problems, such as that of welding a concept of education as the broadening and deepening of the personality with the notion of education as a mould of common citizenship. The times were moving too fast for tranquil reflection. As Sir Philip Morris says of the holders of one old tradition of schooling, 'the tide of industrial practice and scientific advance flowed over them'.

We begin with Bentham and Owen, each with pregnant thoughts on the needful characteristics of reform, each strangely ineffective as a practical reformer, neither an educationist in any satisfactory sense of the word. Both long livers, though of quite different generations, they overlapped one another for sixty years, and during that time the population doubled; the maximum impact of industrial change was being experienced upon the social fabric; the loss of civility in the built-up areas was well-nigh complete when Bentham died; and radicalism, after going almost entirely underground during the fierce and gloomy reaction of a whole nation to the French revolution, became in 1832 at last respectable enough to attempt openly to make up for lost time. However we view the ways and principles of the old radicals—and they could be as different in sympathies and outlook as Bentham and Owen are shown to be in this book—we must admit that the reaction against intellectualism in politics had serious results and that the lost time of the revolutionary and Napoleonic period has never quite been made up. For our educational progress the failure of the contemporaries of Pitt and Coleridge to meet the problems of the blackest period of our scholastic history has been little short of disastrous, since, by reason of a delayed start, no project of school expansion has been able to keep pace with the population's increasing numbers and needs, while every ambitious design for the overhaul and assimilation of divergent elements in our educational life has been held up, sometimes for generations, by discord.

The elements of discord were the products of, first, the industrial advance, which, from the social philosopher's point of view, was too easy and too rapid, and secondly, of an inherited habit of division in attitudes to the relations between religion and the state, which was hardened and strengthened by the events of the same industrial revolution.

Educational revolutionaries have been few, and their audiences small. If the positions taken by the pioneers discussed in this book are closely examined it will be seen that their anxiety was in nearly all cases to overcome the effects of a mere time-lag between common practice and a very moderate degree of progressiveness in the current world of ideas. Newman might have used medieval instruments to overhaul the new knowledge of the universe. And Owen is of course an outright exception to my generalization. By peaceful means he would have turned the world upside down. The utopianism of his views, however, is offset by the practical good sense of his observation of the children in and around the cotton mills and the heartening warmth of his belief that all men are brothers, or that at least by educational means they can be conditioned into brotherhood. As Professor Jeffreys demonstrates, we cannot, even admitting all Owen's weaknesses, afford to omit the contribution of this valiant crusader who fought the sloth and complacency of received opinion and claimed that man could alter his circumstances and with them his outlook on the universe.

Bentham also might be regarded as too much of an originator, too forthright an innovator in thought, to be classified as a mere reformer within the range of the commonplaces of education in his time. He was one of the original makers of the nineteenth-century mind. Yet, as Dr. Hans shows, it was really in the advocacy of various *devices* of a more or less practical nature that Bentham made his personal appeal to educationists. He had to be sure important views, novel in his day, about the reform of school curricula—here the barely readable *Chrestomathia* is his title to respect; but none of his patient advocacy in that field would be worth attention in this volume were it not for the revolution of outlook in law, in administration, in political economy and in social philosophy which he helped to bring about. In an essay in the *Westminster Review* which is an interesting, if somewhat perverse, appreciation of Bentham's greatness, John Stuart Mill gave credit to this originality of attack. Other influential philosophers of the eighteenth century had criticized and destroyed current assumptions.

'They were purely negative thinkers, he was positive: they only assailed error, he made it a point of conscience not to do so until he thought he could plant the corresponding truth. Their character was exclusively analytic, his was synthetic. . . . He was not a great philosopher, but he was a great reformer in philosophy. . . . He introduced into morals and politics those habits of thought and modes of investigation, which are essential to the idea of science. . . . It was not his opinions, in short but his method, that constituted the novelty and the value of what he did. . . . Whatever can be understood or whatever done without references to moral influences, his philosophy is equal to; where those influences require to be taken into account, it is at fault.'[1]

It was Bentham's preaching and the example of his friends which forced men to realize that social investigation and the survey of resources, carried out in a business-like way, must precede educational reform. He and his followers are the patron saints of the blue book, and the blue books of the hundred years following Bentham constitute the best reading on educational developments possessed by any country in the world.

It was the work of members of the school of Bentham, above all James Mill, which had the result of giving social significance

[1] See F. R. Leavis (ed.). *Mill on Bentham and Coleridge* (1950), pp. 46–8.

to projects for the education of the new proletariat. James Mill's practical experiment in systematic home education has provoked censure from all commentators from the auto-biography of its little victim onwards, but it can hardly be denied that his formal contribution to the theory of the subject in his famous *Encyclopaedia Britannica* article on education is one of the best pieces of constructive thinking in our whole edu-cational literature. No student in a training department should be permitted to denigrate the associationist psychology of the utilitarians as a mere old-time behaviourism until he has savoured the logical consistency and brilliance of this remark-able essay, which says so little about practical education and yet so much about the presuppositions upon which practice must do her part.

Discussing psychology, James Mill said, 'I would make the human mind as plain as the road from Charing Cross to Saint Paul's,' and, as a good utilitarian, he meant it, and had no mis-givings. He was one of a group of Benthamite radicals who played seriously, not only with educational theory, but with projects for new schools. In these activities Mill himself worked constantly behind the scenes. In uneasy alliance with Quaker philanthropists, the utilitarians helped to promote the Lanca-sterian movement and to establish it on business-like lines. Their liking for the monitorial school has a scrubby look when compared with Owen's advocacy of skilled class teaching. They held cheapness to be a merit, yet they have been too much blamed for this. In Chapter 2 Sir Philip Morris points out that 'the early stages of industrialization, although they laid the foundations of much subsequent wealth, were in fact years of great struggle for all concerned in laying the foundations of modern agriculture and industry'. The burden of the French wars which fell at this critical time was heavy on all sections of the people. Amid the general apathy of intellectuals of their day, the utilitarians gave generously from their private funds for new experiments, and Bentham offered his garden as land on which to build a kind of monitorial secondary school on 'Chrestomathic' lines. These men helped to promote mechanics' institutions. Their work in support of the scheme for a secularist university on rather Prussian lines was decisive in the founda-tion of University College in Gower Street, which, though some have held it to be a triumph of infidelity, is yet one of the world's monuments of consistent belief in a cause; and they planned a complete system of primary and secondary education, based on statistical investigations of population and needs, for the whole metropolis. Their original keenness was hardly matched by the subsequent onslaughts by Brougham and Roebuck and the later generation of Benthamites and their fellow-travellers on vested educational privilege. The exploits of Francis Place and Edward Gibbon Wakefield in promoting interest in educational reform during the later years of the Napoleonic war have yet to receive full attention from historians. Place's bubbling originality and his unruffled temper were invaluable assets to the philosophical radicals in their attempt, which was at best a partial failure and premature, to establish the view that elementary education for all was a social necessity. He was one of the first Englishmen to talk about the educative value of games.

'The boy who plays at marbles may as well draw a map as a ring, and by shooting at a marble placed on Dublin recollect that by striking it under a certain angle, he will place his "taw" in a situation to attack another marble placed on Cork, Limerick or Belfast.'

Place was also attracted by the idea of teaching boys about the relation between the heavenly constellations by placing stars on the walls of a fives court; but I doubt, from the wording of his plan, if he had ever played fives, which is a fast game and hardly permits Zodiacal reflections.

III

The colour of this country's experience, as we have already noted, was strongly affected, first by the timing and speed of her industrial transformation, and secondly by the peculiarities of her schemes of religious allegiance. A full analysis of the motivation of events would demand that numerous other factors, both of permanence and of change, operating at home and overseas, should be taken into account; but this is no place for such an analysis, and I have only space to refer briefly to these two matters, which together afford so valuable an explanation of the cultural backwardness of England all the while that she maintained her titles to be the leading power and the workshop of the world.

That no tradition of public responsibility for education had ever been established needs to be stated, because this astonishing piece of neglect really calls for explanation. It is well-known that the medieval Church had, where not itself actively engaged in teaching, claimed power of general supervision. The Reformation Church inherited these powers and even made them more explicit in canon law, but none the less the religious orders, teaching, preaching, and contemplative, were all dissolved; and thereafter the secular priesthood was given little encouragement from any quarter to enlarge the activities of parish schools, where such existed, or to preserve learning in grammar schools, and meanwhile the profession of schoolmaster ceased to be a monopoly of the clergy; so that, far from using its new relationship with the sovereign State to improve the controls it already possessed over the affairs of the laity, the establishment chose to operate, in ways which were mainly negative, in order merely to ensure that religious teaching remained under the care of orthodox instructors. Even so, the Church was unable altogether to prevent the setting up of dissenting schools, and by the time—some few years before the outbreak of the French Revolution—that Parliament gave equal freedom to both Roman Catholics and Protestant nonconformists to open new schools, the latter had developed a new type of higher secondary instruction in their academies which provided the best education available to the intelligent child of parents of moderate means. The slight continuing connection between the grammar and public schools of old foundation and the Church of England was not a matter of academic significance at the opening of the nineteenth century. At the most elementary level the Church had a somewhat closer hold on instruction—through charity schools—but no monopoly; and the growth in the earliest years of the century of two parallel lines of school development, through the agency of voluntary subscription societies, of which one was strictly non-sectarian, whilst the other was Anglican in doctrine and proselytizing in intention, was a recognition of the fact that the field was open to all and the Government a willing cypher.

Long before this the Established Church had lost the chance

to use the State in partnership to adopt a forward doctrine of national responsibility for popular instruction. As far as public law was concerned, education was now nobody's or everybody's business.

Meanwhile a number of continental despots, less embarrassed by domestic party interest, by nascent individualism, or by vested rights, had been persuaded to bring the provision of popular education within the sphere of State action. On a later page Dr. Hans refers to the precocity of Peter the Great's national 'utilitarian' policy, and to the sequel under Catherine's management. The direction of opinion to help the fulfilment of national aims is what must be expected from a dictatorial power; though it can hardly be said of the benevolent despots that they wanted more than loyalty and a spirit of obedience. We need not suppose that Frederick the Great, when he ordered compulsory education up to fourteen years, and a periodical inspection, in his regulations for village schools in 1763, or the Elector of Saxony when he followed suit in 1773, had any lofty views about raising the intellectual level of the German peasantry. We know that the Prussian government were content to encourage discharged soldiers of no worth and even poorer types to teach in school. Actually in no part of Germany was the official regulation of schooling very effective in promoting attendance or altering the curriculum before the treaty of Tilsit and the great drive towards Prussian recovery. Thereafter action was brisk, though subject to changes of direction—the result of struggle between ministers who sought administrative efficiency in the traditional Prussian manner, philosophers like Fichte who looked for the regeneration of society by universal education, and kings who feared all measures which might lead to the making of a liberal State.

The important thing to observe in all these reforms is that some time before democratic ideas had begun to touch the common people or even the middle-class intellectuals, long before industry began to leave the domestic workshop for the factory, whilst serfs still worked in the fields, the shadow of State discipline, as an instrument of national policy, began to fall across the schools of a continental Europe still medieval in many of its features. France, from the fall of the monarchy, can be included in this area. The debates in the successive revolu-

tionary assemblies upon the various schemes for the nationaliza-
tion of schools which were put before them covered an almost
unbelievable range of possible public action. They created a
most bitter reaction against 'Jacobinist' ideas in school reform
on this side of the Channel; and they had an important sequel
in the attempt of Napoleon to remodel the whole pattern of the
educational process from infancy to the university in a single
national plan, with power concentrated at the centre, and a set
of rules and principles applicable to all forms of education,
public and private. France's brilliant record in secondary
education dates from Napoleon's time—if not indeed earlier.
And, although the grand design remained ineffective and
shadowy at the lower age levels until Guizot, prompted very
ably by Victor Cousin, carried out sweeping reforms under the
Orleans monarchy, by 1840 there could be no questioning the
argument that France's superiority to Britain was the consequence of deliberate State action, restrained within limits by
a cool understanding with the Church of Rome.

In both France and Germany the building up of public
educational systems was organically connected with the institution of training schools designed to turn out teachers, and to
this conscious State policy, which comes into focus with great
clarity in the opening of the famous Ecole Normale in Paris in
1810, to say nothing of a network of related training institutions beyond it, a part of the practical success in the development of a public service was due.

It was in respect of teacher-training—that nerve centre of
any educational plan—that Britain lagged so sadly behind. All
the school reformers of the early nineteenth century had something to say on the subject. One or two, like David Stow, the
Glasgow philanthropist, identified it with the solution of their
own problems and began experiments. But it was not until the
appearance in the public service of James Kay-Shuttleworth
that the government began very gingerly to play with policies
directed to the supply of professional teachers. In fact the
decision in 1839 to found a publicly owned normal school,
though it failed of exact achievement, really marks the first
stage in the history of State intervention in England. The
beginning of the parliamentary annual grant to elementary
education six years earlier had been no more than an admission

of the existence of a public conscience; and it was a small price to pay for the withdrawal of Roebuck's motion for the erection of one or two schools, with government aid and popular control, in every parish; and it had committed the State to nothing at all.

The selection of Kay-Shuttleworth, the father of the pupil-teacher system and of the elementary training college, as one of the figures to be studied in this book may help to emphasize the importance which the historian of our educational progress must allow to this topic. Both in this field and in his statesman-like handling of the powerful movements of denominationalism his was one of those personal performances the execution of which entitled a man to be called a pioneer; and Mr. G. M. Young has hardly exaggerated his role in the shaping of our national institutions when he says,

'That the late Victorian democracy was not altogether un-fit for its responsibilities, was in the main the work of one man, and, if history judged men less by the noise than by the difference they make, it is hard to think of any name in the Victorian age which deserves to stand above or even beside Kay-Shuttleworth's.'[1]

The industrial revolution in England in its most violent stage; the political witch-hunts and the long reaction against popular movements which were provoked by the Terror in France; the fluctuations of commodity prices and the war-time shortages; the rapid increase in population in those manufacturing areas which were least capable of providing educational opportuni-ties; the failure of housing; the grim spectre of technological un-employment; and the vast increases in unco-ordinated poor-law assistance on the countryside, all these combined to produce a situation in which the undoubted brilliance of the top layer of society hid a depression in the cultural levels of the mass of the people far deeper than earlier generations had known. Had a tradition of State intervention in education stood at hand during these years, there would have been something to resist the great wave of individualism which derived strength from the success of the new industrial techniques. The economists preached non-interference in trade and industry and argued that the human labour-unit should be free to follow his own

[1] G. M. Young. *Victorian England: portrait of an Age* (1936), p. 89.

interest and to accept the rewards set by the operation of an unrestricted market. When Adam Smith had preached this gospel in 1776, skill and a degree of enterprise and self-respect in the working man were still things to be valued, and this wise student of social forces pleaded for schools for all working-class communities at the public charge. Fifty years later many more productive processes had been mechanized, apprenticeship was already a dying institution, the navvy and the untrained labourer made up a large part of an uneducated proletariat, and 'labour' had become an undifferentiated mass of unskilled, illiterate and, in the mind of the governing class, potentially dangerous material, to be kept outside the body politic.

Although it is a libel upon the economists of the period to say that their intellectual community, with its Benthamite associations and its strong sense of social service, was indifferent to the need for educational reform, it is certainly true of most of the people who controlled political opinion that, at the time of the first Reform Bill in 1832, to say that they accepted without remorse the existence of a society split pretty clearly into two divisions, of which the educational requirements were believed to be fundamentally different. The 'two nations' had come into being. And this shocking situation so dominated the outlook of the Victorian pioneers in education that they were constrained to find ways of demonstrating with the strongest emphasis that the maintenance of two communities in one state was unnatural, unchristian, wasteful of human resources, and damaging to national efficiency, and generally to work for ends which must be regarded as broadly social rather than as narrowly cultural. Which is one reason why most of the leading English educational figures had no more than a local reputation —only Jeremy Bentham and Herbert Spencer have a world status—and by reason of their practical preoccupations have had little contribution to make to the growth of pedagogic theory.

IV

All the earliest attempts to persuade Parliament to intervene have certain features in common which betray the difficulties of the innovators. There is the manifest problem of machinery.

To whom shall initiative be entrusted? How are funds to be raised? How administered? Local government existed; some of it was ecclesiastical in origin; some secular; none very satisfactory either on its own merits, or as a scaffolding on which to hang a new public service. The Scottish system of parish schools seemed to some observers to provide a kind of model, but the tradition of social equality, nursed on low incomes all round, which still animated schools north of the border, was too lofty for the would-be imitators; they all came to the conclusion that the best place—perhaps the only place —at which to have compulsion was below the poverty line.

The first abortive attempt, by Pitt in 1796, set out crudely to dovetail a nation-wide system of compulsory schools of industry into the old poor-law framework. Whitbread's scheme of 1807 was also a poor-law measure. He proposed a network of parish schools supported by local rates, but he committed the tactical error of making the justices of the peace responsible for administration. The Archbishop of Canterbury said that a plan for local schools which would not be 'under the control and auspices of the Establishment' violated the first principle of education; and the Bill was lost in the Lords without a division.

The paradox of the whole situation in the first half of the century lies in this, that, while all the time there went on a great deal of earnest discussion of remedies for a defect in the national life which lay open to the observation of all men and women of good will—still nothing happened. It was not merely that the clergy—the high church party at any rate—found it impossible to think of elementary education as something which could dispense with religious instruction (based on the creeds, not a mere reading of the Bible) in any part of the whole range of teaching, there was also a large body of uncompromising belief that any substantial inter-mixture of lay control in the popular school was a betrayal of the Church's 'sacred trust'. This was the most formidable obstacle in the way of national planning. And, all the more because nonconformity was distrusted and feared and despised in these quarters, it was a wrecking obstacle. Until the nonconformists themselves were forced by economic circumstances to lean away from voluntaryism and turn to rate-aid—and the lesson took two generations to learn—a mixture of private charity and public charity was the only compromise available.

The political doctrine underlying the archbishop's criticism mentioned above was maintained for many years as the touchstone which the Church applied to all new measures. Rate-aided parish schools for the poor under clerical supervision would in all probability have become a reality, were it not that the revival of dissent during the middle period of the industrial revolution brought another very strong body of convinced opinion into the arena of discussion. Though nonconformists were individualists by tradition and opposed to State interference in their lives for historical reasons, the principal cause of their furious intransigence on the issue of public instruction was the fear that if the Church's support enabled a parish-school Bill to pass, the clergy would steal a march on them and try to recover in the new schools what they had been losing in the conventicles. When in 1820 Brougham, James Mill's erratic pupil, after a long campaign of purposeful fact-finding, brought in his parochial schools Bill, with a call on both national finances and local rates, he was determined to run no risks with the bishops, and so proposed to give virtually all powers of direction to the vestries and of visitation to the clergy. The result was that Roman Catholics and dissenters raised opposition, and the Bill was withdrawn.

Thirteen years passed before the next major attempt to re-open the subject, this time by J. A. Roebuck, who later helped to draft the Chartist political programme. His proposal ingeniously skirted the difficulties of Church control by the use of central funds and local committees of management; but prejudices were not satisfied, and again politicians were overcome by fears and misgivings and again a workable proposal was withdrawn.

The fate of Sir James Graham's later attempt (in 1843) to turn the flank of criticism by a not very plausible combination in one measure of factory-welfare provisions, poor-rate finance and clerical oversight of schools is discussed later in this book. It provoked the heaviest counter-attack from nonconformity yet experienced by any nineteenth-century government. But by that time the initiative in proposing a national system had for a while almost passed to the working class, which by the middle thirties had developed a half-conscious awareness of its needs and a conviction of their wilful neglect by Parliament. We can see something of the character of the self-help which they adopted when we observe the spread of mechanics' institutes in this period, and the growing enthusiasm for aids to knowledge in cheap periodical prints. Moral-force Chartism actually began with the discussions of a group of class-conscious London artisans with literary and educational interests; and nothing is more surprising than the way in which the somewhat prim plottings of William Lovett and his friends, aiming at reform by gradualism through the use of nationally owned or co-operative schools, were converted and enlarged by the stronger passions of the Midlands and North into an attempt to secure the Charter by violence. In the London Chartist's manifesto—or programme—of 1837 we hear much, for the first time, of the *right* of the citizens to education.

'Society implies a union for mutual benefit, and consequently to publicly provide for the security and proper training of all its members. . . . Is it consistent with justice that the knowledge requisite to make a man acquainted with his rights and duties should be purposely witheld from him, and then that he should be upbraided and deprived of his [political] rights *on the plea of his ignorance*?'

The collapse of Chartism came with the fiasco of the Kennington Common meeting in 1848, the year of European revolution. In Britain there was no revolution: the fear of revolt from below finally disappeared. There was an improvement in economic conditions; and a subdued trade-union movement, based on craft associations, changed its policy and acquired a sort of respectability. The new Liberalism, which looked askance at pure Cobdenism, and came to require working-class support, was in the making before the death of Palmerston in 1865 altered the whole political atmosphere. Matthew Arnold became a State inspector of elementary schools in 1851, and later helped to make his brother-in-law, W. E. Forster, into the pioneer who successfully challenged his own party and imposed an educational system on his countrymen in 1870.

It is, of course, only a strange coincidence that on 10th April 1848 Charles Kingsley came up from the country, and with J. M. Ludlow walked over Waterloo Bridge in the rain and saw

the wet and unhappy remnant of the Chartist demonstrators
returning home. That day they talked with Frederick Denison
Maurice, and Christian Socialism was born. The significance of
this is that the middle class was now sure of its strength, and its
attitude to the poorer classes was changing from fear to a much
more complicated emotion.

V

Newman, Arnold, and Spencer, each in his fashion contributed
to the downfall of the scale or system of values which, if it had
called into being the educational institutions of the first half of
the nineteenth century, helped to maintain their worst features
and to leave barren the gaps between them which might have
been filled. To say that together they helped to build a new
conception of education's role within the framework of society
would be true in some measure, since all three had strong views
about the unity of education, especially in relation to what
Spencer called First Principles. Newman had perhaps the
strongest intuitive understanding of the place and art of teaching, and he is one of the few English writers to have given us a
complete analysis of the nature of that which is the common
ground between teacher and pupil when they have come
together on an *intellectual* plane.

Arnold understood, as the others did not, the problems of
school organization and the important connections between the
school and all the forces of social harmony and social tension.
He knew, or should have known, the elementary schools and
the difficulties of their teachers inside out. At the same time, by
reason of his upbringing, and by an acquired keenness of insight, he was able to feel himself into and criticize and describe
in words the ethos of the public schools in their current stage
of transformation. He had a better knowledge of contemporary
educational systems abroad than any other Englishman of his
day, and could have put this equipment to even better use had
he been pleased to treat his chosen bread-and-butter trade as
a calling which demanded a little more systematic application
and a little less disdain.

Spencer knew least of practical education and its ways of
thought and action — in fact he knew very little. Yet of the three
he made the strongest impression, because he was able to say,

in the arresting, unequivocal expression of one who has himself made new discoveries, a large number of sensible things about educational method and the subject matter of education, which had indeed been said by others whose writings he had not had the leisure to read; things which nevertheless had not for the most part been said before in the idiom of his generation. Some of his thoughts were novel; all of them *seemed* new and fresh; though even sympathetic students of Spencer must have been worried by his excessive dogmatism. If today his views on education sound too much like platitudes or downright wrong-headed, that is because we have mastered the chief of Spencer's lessons or lost interest in his too plausible analogies.

If we look for action in full alliance with thought, Matthew Arnold was the most considerable figure in the mid-Victorian world of education. Yet in precisely what his contribution consisted no-one has yet been able to say.

There is hardly an aspect of school or university activity that he did not touch. But the touch is so often an oblique one, and contradictions are so liable to crop up, that, rather than try to tabulate his specific recommendations, the inquirer must often be content to estimate the effect of Arnold on the outlook of his generation; and even this is hazardous. As Professor Pattison remarks, 'it was the end rather than the means on which Arnold continually insisted . . . the alternative to Culture was Anarchy, with the collapse of all civilized tradition and "the beautification of a whole nation through clap-trap".'

He always had a point of view and, because he worked out the value of everything he saw, he is one of the historian's best aids to a sympathetic understanding of the triumphs and the miseries of the schoolroom in the period before and after the imposition of Robert Lowe's revised code, which he attacked with such generous ardour. Yet, in regard to what he called 'machinery', which seems to have included virtually every practical concern of an inspector of education, his interest for us today is probably much less compelling than in regard to the way in which he spoke to his age about culture and the concept of social usefulness. Professor Pattison condenses this message with admirable terseness when he says that Arnold's desire was 'to encourage an inward condition, a critical habit, which would concentrate not on doing, but on being, and

26

evaluate whatever was done by some more durable standards than desire or efficiency.'

In the popular schools the real matter for Arnold was the degree of civilization to which the children could attain, not the ability to spell their way through a prescribed book. Still, in approving this attitude, we may sometimes be tempted to over-look the great advance which even the most mean-spirited of the government regulations secured whilst Arnold continued his school visits. Arnold himself, in spite of grave doubts about policy, 'could see [in 1879] that the cause of popular education was safe'. During the thirty-five years of his inspectorship some of the most significant stages in the growth of our primary system were passed, and when at last he retired in 1886, the reforms of Mundella, in securing compulsory attendance, in humanizing the elementary-school routine, and in setting technical education on a sounder foundation were showing the changes in the country's outlook which Arnold was doing so much to influence. As Mr. Armytage in his chapter on the liberal reformers hints, things had reached a turning point when Mundella took note of the *Lancet's* statement that 'the educational system is not overworking children, but demons-trating that they are underfed', and urged local authorities to provide cheap meals for pupils.

Though he saw in education a future means of overcoming class barriers and creating something near to cultural homo-geneity, Arnold was a realist in recognizing the moral and political ascendancy of the Philistines, that is, the middle class, and the urgent priority of its claims upon educational states-manship—'the work,' indeed, 'of raising its whole level of civilization'. He admired the older public schools to which the Barbarians sent their sons, and their humanist traditions, even though he despised their grammar-grinding and their neglect of opportunities for aesthetic training with the aid of classical literature. He quoted Talleyrand, himself an educational reformer, who had 'truly said that the education of the great public schools was the best in the world. He added to be sure, that even this was detestable. But allowing it all its merits, how small a portion of the population does it embrace!'[1]

[1] *The Popular Education of France*, pp. 74–5, cited W. F. Connell, *Educational Thought and Influence of Matthew Arnold*, pp. 244–5.

For the integrity of the middle class and the prospects of professional competence the existence of the public schools was indeed something of a danger, because of the narrowness of their intake. Arnold was one of the first to recognize the significance of the cultural distinction between the upper and prosperous ridge of the middle class—Mr. G. M. Young's 'new patriciate'—which joined with the landed aristocracy in producing leaders and intellectuals, and the business community in general which was for the most part ill-educated in indifferent schools run by private enterprise.

'So we have amongst us the spectacle of a middle class cut in two in a way unexampled anywhere else; of a professional class brought up on the first plane, with fine and governing qualities, but disinclined to rely on reason and science; while that immense business class, which is becoming so important a power in all countries, on which the future so much depends, and which in the great public schools of other countries fills so large a place, is in England brought up on the second plane, cut off from the aristocracy and the professions, and without governing qualities. . . . Short as the offspring of our public schools and universities come of the idea of science and systematic knowledge, the offspring of our middle-class academies probably come, if that be possible, even shorter. What these academies fail to give in social and governing qualities, they do not make up for in intellectual power. Their intellectual result is as faulty as their social result.'[1]

The State must provide or, failing the will to provide, must 'organize'.

'The system was not to be remedied', says Arnold's latest biographer, 'until England made for herself an organic system of education. And in such a structure the keystone was an adequate supply of properly guaranteed secondary schools for the middle classes. Below them, primary education was a truncated, uninspired thing without a well-developed secondary system, and, above them, the universities were similarly weak without the foundation of good secondary education on which to build.'[2]

What the Taunton Commission, ably advised by Arnold,

[1] *Report on High Schools and Universities in Germany* (1874 and 1892), ch. ix.
[2] Connell, op. cit., p. 269.

recommended to the nation in 1868 might have produced results of this order; though the Commission did not quite conceive of a 'ladder'. But, as Mr. Armytage shows in his chapter, W. E. Forster, given his first task as the minister responsible for education in Gladstone's first government, failed to find the support to see the programme through. This was a serious setback to the views of progress for which Arnold stood; and by 1902, when the remedy came, public action had unpleasant associations for the middle class: some of the opportunities for integrating the whole system and cutting out the stigma of board-school segregation had been lost for ever.

VI

We are creatures of our time. Had these lectures been written before, say, the preparation of the Hadow report, much less attention would probably have been given to the social implications of the educational proposals with which we are here concerned, Arnold's views among them. We should, in his case, have felt it desirable to say more about his attitude to the lively controversies concerning the place of God and morals in education, to examine his bewildering and rather pusillanimous handling in public of his own theological compromise, and at the same time to consider his position among the parties of the cold war which was in progress between the defenders of the humanities and the supporters of 'modern' subjects; and we should note that behind the cold war of the curriculum was a hot war between the theologians and the scientists which had a somewhat baleful influence on the progress of the schoolmasters' disputes.

Herbert Spencer and John Henry Newman are natural foils. They had little in common in relation to our present inquiry except perhaps that both failed to share Arnold's concern for education as a class solvent and as a constructive force in society.

From questions of social dynamics, State provision, and ladders of opportunity, Newman always preserved a certain distance. He said, when a very old man, that he 'had never considered social questions in their relation to faith, and had always looked upon the poor as objects for compassion and benevolence'.

Spencer deliberately refused to education a place among the organized activities of a civilized community. In any case there was little that he could see, when he was writing his famous essays, to admire in the State's first efforts in this direction; and when it comes to political theory, we must accept as one of his most firmly held principles that this kind of interference with the liberty of child or parent was a sign of retarded development in the great ordered swing of society towards the goal of harmonized individuation—when *enlightened* selfishness, free from arbitrary 'rule-teaching' would reign supreme. 'Always towards progress is the mighty movement—towards a complete development and a more unmixed good.' Evolution was progress; progress was necessity; progress was the triumph of the individual.

In the struggle between revealed religion and rationalism Spencer's position is uncertain. He was a biological evolutionist before the scandal came to a head in 1859 with the *Origin of Species*. He had no place for special revelation, because the ultimate cause was thrust back into the region of the Unknowable. But he endowed the Law of Nature with a peculiar moral vigour, so that it seemed to transcend the ordinary workaday nature in which the individual tried to get his local bearings; and it is arguable that Spencer's great appeal to the generation which tried to profit from his teaching was due to his ability to invest arguments which tend to support a rather commonplace optimism concerning the future of a society a little dubious about its foundations with a fine assurance of natural sanction.

Certainly in the matter of education the attractiveness of his teaching can be explained in this way. It is always difficult to discover the principles which should underlie a sound educational method or programme. The subject appears on one day to be a department of morals, on another a corner of political science, on a third even an offshoot of psychological theory—in any case the plaything of concerns outside itself. When Spencer ties up all sciences under one great underlying principle, and when he shows that a certain succession of subjects in the child's order of learning can be supported by a law of recapitulation;

when he asserts that biology is the science of life, and it cannot be doubted that self-preservation, by direct or indirect means, is its great lesson, then at least we have a guide to the subjects fit for useful study. When he proves, or rather opines, that Nature has no place for altruistic motives (which are notoriously difficult to take at their face value), that the suppression of error by human judgement is dangerous to life, and that, if we need guidance, or indeed discipline, Nature will provide it in the form of reliable checks and lessons, as when the child lays hold fire-bars, then a simplicity is imported into educational principles which many have found to be irresistible.

By such means as this the British public came to learn something of the importance of self-activity in infant teaching, of the essential part which physical training must play in a balanced scheme of education—a badly needed lesson—and of the fact that work in the newer natural sciences had proceeded far enough to bring their subject matter into the ambit of the secondary-school curriculum.

As Professor Lauwerys quite fairly remarks in his closely reasoned analysis of the four chapters on education, Spencer 'has no very original ideas to express. . . . Chiefly he attacks existing and dominant educational ideals. He proposes to re-place a one-sided literary and humanistic bias in secondary and higher education by an equally—though no worse—one-sided scientific and factual bias'. Yet 'the impact of his thought and writing was very great'. An account of the remarkable success of his educational thought is given by Professor Lauwerys in Chapter 7, and we are persuaded that, in spite of the oddities and incongruities of Spencer's argument, the good points were well taken by his readers.

Newman's message to the same generation of readers was of a different nature. To move over from Spencer's essays into the discourses given in Dublin is to enter a new climate of thought. Newman enters our small company on the claims of his own merits, with as good a title as any, although the range of his practical interests was of course rather limited. It extended but a little way beyond the question: to what course of university tuition shall the professional classes—or at any rate those habitually using these institutions—be exposed?

The subtlety and depth of his treatment of this question about the function of a university was such however that almost every attempt at interpretation by commentators has placed the emphasis in a different way; some being willing to argue that his concern was to implant Oxford ideals among the Catholic Irish, and so to civilize them; others holding that he wished to demonstrate how narrowly the limits of university study must be confined to purely intellectual matters by reason of the Church's exclusive control of faith and morality; others that he was preparing the way for the creation of a secluded forum, undisturbed by any near spiritual authority, for the free discussion by forward-looking Catholics of current problems and current trends; others again that he really was attempting to vindicate the claims of liberal education against crude utilitarians like Spencer (*alias* Antichrist) on the one hand, and obscurant seminarists on the other, whilst enlarging its bounds and providing for a creative reconciliation of all *scientiae*, humanist and non-humanist, architectonic and peripheral, under the presidency of the queen of sciences, theology. '*Cor ad cor loquitur*,' Monsignor Knox once flippantly remarked, quoting the Cardinal's heraldic motto, 'and he [Newman] must be content to be at the mercy of the receiving instrument'. I think he could hardly be discontented with his interpreter in Chapter 6. Mr. Beales makes it clear that in his judgment the chief intention was to define the aim and the area of studies at the university level, whilst providing against injury to the spiritual health of Catholic believers by dispositions and balances within the field of non-moral instruction.

It has been said that Newman's influence belongs to this age and not to his own, and, as Mr. Beales shows (indicating the rich content of the whole discussion of a truly *integrated* curriculum), there is immense profit to be had from a study of Newman's lectures, whether the man's educational thought is studied within the frame of the historical personality, or even outside it. We are not, it appears, able properly to assess the effect of Newman's lectures on his own time, in the living word or in print. They certainly did nothing to maintain a rachitic little Irish university on its wobbling legs. Today they are still of vital importance to anyone who is concerned with the way in which an intellectual élite is created and fostered. And even today the attempt of this Roman convert, with his ultra-conservative past and his newly, as it seems, enfranchised outlook (for in Dublin he took up the cudgels for sweetness and light against darkness and obstinacy), with his ideal of a liberal education which set no limits to the operations of the under-graduate's soaring mind—yet conducted in reconciliation with the claims of a religion in which matters of faith and morals were established beyond argument—this attempt is a fascinating performance. For, admitting as he did all the rights of physical science and evolutionary physiology to develop their claims and to live on terms of harmony with theology and speculative metaphysics in the same quadrangle,[1] he seemed to make non-sense of the shrill disputes which were then, in 1852, working up between the evangelical, and other, supporters of a scriptural Adam and the *avant-garde* of the terrible new sciences of geology and biology, a party which was even then sacking the respect-able Christian universe of Newton and Paley and Bishop Usher.

The ideal educational establishment which Newman puts before us, with his distaste for research and for vocational specialization, is a place where intelligent and somewhat dis-interested people can enlarge their minds and continue to argue in the interests of truth. The ideal can without too much distortion be extended from the university to the higher secondary school; and we have indeed recently observed the high master of Manchester Grammar School, with a number of cautious adjustments which recognize the passage of a hundred years and the strong reaction of our times against the privileges of a leisured class, defend a point of view similar to Newman's within this very frame of reference.

The notion of the creative employment, during the edu-cational process, of the instruments derived from liberal studies

---

[1] I do not think Newman would have agreed with the following statement by Dr. Emil Brunner in his 1948 Gifford lectures (*Christianity and Civilization*, ii, 22), but it does at any rate set out very neatly the attitude which Christian schoolmasters are now at liberty to adopt. 'The word of God in scripture is no divine text-book of astronomy or anthropology. God's revela-tion in His word is given to us by men who lived in the pre-scientific ideas of their time. . . . Science and faith are on different planes, perhaps we may say on planes standing vertically at right angles to one another, and having therefore merely a common intersecting line. . . . It is equally stupid not to believe in God for scientific reasons and to oppose science for reasons of faith.'

—the use of that which by Newman's definition is useless—is so foreign to most continental ideas of advanced education as they have developed since the eighteenth century, that we may be tempted to regard Newman as the most English, perhaps the most *typical*, of our pioneers. As we glance over the names of the people in this book—Bentham and the elder Mill, Owen, Kay-Shuttleworth, Spencer, Arnold, Newman, Forster, Mundella, Acland—it seems that only one, Newman himself, had any religious passion, and that even he contrived an educational programme which aimed to keep worship and the teaching of morality out of the classroom.

Thus in the sphere of education our native wood-notes wild seem, rather surprisingly perhaps, to echo little concern with the problems which exercised so many men and women in the arena, such as that of the place of dogma in the classroom and the conflict between a divine order of things and the claims of scientific rationalism. Have we been partial in our selection? Or would it be right to argue that the creative minds have been just a little bored with these matters? I think the note of restraint was sounded by Maria Edgeworth and her father when, with characteristic prudence, they eschewed the religious issue in the construction of one of the lesser monuments of our educational thought.[1]

Whether it can be claimed that the English have dealt more effectively than other nations with the questions posed by religion to a secularist State is one of the hardest questions for 'comparate education' to handle convincingly. The circumstances for the English have been peculiarly difficult. Thus through usage we have become skilled makers of formulas. Some of them paper over the cracks—and it is yet too early to be sure about the cracks below the surface of the Act of 1944; and others miraculously perform the task of chemical welding. The full effects of the arrival of the evolutionary theory and historical materialism could not be dealt with in our lectures, for they are only now being experienced; and they are turning

[1] In the second edition of *Practical Education* (1801) they rally against one of their critics who has said they neglected religion. 'Can anything material be added,' they coolly ask, 'to what has already been published on this subject? Could any particular system meet with general approbation?' They think it well, however, to disavow in explicit terms the design of laying down a system of education, founded upon morality, exclusive of religion.

34

the world upside down. It may be argued that, if life could evolve, so could forms of society, and also the *mores* of society. What then becomes of absolute values? Where, as the Sophists used to ask, is the standard of justice? Lord Acton, who had an uncomfortable way of probing to the marrow of this kind of problem, once said:

'It was a very short step from the suspicion of Protagoras, that there were no gods, to the assertion of Critias that there is no sanction for laws. If nothing was certain in theology, there was no certainty in ethics and no moral obligation. The will of man, not the will of God, was the rule of life, and every man and body of men had the right to do what they had the means of doing.'[1]

The schoolmaster, whether he wishes it or not, must ever be a moralist, and no one can doubt that in days when the 'highest common factor' is all that a combined syllabus or a government hand-out will provide, the schoolmaster must be desperately in need of help and advice. If relativism in moral and spiritual matters is to be our portion, only Bentham among the figures in our gallery is likely to offer much help; and I am inclined to think that if educational theory can claim no better fate than to be the spoil of nominalists, we might go farther than Bentham and fare a good deal worse.

VII

It is much easier to produce a list of modern developments in educational thought and technique in which we in England have put up no more than a second-class performance than to indicate the models in the exhibition which seem to demand the award of first-class diplomas. In the former we must of course regretfully include technical education. The various endeavours to keep up through educational devices with the technological developments and institutional forms which have flowed from the industrial primacy we so ungracefully accepted in the days of Owen and Kay-Shuttleworth have one and all been pathetic in their ineptitude. Although there have of course

[1] 'Sir Erskine May's "Democracy in Europe",' *Quarterly Review*, cxlv, number 289 (1878). Since reprinted more than once.

been brilliant individual attempts to form a public mind and to get results, the story of the pioneer ventures would hardly have adorned our tale.

The story of secondary education in England is a mixed one. The 'religious question' made State intervention impracticable for many years in the elementary schools, and while that difficulty remained it was hard to think about a national educational service at any higher level. And indeed the survival of the poor-law mentality for a long time prevented people from questioning the assumption that the middle classes could and would in some unexplained fashion provide their own centres of instruction as and where required. *Laissez-faire* politicians preached that in a free country schools ought to be free from control. The strength of the notion that secondary education was essentially a middle and upper class activity was a consequence of the same play of circumstances, and the belief did not die earlier than the Bryce Commission's report of 1896. Between Forster's attempt in 1869 to secure a national policy in regard to secondary schooling and the Act of 1902 there passed an interval of about the same length as that which elapsed between Kay-Shuttleworth's preliminary efforts in the primary field and their realization in 1870. 'The ghosts of a century's neglect could not be so easily exorcized or reasoned away.' As Mr. Armytage demonstrates in Chapter 9, all the intervening years between Forster and Balfour were required for the maturing of opinion, and for the securing of a framework fit to carry the weight of a national scheme for secondary schooling in the pattern of partnership already developed between local ratepayer and Whitehall official in the old school-board setting.

Only then, in 1902, when as Sir John Maud says, 'education was first brought into the main stream of local government', did the concept of public *enterprise* as the dominant element at both levels of instruction become established—a point at which Sir John's theme concerning the rôle of the administrator, which he develops with a civil servant's modesty in Chapter 10, sets our mind working on a new train of thought.

In counting losses and gains we must not fail to notice the unique phenomenon of the rise and spread of the public schools. Their existence, the fact that in a narrow sector they achieved a most marked success, no doubt damaged the prospects of the orderly advance of a nationally centred policy over many years. This has already been hinted at in reference to Arnold's opinions. But it provides no good reason for denying that for a few thousand boys in each decade the British maintained the type of one of the best educational societies in the world, and moreover actually *created* it, in the period covered by this book, on the decaying foundations of the 'great school' of an earlier time—as the result of the work of two generations of headmasters, all of them uncompromising individualists, who certainly could claim with justice the title of pioneers; though that in fact is the last thing these tradition-loving teachers were willing to do!

Thus in some ranges of our practice in handling young people we could display our exhibits with a certain pride; though they may look odd in any international setting—odd just because we have been blind nearly always to the continental examples of purposeful scholarship in secondary schools, and on the rare occasions when we have looked for assistance we have not selected suitable models.

If we choose on the other hand, as I think we do in this book, to be judged by home-fabricated standards, then the tempo and the phases of development in these different branches of activity should be studied in relation to obstacles and frictions.

Out of the solution of a long series of problems there has emerged a ground-work or plan, of somewhat unsystematic aspect, made up of checks and balances, rights of way, and a queer fabric of conventional relationships, embracing not only various public authorities but also associations of employers, teachers, and other interested parties. No one can truly say where sovereignty in the promotion of initiative at present lies, any more than he can explain to the foreigner the virtues believed to exist in such an ingeniously bred monster as the controlled voluntary school. Pioneers are not currently in much demand; but they can still find scope at all levels. This is especially true of life at the working face where the educator himself experiments with new tools and formulates his ideas. Although private enterprise is almost a thing of the past in many sections of our educational world, we teachers have retained in essentials a large part of the freedom which the

Victorians believed (wrongly) to be their birthright, and in some respects have amplified it.

This is not the place for definitions; but it is, of course, a commonplace that the English teacher has long been particularly concerned with that part of education which can be described as the art of *developing capacity* in his pupils; and that the cultivation of this art has been connected in some obscure way with the teacher's own liberty of action. We have maintained a claim to teach, within wide limits, what we thought fit; also to choose the books and equipment to be used by our pupils, and to determine our own methods of instruction. If serious persecution had raised its head, martyrs for the freedom of teachers would no doubt have been forthcoming. Fortunately the potential martyrs have been allowed to get on with their work, because administration has been, generally speaking, on their side. And Sir John Maud's concern in Chapter 10 of this book is to show how the marriage of public policy and anministrative expedience since the Balfour Act has safeguarded this liberty of the teacher as well as the rights which, within the British democratic pattern, have been acquired by local authorities and made over to itself, through parliament, by the central power.

There is an extensive literature on the sphere of official action in education. Yet the activities of the members of the administrative grades in the public educational services, in their constructive work as builders, as midwives, and as inspectors of standards, is not often discussed. To these people none the less belongs the principal credit of the pioneering work, sometimes informed with genius, which has been responsible for the changes in the last fifty years. We did not feel that we were going beyond the plan proper to our operations when we asked Sir John Maud to discuss the spirit and outlook of these anonymous characters and to provide a glimpse of the milieu in which they have operated.

It is sometimes said to be one of the great merits of the 1944 Act that it brought together and forced together in amity all the constructive elements derived from public and private initiative inherited from the previous hundred years. This is by no means the whole of the matter, for we can still remember some of the historical elements which went unlamented into discard. But it is true, if we look closely at the provisions of the Act and the consequential decisions of the Minister's advisers, or rather through them and beneath them, that the documents are palimpsests in which the work and ideas of figures as remote as Kay-Shuttleworth can still be seen. We note for example the devolution of responsibility from the central office, and the sense of forbearance it learned to show in respect of direct action. We note the presence of financial sanctions in support of uniformity; and even the employment of building allocations (which we look upon as new) as an instrument of central control. We note the invention in due course of the 'chosen instrument' as draughtsman of new policy whereby, in Sir John Maud's words, 'the central administrator seeks to avoid both the appearance and the character of a dictator;' and the close alliance of the State with voluntary or quasi-voluntary agencies—from the Home and Colonial Infant School Society down to the National Foundation for Educational Research; and, from the first days, the powerful directing work of the inspectorate. Whereas Kay-Shuttleworth looked forward in thought, often with qualms, to the distant results of his inventiveness, Sir John Maud (who has himself instructed undergraduates in constitutional history) is able to look backward and appraise them. Sometimes he has had his precedessor consciously in mind; as, when formulating teacher-training plans for the late emergency, he and his colleagues have 'followed the second thoughts of Kay-Shuttleworth'.

Most readers will be glad to be reassured about the existence of principles in the management of the public sector. They will be pleased to have them identified, and interested in the way in which Sir John allows such ruling ideas as 'the wide dispersion of decision', the multiple 'mandate', consultation, and the use of voluntary services, to disclose themselves in their historical setting. When we realize that the central administration has to consider when and how 'action should be taken to meet the needs revealed by prophecy', and 'to contrive', in looking forward, 'that the national interest is so served that both local authority and teacher have as much as possible of the freedom each wants—and all the freedom that each really needs', we can see that 'value judgments' are all the time having to be made. When we are permitted to infer that the local administrator is not conceived to be doing his work unless he knows that he is 'more than a trustee for the interests of his legal master' the local education committee (whose mind he has often been engaged in making up), and that, with his moral trusteeship for the teachers and their pupils, he may be regarded as the king-pin of the twentieth-century educational structure, we appreciate the importance of staffing our most sensitively trained public service with great care.

There is an element common to both the beginning and the end of the period dealt with in this book: the problem of the shortage of personnel. In Bentham's time the clerics, who in happier circumstances could have inherited the educative rôle of the medieval clergy, had virtually abandoned school-keeping. They had taken to the country parsonages and were being absorbed into the squirearchy. Lay teaching was not an established profession. There was hardly any vocational tradition in the schools at a time when educational developments of wide extent were called for. The country needed what the sociologist Max Weber called a 'status group of *literati*'. The failure of any powerful element in society, and of the State itself, to intervene and create reasonable conditions for the growth of such a group was a tragedy. At every stage thereafter—certainly until 1902—the provision of an appropriately trained personnel was more important than buildings and equipment.

Some of these troubles are still with us. It is well-known that our ability to tend the requirements of the young population of the 'post-war bulge' will depend on the entry of many more women teachers, and that this in turn is going to be a charge on the capacity of our secondary schools to give inspiration to potential teachers in their upper forms. The provision of new entrants to the higher ranks of educational administration is a constant drain upon the very best level of talent in the teaching profession. There are times when those whose task it is to feed new entrants into the body of the profession are forced to resent the need for a haemorrhage so constant and so weakening. Sir John Maud's chapter provides the answer to such criticism: the inspector and the official must know much about teaching from classroom experience before they can be fully trusted.

If it were possible to argue that we are adequately equipped to produce the professionals in the schools and the offices there would still remain the problems of the unpaid services and of building up the unorganized ranks of the friends of the schools, the supporters of the youth club and the educational settlement. Here may be found the weakest joint of a delicately balanced system of dispersed power and decision depending so essentially on the proper functioning of local democracy. At the present time the pioneer most in demand is he or she who will organize citizen opinion around the community school and the new educational project, and coax the neighbours into taking a warmer and more intelligent interest in what is going forward. Even uninstructed observers notice that so far, since 1944, no spectacular success attends the progress of our revised schemes of school management by boards of citizen governors, and of ratepayers' control on a divisional basis. Our paid officials have not yet discovered how to recruit school managers possessing any reasonable combination of knowledge and zeal, or how to build local enthusiasm round the fortunes of a small group of schools. Perhaps after all the fault lies not with them but with the rest of us, the members of the public.

2

THE ENGLISH TRADITION IN
EDUCATION

*

SIR PHILIP MORRIS

*A lecture delivered at King's College on 15 January 1951;
the Principal of the College in the chair.*

The City of Bristol, which sent Burke to Westminster and
in which so many adventures of exploring Elizabethan
mariners were planned, is not likely to produce a lecturer
who underrates the importance or the value of tradition. Nor
is a city with such a picturesque and varied history of great
achievement, high endeavour, and art and culture likely to
produce a lecturer who regards tradition as being a matter
solely of principles and ideas inherited from the past, accepted
unquestioningly and observed meticulously. Bristol is a city
which has been a closed fortress with a flourishing monastery,
a centre of world trade, the starting place of the discoverers of
new worlds and the centre of industries both old and new. It has
reached heights of civic responsibility and dignity and the
depths of municipal corruption. It has known great public
spirit and all the graces and dignity of a medieval corporate life,
and it has had in its day, and at an important period in the
history of the country, inactive oligarchs who have been described as being 'so well accustomed to neglect their old duties
that they were not likely to attend to the new'. Living in a city
like Bristol, you are surrounded by the past in all its great
variety, inevitably influenced by it, but incapable of being its
willing slave. Thus, despite the subject of my lecture I cannot

42

treat the great tradition which is ours from any abstract point of view, nor can I regard our educational tradition as being distinguishable or separate from the main course of developments in a growing modern society. Without depreciating our great achievements in the field of education it can still be truly said that we have not hitherto been a nation of great educational thinkers. In what we have done educationally we have almost always been meeting new situations caused by changes and developments in society at large, always greatly influenced, sometimes much too much so, by the past, but always at the same time trying to devise means which would achieve definite and relatively short-term objectives.

I was visiting universities and university cities in Australia and New Zealand last summer and the power of what we call our tradition is perhaps more strikingly observed in another clime at a great distance from home than in any other way. In Southern Australia in a house constructed from materials which the original settlers of two generations ago had taken with them from this country, their grandchildren greeted me, a stranger, as a visitor from Home, although they had themselves never set foot in this country. All my latent interest in our own history was reawakened even more in Christchurch in what used to be the province of Canterbury in New Zealand, where I suddenly felt that I had been transported back to the Canterbury of my youth. A newly awakened interest in the development of Canterbury, New Zealand, left me wide open to the temptation of inaugurating this present series of lectures, particularly when I saw the excellent programme of lectures which had been planned.

The history of Canterbury is an excellent example of the good fortune which has so often attended us by the coming together of people widely different in background, ideas, and temperament, but capable of an equal interest and enthusiasm for a particular project. No modern planner, looking for two people to act in partnership in founding a new society, would have selected two such different and unlike persons as Edward Gibbon Wakefield and John Robert Godley. Wakefield's colourful but not entirely creditable matrimonial experiences had resulted in enforced leisure in prison, which he had used to conceive and nourish a passionate enthusiasm for colonial

43

development. Some would say that his far from blameless past was a disqualification in the founder of a new society and an impossible bar to effective co-operation with Godley, an austere and high-minded young squire, supported as he was by the most respectable names and institutions both in Church and State and armed with the name of a great Oxford college. Not for the first time in the English tradition two entirely unlike personalities and standpoints met together, accommodated themselves to each other and achieved much. It was not due to either Godley or Wakefield that the development of this new society diverged from the original lines laid down for it. The arrival of sheep rangers from New South Wales owing to reasons wholly unconnected with the nature or intentions of this new-found society, introduced new ideas, taught the original settlers new tricks and changed the course of Canterbury's history.

The programme for this course of lectures suggested to me that those who had planned it had had in mind a similar con-fluence of different standpoints, which were brought together by agrarian and urban developments at the end of the eighteenth century. I saw the nineteenth century from the educational point of view as being a century spent, not without its great achievements, in struggling with vast social problems. Only with the greatest of difficulty and frequently for the time being wholly without success, men of very different religious, intellectual and political views were struggling to discover immediate objectives on which they could find sufficient common ground for progress to be made.

Any lecture about the English Tradition in Education which is to serve as a satisfactory introduction to this particular course must display the English tradition at work. It cannot mention all the important influences which have shaped men's minds in this island, which for a thousand years has been free from the invader and able to find peaceful means of accomplishing changes which have involved revolution and bloodshed in less happier lands. What I have tried to do is to look at the course of educational development over the past one hundred and fifty years and see in it how our tradition has operated in the field of education. I have already said that the educational arrangements of a society are only one manifestation of its social convictions and ideals. The development of its educational

44

arrangements can only be appreciated if it is seen, not merely as one aspect of general social development, but rather as part of the very texture of society throughout the period.

Nobody looking at this course of lectures and observing from what varying fields of experience and achievement the great men chosen as subjects for lectures come can doubt what is, in fact, true, that great educational interest and activity was found in many walks of society. Certainly until the end of the nineteenth century, education was not primarily, or even to any important extent, a professional activity. Throughout this period all men of responsibility in society were obliged to know and do something about educational affairs, and it is, I suppose, still a part of our tradition that everybody tends to regard himself as an educational expert.

A new civilization was being born at the end of the eighteenth century. The application of scientific knowledge to the ordinary activities of mankind, which had been developing slowly for a century or more, suddenly took on a spurt and began to acquire more and more force, encouraged by its immediate success. The thinkers of ancient Greece, content to leave the industrial arts to slaves and despising the application of the results of pure thought to the satisfaction of immediate needs, had avoided initiating a social revolution and at the same time set limits to the advancement of their own scientific knowledge. In the circumstances of his own day Newton, inspired by Greek philosophic and scientific thought, but also reacting against it in his denial of the utility of conjecture, had started a train of thought congenial to the ordinary matter-of-fact Englishman. Scientific knowledge could be applied to the satisfaction of men's needs and be itself advanced in the course of its application. The end of the eighteenth century, because of this new standpoint, saw not only the breakdown of a rural society, but also an urban revolution. These great changes occurred during the strain of the Napoleonic Wars and largely enabled us to withstand the Napoleonic threat to our freedom to pursue, in ways more congenial to us, lines of development very like those which were much less successfully pursued, with so much bloodshed and upheaval, by revolutionary means in France.

No study of the educational history of the nineteenth century is genuine unless it takes fully into account all that was involved in the change which came over the face of the country in a period of time not much greater than a single generation. Men and women accustomed to living on and in the country, brought up in the atmosphere of the countryside, found themselves in rapidly developing towns built as widespread lodgings for men, women, and children at work in the prison-like conditions of the early factories. Those who were left behind in the country-side found that the beginnings of scientific farming gravely affected their means of subsistence. For instance, the gathering of conies became, after the enclosures, the crime of poaching which was so rigorously treated and dealt with and at the same time often secretly applauded by rural magistracy. Probably few other countries could boast an activity which was at once so natural, so much denounced and so much admired, and probably no other country in such circumstances has produced a song like 'The Lincolnshire Poacher'. The great economic difficulties which overcame the countryside were in their own way as serious as the different problems which arose in the rapidly increasing towns.

The Speenhamland magistrates gave the administration of the Poor Laws an entirely new turn. One of the results was that the development of elementary education was very closely associated with the administration of the Poor Law and, as regards a large number of children, co-extensive with it. Pauperization was at work in the countryside, and exploitation which, it is true to say, was initially due to economic factors rather than to lack of humanity in the towns, was accompanied by a rapid increase in the whole population of the country, con-tributed to both by a considerable increase in the expectation of life and by an increase in the birthrate. A state of affairs had come into being in which the habits of thought owing so much to the Greek tradition found themselves in circumstance wholly different from those of the Greek thinkers. A new society was in the making in which those engaged in agricultural and industrial pursuits had inevitably, in the course of time, to be given the privileges of full citizenship. It was no use continuing to rely solely upon the intellectual achievements of men for whom the practice of the industrial arts was the affair of slaves, for whom it was only necessary 'that they (the poor) should obey the law and not even desirable that they should know or understand it'. The first symptom of the inevitable change which must come over the standpoint of educated men was the almost wholly unsuccessful repressionist policy of the early years of the nineteenth century, during which the foundations of our elementary education system were being laid.

It is not my intention to give a historical lecture, but rather to revive in those who have already known it and to awaken in those who have not yet experienced it an interest in the varied social history of the country which is a more rewarding study than concentration upon our rather exiguous explicit educational thought. We possess an educational system which was forged upon the anvil of social necessity, in the heat of political and religious controversy, and not a planned system thought out in principle and detail and then continuously and painstakingly carried out. Few of our great educational ventures have turned out exactly as was intended, and many protagonists of different views have found themselves in due course cooperators in the achievement of particular objectives. This is true even of what we usually call the public schools. Some of them found their origins in the grammar schools of the sixteenth century and earlier, while many of those which are great educational institutions today were brought into being by the necessity for a secondary education for the children of a new society, existing facilities for which were too sparse, too parochial, and in a large number of cases, it is sad to say, very inactive. Their curriculum owes much to the traditional curriculum of the Renaissance, but during the last fifty years, at any rate, and in some cases for a longer period, the tide of industrial practice and scientific advance has flowed over them. Through all the changes which have come upon them they have continued to place the highest educational importance upon the establishment of powerful communities with an ordered way of life, giving many opportunities for the acquisition of informal but profitable social and intellectual experience.

They have been fortunate, during a period of such rapid and revolutionary change, in having been able to preserve these characteristics. They stand today, when our problem is clearly the invention and provision of a satisfactory secondary education for all the children in the land, as witnesses to the necessity in education of good living and facilities for good social experience, allied to good teaching. They continue to remind us that education is not an affair only or even primarily of classrooms, books, and apparatus, but rather of educational institutions, expensive to provide and maintain, with space in which to live spaciously as well as rooms adequately equipped for efficient teaching. Important as our public schools are, it is nevertheless true that during the nineteenth century they had little interest in or contact with the rising tide of educational development which has given us the educational system of today. So long as the implicit policy in educational development was to restrict the education of the masses to a rudimentary elementary education and to prevent elementary schools from developing a secondary stage—and this was the case until the end of the nineteenth century—there was naturally no field of common endeavour or of common problems. This position was changed to some extent by the Education Act of 1902, which initiated the publicly provided secondary school system, and has been changed even more by the Act of 1944, which gives statutory recognition to the obligation which rests upon society to provide a secondary stage of education for all children. Some interaction and relationship between the public schools and the education system at large is for the future inescapable. On this theme I must not venture further.

The widespread interest in education for the sake of educational progress which exists today was not a characteristic of the nineteenth century. The general climate of opinion can be gauged from the reception of the Bill introduced by Mr. Whitbread in 1807. The proposals in the Bill followed naturally upon the great humanitarian and religious movements at the end of the eighteenth century and contemplated the provision of education as an indispensable preliminary to any sound Poor Law administration and to the amelioration of the lot of children employed in industry. The question whether it was a good thing to disseminate education amongst the uneducated masses quickly arose. The fate of the Bill and the arguments which led to its final rejection clearly showed that informed opinion of the day was not ready 'to accept the risks of making the poor discontented'. The Bill served the valuable purpose of making clear to all thoughtful people some of the many problems which were essentially bound up in the provision of elementary

48

education for the children of the country. It became clear, for instance, that the time spent in education, must be taken from gainful employment and that, so far from continuing to be a financial asset, children would necessarily become the object of both individual and general sacrifice. The obvious necessity for the use of compulsion to free children from one kind of life in order that they might be better brought up and educated initiated a conflict between those keen on social progress and the 'voluntaryists' who in rightly emphasizing the importance of spontaneous effort and willing service in the cause of education entirely overlooked the fact that spontaneous and willing effort could not rescue the children of the masses from the condition in which they found themselves.

It is not surprising that the question of the cost of establishing the universal provision of rate-aided parochial schools should also arise. The early stages of industrialization, although they laid the foundation of much subsequent wealth, were in fact years of great struggle for all concerned in laying the foundations of modern agriculture and industry. It is not therefore surprising that much time and energy were spent on discovering how cheaply rudimentary elementary education could be provided. Bell and Lancaster had, independently of each other, rediscovered the monitorial system and, relying largely on the principles underlying this sytem, it was used as an argument in favour of the Bill that education could be provided at a very cheap rate. An insistence upon the cheapness of elementary education is to be found running like a constant refrain through the official documents of the nineteenth century. Bell had said in 1808, 'Parents will always be found to educate at their own expense children to fill the stations which require higher qualifications'. Thus the division of education into one compartment for those who were so placed as to be able to obtain it for themselves, and another for those who were not only powerless to demand it but also frequently unwilling to accept it was established. As we have seen, this division of education into two parallel compartments persisted throughout the century, was reinforced by the Act of 1902 and did not disappear until the Act of 1944.

The provision of rate-aided parochial schools as contemplated in Whitbread's proposal also gave rise to strong opposition on the part of the Church. That there was an interest in education at all at this time was a direct result of religious and philanthropic enthusiasm, but the historical claim of the Church that it had a commission to educate the whole nation gave rise to great difficulties. The general argument that elementary education could be cheap tended to conceal the immense cost of establishing a system of universal education and so concealed also the very great difference between the material resources of the Church and its spiritual mission. This religious controversy is clearly seen at the time of the attempt to introduce a kind of Board of Education in 1835 and 1838. This proposal raised the opposition of the Church and religious interests to a high pitch and contributed one of the most unfortunate of all elements in our educational tradition. It appears inevitably, but not necessarily justly, that the Church was opposing educational progress. Also, at a time when Nonconformists and Roman Catholics were suffering severe educational as well as political disabilities, sectarian bitterness was greatly increased and many who did not doubt that the foundation of education was essentially religious found themselves driven into undenominational or even into avowedly secular movements. Understandable as the position adopted by the Church in the light of its past history is, it cannot be denied that this particular controversy has exercised and still exercises a very powerful influence upon educational thought and is still responsible for much confusion and misunderstanding. A standpoint which is much more in keeping with the outlook of today was cogently expressed by Macaulay in 1847 in the following words: 'I appeal with still more confidence to a future age which, while enjoying all the blessings of state education, will look back with astonishment to the opposition which the introduction of that system encountered and which will be still more astonished that such resistance was offered in the name of civil and religious freedom'. Nevertheless the great controversy started by the proposal to establish a kind of Board of Education gives us another opportunity of seeing our tradition at work, because the original proposals were withdrawn and a Committee of the Privy Council established by administrative act, thus leading to a very similar result by an obviously different route.

Notwithstanding the birth pangs of elementary education provided at the public expense, great progress had been made by 1870, when it became possible to contemplate not only compulsory universal attendance at school, but also the establishment of School Boards for the purpose of providing elementary schools at the public expense. The old controversies still continued and embittered much of the work of the School Boards at their inception, but from 1870 onwards it was clear that the climate of opinion had sensibly changed and that two new ideas had already begun to emerge. First, the conception of elementary education was broadening into something much less rudimentary and much less cheap, and second, the need to develop and extend the provision of higher elementary education for the children of parents who could not afford to pay for it was being stated and increasingly recognized. Thus during the last thirty years of the century many varied kinds of higher education, going far outside the statutory intention of elementary education, began to appear, some of them at the instance of religious and voluntary societies and some of them at the instance of the School Boards. These experiments in universal post-primary education were the subject of great criticism and eventually the legality of the provision of anything except rudimentary education was challenged and it was held to be against the law of the land. Thus the nineteenth century had seen not only the development of a system of universal elementary education but also adventurous and, as it turned out, illegal experiments in the provision of post-primary education. The twentieth century was thus ushered in with a new and difficult educational problem to face.

Meanwhile, although a large number of the local grammar schools of the country in the early years of the nineteenth century were inactive and standing upon the ancient ways, there was much movement and progress in a variety of directions in the field of post-elementary education. One of the serious social effects of the breakdown of life in the countryside and of industrial development in the towns was to be seen in the breakdown of apprenticeship in large sectors of the field in which apprenticeship had become well-established and a vital educational force. A natural urge to self-improvement, combined with the demands of developing industry and social

change, encouraged and gave new importance to apprenticeship schools and many other similar educational movements.
The importance of the new knowledge to industrial and social
change, which for many years escaped the attention of the
grammar schools and the universities of old foundation, gave
rise to new institutions and also gave new importance to old
movements.

It was in this soil that the germs of the movement which led
to the development of technical colleges and the foundation
of university colleges found nourishment. Much of the strife
and controversy which has already been noted in the growth
and development of elementary education was reproduced
in this educational movement which, starting somewhat later,
gathered force more quickly under the powerful influences of
the times. Thus the unwillingness on the part of old institutions
to interest themselves in the sciences and a determination on
the part of those steeped in the medieval tradition of scholarship to resist the enlargement of fields of study, together with a
tendency to see in all new knowledge a threat to the religious
foundations of life and society, caused not only the establishment of rival institutions, but also much strife and controversy.
Later in the century a new problem, that of the emancipation
of women, arose, and the obvious justice of equal educational
opportunity for men and women was accepted neither quickly
nor without much heartburning and difficulty. Indeed, it was
left for the twentieth century to carry this movement over some
of its most important and difficult obstacles. While, however,
the rights of women were being tardily accorded and defined
in the universities by administrative act and almost in a fit of
absence of mind the secondary education movement initiated
by the Education Act of 1902 proceeded without question or
difficulty upon the basis of equal provision for boys and girls.
The importance of this decision, or accident—and which of the
two it was we shall never certainly know—in the educational
development of this century cannot easily be overestimated.
For instance, all who now survey the contemporary educational
scene cannot fail to recognize that much of the educational
improvement which we desire can only be secured by a still
further increase in the already very large number of women
who teach in the schools.

52

The older universities for almost half the nineteenth century preserved their own way of life and became increasingly detached from the large social and educational movements which were proceeding in society at large. The pressure of events was bound, however, in due course to have its way and the reform of Oxford and Cambridge, with much support from within and with increasing pressure from without, was eventually undertaken. From that moment the new knowledge, which had already found a home in new institutions, began to transform the older universities as well and religious disabilities were reduced and eventually wholly removed. Once again our older universities were in a position to consider and study everything of significance to the life of the country and the problems of humanity. Had the reform of Oxford and Cambridge been much longer delayed, the great progress in university education which has been of such importance to society in the last century would inevitably have taken different lines and might easily have suffered the loss of the ancient tradition of the older universities, which has done so much to shape and inform the new.

I deliberately do not enlarge upon the development of universities because members of the University of London and especially perhaps members of King's College, an institution so intimately concerned in this movement throughout the nineteenth century and exercising such a powerful influence today, can be in no danger of underestimating the central part which universities must always play in the maintenance of the educational verities, of standards and of educational progress.

The history of educational progress in this century, so recently brought back to our minds by the discussions which preceded the passing of the Education Act of 1944, should need no description. A tribute should, however, be paid to those responsible for the measure for maintaining the religious foundation of education without causing a denominational storm. It is, also, an opportunity which should not be missed of reminding ourselves that the official publications of the Committee of the Privy Council, and subsequently of the Board of Education, are amongst our most valuable and important educational documents. Perhaps chief amongst these is the Report of the Consultative Committee under the title *The*

Education of the Adolescent, which appeared in 1926. This magnificent document, which has too soon fallen into disuse, provides at once a brilliant recapitulation of the history of the development of public education and a vivid statement of the educational progress of our own day. Not only does it insist that the division of education into parallel compartments is outmoded and untenable, but it also reminds us in vivid language of many of the vital things about education of which we too infrequently remind ourselves. The scheme which this report advocated was the substantial basis of the 1944 Act and, as the Committee themselves said, could 'be simply stated'. The difficulty of stating the ideals which should inform and bring the scheme to life is emphasized by this Committee, but their attempt to do so in the following words effectively epitomises a hardly acquired educational ideal:

' . . . It is less easy to state the ideal which lies behind our scheme. But there are three great ends of human life and activity which we trust that our scheme will help to promote. One is the forming and strengthening of character—individual and national character—through the placing of youth, in the hour of its growth, "as it were in the fair meadow" of a congenial and inspiring environment. Another is the training of boys and girls to delight in pursuits and rejoice in accomplishments—work in music and art; work in wood and in metals—work in literature and the record of human history—which may become the recreations and the ornaments of hours of leisure in maturer years. And still another is the awakening and guiding of the practical intelligence, for the better and more skilled service of the community in all its multiple business and complex affairs—an end which cannot be dismissed as "utilitarian" in any country, and least of all in a country like ours, so highly industrialized, and so dependent on the success of its industries, that it needs for its success, and even for its safety, the best and most highly trained skill of its citizens.

'The forming and strengthening of character; the training of the tastes which will fill and dignify leisure; the awakening and guiding of the intelligence, especially on its practical side —these are the ends which we have had in view; and it is in their name, and because we think it may serve, in its measure, towards their attainment, that we commend this report to our readers. Not the least among these ends is the forming and strengthening of character, both individual and national. It is here especially that a national system of education may serve to elevate a nation. Great Britain, like other countries, but perhaps more than most, is passing through an era of industrialism. Industrialism has its grave effects on national life. It demands, only too often, a narrow specialization of faculty; it produces, only too readily, a patterned uniformity of work and behaviour; and it may, unless it is corrected, infect the minds of men with the genius of its own life. Education can correct industrialism, by giving to the mind the breadth and the fresh vitality of new interests, as it can also make industry more effective; and we believe that the teachers of our country—given their opportunity—can bring the discipline of the school to aid the influence of home in making a new generation which alike in character, in tastes, and in trained skill will justify them abundantly of all their labours.'

The development of educational thought in this country, as I have already said, has been implicit in educational movements and in educational expansion rather than explicit in the development of educational theories or educational plans and policies. The ideas which have inspired educational movements in this country have come from all walks of life and from all sections of the population. Our educational tradition has something vital and even organic in its nature. At no time have past achievements exerted little influence, and yet at no time has the past provided dogmas which successfully confined and prevented developments and the growth of new movements. The fact that our tradition is essentially composite of what is inherited and what is transmitted is its most distinctive quality and makes it difficult to analyse, and something about which it is wholly inappropriate to dogmatize. Our great and adventurous thinkers have almost always been steeped in the influences of the past and also capable of asking themselves not only whether some new proposal has been tried before, but also whether there are compelling reasons for trying it now. Thus, while there have frequently been quite fundamental changes in our educational objectives and in our educational arrangements, there have been no abrupt breaks with tradition. The

lectures which are to come in this series will show in a particularly appropriate manner from how many watersheds of
human experience the stream of educational progress has been
fed and by what a variety of accidents great contributions to
education in this country have been continuously made from
other fields of human activity and experience.

If the accumulated experience of society is to be available
for the enrichment and development of society, it must be continuously being studied and rediscovered. The accumulated
knowledge of society becomes available to successive generations as they are born, however, not only by study and teaching
in educational institutions, important as these activities and
institutions are, but also through the normal workings of
society. For example, the gradual emergence through much
tribulation and difficulty of teaching as a learned profession
would not have been possible without the example of the other
professions, which had earlier found their bonds of unity and
techniques of professional association. Dependent as professions
mostly are, for their standards and repute, upon the nature and
quality of the training for them, it is interesting to note that the
first minute of the Committee of the Privy Council on its establishment, which raised a storm of controversy, provided for the
establishment of a teachers training college. You will inevitably
hear about this later in the series because Kay-Shuttleworth
had no little responsibility for the decision and, notwithstanding the reconsideration of the minute owing to the storm of
criticism it caused, was in many ways the originator of training
for teachers. Without this development of a teaching profession,
one of the greatest elements in our educational tradition, the
liberty of the teacher must inevitably have been one of the
casualties of educational expansion.

It is not only in the educational sphere itself that the ideas
which chiefly inspire our educational tradition are continuously
revived and reborn. The gradual emergence in the nineteenth
century and the rapid development in our own day of many
kinds of industrial and commercial training within commerce
and industry is another important example. The days when the
majority of the workpeople in industry or commerce could be
regarded as mere hands or instruments have long passed and
the complexity of industrial and commercial organization has

made inevitable a much greater participation by ordinary people in matters of organization, management, and policy. The lion's share of the credit for new ideas in these directions can justly be accorded to the great influence which the Quaker movement has exerted not only upon industrial and commercial life, but also upon education itself.

The most important vehicle of the English tradition has always been the domestic atmosphere in which boys and girls were brought up. Before the idea of providing schooling in any formal sense for the majority of children was first conceived, the main place of the education of children was the home and the community in which children were brought up. Before systematic agriculture and industrialization changed the whole face of the social scene in England, boys and girls, particularly in the countryside, acquired at home and in the compact social structure in which their homes were placed their training in morals, manners, and skill. In the towns, also the private corporations and guilds exercised an important influence upon the quality of home life and the social and moral training of young people. It was, e.g., the general rule in the old apprenticeships for the master to whom an apprentice was bound to become responsible not only for his training, but also for his moral and social development.

Schools then came into existence in an atmosphere in which all these responsibilities were still exercised in their own spheres by landlords, guilds, and corporate bodies, and the necessity for ensuring the continuation of a moral and social tradition had a very considerable influence upon the early ventures in the provision of elementary education. This influence is still more marked, perhaps, in the objectives and outlook of the early institutions for the training of teachers. At the root of all these ideas was the fundamental notion that the home and its atmosphere was at least as important an element in the education of boys and girls as any other educational institution. The many complaints which are made from time to time of the inadequacies of home influence and of an alleged deterioration of standards tend to make us lose sight of the immense strides which have been made in establishing a new and altogether more satisfactory level of family life, both material and social. No one who mixed with young men in the armed forces during

57

the war could fail to be impressed by the overwhelming anxiety shown by all of them for a hearth and home of their own, or by the great influence which their own home environment was still exercising upon them when they were far away and exposed to strong and novel temptation.

It is probably because our provision for universal education struggled into existence in a social environment in which great reliance was placed upon the unconscious acquisition of good social and moral habits, that we have in this country schools which at the best reinforce and at the worst replace the moral and social teaching of the home and which have been instrumental in strengthening and improving out of all recognition the way in which young children are cared for and brought up. It would be wrong to be complacent about the present state of affairs, full as it is of weaknesses and shortcomings, but it would be even more wrong to fail to recognize the great improvement in the ordinary lot of children at home in both town and country which has come about during the last hundred years. It is a vital part of our tradition, which the educational system has on the whole strengthened and certainly continuously revives and transmits, that however much schools can do, they cannot be regarded as substitutes for homes.

Lastly, education in this country has always been, and I rejoice to think it still is, more a movement than it is a system. As we have seen, the great religious and voluntary movements, combined with local initiative, can rightly claim to have been pioneers in education. So in our own day the tradition persists by which a great variety of people in churches, universities, industry and commerce, and in many fields of experience are involved at all levels in the government and development of education. There is no other country in which so much voluntary work is willingly placed at the disposal of an educational system and at the same time so willingly accepted and effectively used. It is partly for this reason that perhaps the most important documents relating to educational developments are official reports which, far from being the reports of officials, are the work of committees and groups of people brought together by officials for the sake of pooling experience and ensuring that changes as they are made should observe that continuity which is so essential to education in all its aspects. In the course of working out so many techniques, by which so much experience could be made available for educational purposes, we have also provided ourselves with educational officials who are unequalled in the rest of the world for their breadth of interest, their versatility of technique, and their unassailable integrity, both of intellect and of behaviour.

It was inevitable that I should set aside all temptation to to give a complete and rounded analysis and evaluation of our educational tradition. I shall nevertheless not escape criticism for having devoted so much of my time to expansion, development, and the provision of educational facilities and too little to the educational process itself and to the ideas and principles involved. I have deliberately taken this risk because, as I saw it, this series of lectures was planned so that each lecture as it came might provide one or more strands in the complex pattern of ideas which underlies all true education everywhere. My more limited objective has been to show from the beginning that this carefully planned series of lectures had unity as well as diversity and that the evident diversity of people and of apparent subjects was a reflection of the diversity of our educational tradition. I cannot, however, resist the temptation myself to refer to a few of the fundamental ideas which seem to me to be distinctive of our English educational genius.

We have throughout our history at all times thought more in terms of developing institutions than of principles of organization. It is this concrete approach to the human problem of enlarging ideas and making them flesh which has given us such a rich variety of institutions, educational, and otherwise, of which we are so justly proud. Further, throughout our history we have regarded an institution as being all the stronger because it included not only a variety of people, but also differences in ideas and beliefs. This has been a powerful influence in all our educational endeavours as well as in our political and constitutional development. The basic conviction shared by every Englishman that ultimate political power rests with the King in Parliament and not with the government of the day is of fundamental importance to our way of life and to the development and safety of the growing idea of democracy, which more and more possesses us as it is brought under attack from any quarter. The fundamental importance of His Majesty's Opposition which is realized in this country not least by the Government itself, finds its parallel throughout all our educational institutions. Within our educational institutions themselves there has been, over the past half-century and for even longer than that, a notable movement towards the sharing of the responsibilities of institutional government, and this is an important movement which needs encouragement from all quarters.

It is this institutional idea which has kept before our minds, notwithstanding occasional waverings, that what we want in this country and intend to have is enough good schools for every child and not, except by accident, an educational system which is completely systematic. When the visitor from overseas regards our educational arrangements as constituting an incomprehensible patchwork, he is in fact being brought into contact with the source of their educational strength and not with the defects of an educational system. It is vital to our future that we should never overlook the importance of the school as the essential and indispensable unit of education and that we should systematize only as far as is necessary and then only if it is possible to do so without doing violence to the integrity of the school.

Notwithstanding the rapid expansion which circumstances made inevitable and the development of our educational arrangements in almost wholly separate parallel streams, we have never for long departed from a deep-rooted belief in the importance of the individual. We have always so far seen education as being chiefly concerned with the all-round development of persons and not merely as a matter of the instruction of classes. The survival of this vital and fundamental idea is something in which we can take an immense pride, especially when it is remembered how large have been our classes, how much mass teaching has had to be done and how nevertheless the collection of children and teachers together for the purpose of education has resulted in the foundation of schools which are real communities. In the present difficulties with which the schools are inevitably struggling this fundamental idea of the supreme worth of personality will not suffer, largely because of the ideals which inspire the teaching profession. It may well be that in many schools less can be done for the all-round development of personality than teachers would like to do, but this must and should not mean that the desire to do more and more as opportunity offers in any way weakens. In the world of today and in the world into which we are moving no amount of instruction will help us to face our problems if it proceeds at the expense of or in the absence of the inculcation of principles and a sense of responsibility and purpose in living. The religious controversies of yesterday must not blind us to the fact that knowledge without a faith by which to use it is valueless, and that faith without the knowledge to give it expression in acts and deeds is impotent.

Our old traditional idea of the teacher surrounded by his children has, notwithstanding almost insuperable difficulties, remained with us. We have maintained obstinately, and I think rightly, the view that it is the teacher and his relationship with children that matters and that the curriculum, important though it is, has an importance of a lower order. The liberty which teachers enjoy in their choice of methods, in their working out of objectives, and in the establishment of their relationships with each other and with the children, is a priceless possession. In no other country would the main publication of the central Education Department about the curriculum be entitled *Suggestions for the Guidance of Teachers*. A whole tradition is wrapped up in this simple phrase. It is still, I am glad to say, the teacher who carries the main responsibility and it is in schools and in educational institutions that the curriculum ought to be fashioned. At times in our history, for instance, during the period in which detailed and restrictive codes were issued, the shaping of the curriculum of the schools has been done in spite of regulation, and more recently external examinations have achieved great and even in some ways excessive influence, from which it is to be hoped the schools will similarly free themselves.

The very tenacity with which the traditional medieval curriculum has been defended and the fierce struggle against the addition of new subjects is itself an indication that we have always maintained a distinction, without being able to define it, between general education and specialized instruction. The rapidity with which knowledge has advanced and the comparative speed with which subject after subject has fought its way into the schools have done much to produce confusion in our thinking about the nature of a general education. Pre-occupied as we have been with adding new subjects and looking at the curriculum in terms of balancing subjects and finding time for everything, we have not unnaturally fallen into the danger of confusing the subjects themselves with the function of subjects in the education of children. The reasons for this would take not one lecture, but a whole series of lectures to outline. A new and perplexing educational problem was created when Bacon and Newton gave a new turn to the direction of thought in this country similar to the turn which the Cartesians gave on the continent. Those who found these new ideas anathema to them became more and more entrenched in their view that there was a hierarchy of subjects and rejected the claims of new fields of knowledge. In the education of children, however, what matters most and should command our attention is the use of subjects for the purpose of education. We must reject a strong tendency to regard education as the inevitable by-product of the efficient teaching of subjects and recapture an older but sounder view, that the education of persons is the root of the matter and their training in subjects an indispensable ingredient in it.

I have read many lectures on our educational tradition and they have been devoted largely, and I am sure rightly, to the debt which all education owes to Greek thought, the Christian religion, and the achievements of the early Fathers and of the Church. In having taken an entirely different line I do not wish to seem to underrate the great importance of all these powerful and indispensable forces. Indeed, whatever mistakes I may have made, I hope I have done nothing to deny what I believe to be the truth, that there are eternal principles which, being the alpha and omega of all education, cannot themselves ever be perfectly defined or completely understood. I have concentrated more upon showing in what changing modes and by what different methods these eternal principles have found expression according to the problems of the day. In appealing in an amateur fashion to history to inform and guide us, I have not taken and do not take the view that history is an evolutionary process of which Man is the slave. On the contrary, I hope that I have succeeded in showing that I regard it as Man's duty and high privilege to make history, and his plain duty to study the struggles and achievements of the past in order that he may, if he can, give more fitting expression in his own day to the eternal and unchanging principles which he shares with his forebears. The rest of these lectures, concerned as they are with the achievements and disappointments of men who contributed much, will, I have no doubt, confirm this point of view.

3

ROBERT OWEN

*

M. V. C. JEFFREYS

A lecture delivered at King's College on 22 January 1951;
Professor A. V. Judges in the chair.

I

A man whose long life spans the gap between Oliver Goldsmith (d. 1774) and George Bernard Shaw (b. 1856) Joseph Priestley (d. 1804) and Oliver Lodge (b. 1851), Adam Smith (d. 1790) and Sidney Webb (b. 1859), George Washington (d. 1799) and Woodrow Wilson (b. 1856) —a man, moreover who at one time or another met almost everyone of contemporary importance in Europe and America and who numbered among his friends people like Jeremy Bentham, Francis Place, and Henry Brougham—such a man must have seen a good deal of history in the making.

Robert Owen was born in 1771, two years after the patenting of Watt's steam engine and about the time of the inventions associated with Arkwright and Crompton which necessitated the vital change in the cotton industry from the domestic to the factory system.

Owen was an infant when we were losing the American colonies. The year when he went into partnership on £100 of borrowed capital to manufacture spinning mules was the year in which the French Revolution broke out—not that Owen paid any attention to the event. And he was married and bought the mills at New Lanark in the year when Napoleon became First

Consul and the English Parliament passed the Combination Laws.

During his life the population of Great Britain increased from 7,500,000 to 23,000,000, and the great economic revolution took place which subjected English society to unprecedented strains, but without which that mounting population could never have been fed. When Owen was born the application of coal to iron-working, and the industrial development of the Black Country, was in full swing. He lived through the rise of the Lancashire cotton trade. He saw fortunes made and made one himself; he beheld the nightmare misery of the factory towns and watched the early struggles of organized labour. He was sixty before Parliament was reformed, factories were inspected, or education was assisted by public money. He outlived Chartism and saw modern trade unionism founded by the establishment of the Amalgamated Society of Engineers in 1850. When he died in 1858 at the age of eighty-seven he could look back on the building of the Crystal Palace and the Crimean War.

II

Up to the age of thirty Owen's career followed the romantic pattern of the successful self-made business man.

Son of a Welsh tradesman, he learnt to read and write in the village school. By the age of seven he was acting as assistant to the schoolmaster and was reading everything that he could lay his hands upon. But he was no mere book-worm. He was a fast runner, good at games, and was popular among his companions. He went to work at the age of nine.

He was a precocious child. At the age of ten, having reached the conclusion that there was something wrong with all religion as then taught, he set out for London with forty shillings in his pocket over and above the coach fare.

A married brother in London found him a job, and for the next eight years Owen worked as a shop assistant in Stamford, in London, and then as a draper's assistant in Manchester. At Stamford 'with the greatest reluctance and after long contests in my mind' he was 'compelled to abandon my first and deep-rooted impression in favour of Christianity, but my religious feelings were immediately replaced by the spirit of universal charity, not for a sect or party or for a country or a colour, but for the human race and with a real and ardent desire to do them good'.

The clue to the whole of Owen's career is in these words. The ardent desire to do people good was the prime moving force throughout his life, and the universality of his early philanthropy was characteristic of all his thinking. There was a doctrinaire grandiosity about all his schemes which made their practical realization impossible.

He came to Manchester at the time of the rapid expansion of the cotton trade when the cottage workers could no longer afford to compete against the machinery installed by the capitalists. The population of Manchester multiplied by almost a thousand per cent from 25,000 at the time of Owen's birth to nearly a quarter of a million half a century later.

At eighteen Owen set up in business in Manchester. Within a few years he became manager of a spinning mill with five hundred work-people and then managing director of the Chorlton Twist Company. Journeys to Glasgow led in 1799 to his entry into a partnership for the purchase of the cotton mills at New Lanark. These were the first important mills in Scotland and had been founded by Dale and Arkwright. Thus Owen found himself the patriarch of an industrial village at the the age of twenty-nine. He married Dale's daughter in the same year.

At New Lanark he made a fortune. He was never interested in money for its own sake, but only as a means of putting into practice ideas which had long been forming in his mind. The first task that he set himself at New Lanark was to remedy the state of affairs among the 2,000 work-people, whom he found 'ignorant and destitute . . . indolent and much addicted to theft, drunkenness and falsehood'. Twelve years later he recorded that they had become 'conspicuously honest, industrious, sober and orderly'.

It is with Owen's educational thought and work that we are chiefly concerned. At the same time it is impossible to ignore his life as a whole. There is a unity of idea and of ultimate purpose running right through the adventures and vicissitudes of his career and Owen would have every right to protest against the taking apart from one another of the chapters of his life.

During the first quarter of the new century Owen's rôle was that of the enlightened and philanthropic employer. After a dozen years' patient and persistent labour in improving conditions of housing, sanitation, and work in the village, he published his *New View of Society* in 1813, and in 1816 opened his Institution for the Formation of Character. New Lanark suddenly became famous, and Owen himself an important public figure. It says a good deal perhaps for the ideological susceptibility of the early nineteenth century that the *New View of Society* went through five editions and was translated into French and German. Owen's central thesis was that human character is formed by environment and education is therefore the key to the re-making of society. In 1815 the government was concerned about post-war social distress and unemployment. Owen got a ready hearing for his interpretation of the slump—that the national power of economic production, enormously increased by the mechanization of industry, was left in mid-air when the war ended and markets shrank. His solution was the provision of useful employment in Villages of Co-operation founded by public money, to supersede the existing demoralizing system of poor relief. Owen believed that each village could produce a surplus and that the labourers could receive a fair remuneration.

Within two or three years, however, the government was no longer seeking remedies for unemployment, but was concentrating in some alarm upon the suppression of disorder. The Luddite riots were followed by the Six Acts and the strikes of 1818–9. Owen saw that there was now no chance of his plan being accepted by the government and in his very natural exasperation he gave full and indiscreet expression to his views about religion. Owen always dramatized himself and there is no doubt that he greatly exaggerated the importance of this famous denunciation of all religion in 1817. Nevertheless, his action finally destroyed any remaining prospects of support from the respectable classes, and Owen turned his mind to the possibility of organizing a working-class movement. He had already in his *Report to the County of Lanark* enunciated the doctrine that 'manual labour, properly directed, is the source of all wealth'.

The working classes at this time were beginning to shake

themselves free from the tutelage of intellectual radicals, and spontaneous working-class movements such as the Mechanics Institutes were beginning. Owen's doctrines were eagerly seized upon and many societies (300 of them by 1830) sprang up based on Owen's principles.

This rapid growth of Owenite societies, however, owed little or nothing to Owen's personal direction. For Owen was out of England at this critical time. The years 1824–8 were occupied by the unfortunate American interlude, as a result of which Owen lost three-quarters of his money and a great deal of his reputation. Attracted by its low price, and, as he thought, its unlimited possibilities, Owen bought the property of the Rappite community in Indiana and founded New Harmony as a model co-operative community, based on agriculture and textiles with strongly developed educational activities. After several secessions and five re-organizations the settlement failed for the simple reason that it never produced, nor was likely to produce, a surplus. Owen's two elder sons Robert and William did their best to rescue the scheme from mismanagement, and ended by becoming American citizens. It is worth noting that the survival of communitarianism in America was due not to Owenite influence, but to the religous movements (e.g., the Shakers and the Rappites) which already existed before Owen went to America.

When Owen returned to England the great topic of public interest was parliamentary reform, for which Owen never had any enthusiasm. He worked hard at the promotion of co-operative societies, many of them connected with trade unions and most of them including educational activities. The Reform Act of 1832 brought no advantage to the working classes and their disappointment was Owen's great opportunity. He lectured all over the country and emerged as the leader of the Trade Union movement—a somewhat ironical position for one who always thought and wrote of the working classes as 'they'.

Always a believer in going the whole hog, Owen organized the Grand National Consolidated Trades Union in 1834. The members of this mammoth conglomeration, most of whom already belonged to some local trade union, numbered over a million in only a few weeks. The plan was to carry out a general strike at the psychological moment and to encourage a new order of society by co-operation among the productive classes. Inevitably the ambitious scheme collapsed.

Owen never accepted defeat. At the failure of the Grand National Consolidated Trades Union he once more switched his policy and embarked on a purely cultural campaign for the regeneration of society. The text of this phase is *The Book of the New Moral World*, published in 1836. In this last and most apocalyptic stage of his development, Owen approached the great revolution 'only by truth, charity, and kindness' and he still believed that truth had but to be proclaimed in order to be received and acted upon. The names of Owen's organizations in this period became even more kaleidoscopic and portentous. He tried to gather all Owenite societies together in the British and Foreign Consolidated Association of Industry, Humanity, and Knowledge, and later in the Universal Community Society of Rational Religionists under which the country was divided into twelve missionary districts. To this period belongs the Settlement at Queenwood, of which the school was the best feature.

Owen had travelled a long way from the days of his shrewd and efficient management of a cotton mill. In these later years he had almost completely lost his grip on reality, but astonishingly had lost none of his energy. At an age when most hardworking public men are deservedly and respectably dead Owen was calling world congresses and delivering addresses to the faithful few who came to hear him, undefeated and irrepressible to the bitter end.

III

'Rarely, if ever, has education been given such unqualified primacy in social reform. Rarely, if ever, has it been conceived of so completely in social terms.' In these words A. E. Bestor, in his *Backwoods Utopias*[1], emphasizes the essential unity of Owen's conception of social regeneration. Owen's central idea, which was implicit from the outset, though he went on developing it throughout his life, was the creation of a new order of society by suitable control of environment—that is to say, by education. He states his doctrine in the first essay of *The New View of*

[1] P. 140.

Society (written in 1813 when he was thirty-two): 'In general character, from the best to the worst, from the most ignorant to the most enlightened, may be given to any community, even to the world at large, by the application of proper means; which means are to a great extent at the command and under the control of those who have influence in the affairs of men.'

He claimed that his discovery of this fundamental principle was based on 'extensive experience for upwards of twenty years, during which period its truth and importance have been proved by multiplied experiments'. The experience, to which he refers was substantially his work at New Lanark, the success of which was impressive. It did not occur to Owen, however, to question whether the achievement at New Lanark really proved his doctrine about the formation of character, and it is clear from his writings that, having once conceived his idea, he regarded it as a self-evident truth. 'In preparing the way for the introduction of these principles, it cannot now be necessary to enter into detail of facts to prove that children can be trained to acquire any language, sentiments, belief, or any bodily habits and manners, not contrary to human nature. For that this has been done the history of every nation of which we have records abundantly confirms; and that this is, and may be done again, the facts which exist around us and throughout all the countries in the world prove to demonstration.'[1] 'These principles require only to be known in order to establish them selves.'[2]

The seductive half-truth which formed the mainspring of Owen's thinking seems in fact to have commended itself to him *a priori* rather than on any systematic examination of evidence. There is no record of his having picked up the idea from his reading. He had the kind of mind which having once fastened on an idea of this kind readily convinced himself of its truth and converted his experience into evidence to support it. The famous incident of the flummery with which he scalded his stomach at the age of five is a striking example of the lengths he could go in finding evidence for his theory. After the scalding episode he always had to be careful about his food. 'This made me attend to the effects of different qualities of food on my

[1] *First Essay.*   [2] Ibid.

changed constitution, and gave me the habit of close observation and of continual reflection; and I have always thought
that this accident had a great influence in forming my character.'[1]

There is no doubt that the Islamic simplicity of Owen's
revelation was a most effective dynamic for action. It delivered
him from all manner of philosophic doubts and gave him
enormous confidence. 'This knowledge of human nature gave
me for a long period an unconscious advantage over others.'[2]

Owen seems never to have perceived the double fallacy of his
theory. In the first place he did not see that if we are wholly
the products of nature and circumstance, and if indeed no man
can be held responsible for his own character, moral responsibility disappears and good and evil cease to have any meaning.
It is remarkable that a man with such a strongly developed
moral sense and so full of zeal to do good to his fellow men
should have based his life upon a doctrine which by implication
destroys morality.

In Owen's defence it is often argued that it was the collective
character of a community, rather than that of individuals as
such, which he believed to be the product of environment.
And it is pointed out that he urged the educational importance
of studying each child as a distinct individual. There seems to
me to be no need to invoke this dubious distinction between
collective and individual character. The truth seems to be that,
like many reformers, Owen was inconsistent. On the one hand
he plainly states that 'the character of *each* of our race is
formed by God or nature and by society; and it is impossible
that any human being could or can form his own qualities or
character.'[3] There could scarcely be a more uncompromising
denial of moral responsibility. On the other hand his desire to
benefit mankind implied a lively recognition of moral value
and his interest in his fellow men and individual human beings
saved him from thinking of humanity in merely general terms.
The clue to Owen's inconsistency is not far to seek. Desiring,
as he did with all his heart, the regeneration of the human race,
it was necessary to eliminate from the picture anything that
would make that regeneration impossible. He must deny
Original Sin and must believe that all human wickedness and

[1] *Life*, pp. 2–3.   [2] Ibid., p. 30.   [3] Ibid., pp. 58–9.

misery proceeded 'solely from the ignorance of our fore-fathers'.

This is in fact Owen's second fallacy. He failed, as did Roussseau, to see that he was involved in a contradiction about the nature of history and society. If human beings are by nature rational—if, as Owen believed, it is necessary only to perceive the truth in order to pursue it, and if, moreover, history presents an inevitable progress 'from ignorance to intelligence'—it is impossible to account for the irrational elements in human affairs to which is attributed the corruption of civilization from which man needs to be delivered. In other words, if it were really as easy as Owen thought to put the world right it is the more difficult to explain how the world has got so wrong.

Owen's view of education followed directly from his doctrine about the formation of character: 'Train any population rationally, and they will be rational.'[1] In dealing with a corrupted society the first step is to remove those environmental circumstances which generate bad habits and the second stage is to educate positively for right living. In the education of the individual child the first step is to train the child from the earliest infancy in good habits, and the next stage is to awaken the child's rational understanding of the true principles of living. It is worth bearing in mind that Owen always appreci-ated the importance of adult education together with that of the education of the children. He fully realized that it was a waste of time and effort to educate children unless the adult members of the community were also made intelligently aware of their responsibilities.

Owen states his view of the raw material of education in these words: 'Children are, without exception, passive and wonderfully contrived compounds; which, by any accurate previous and subsequent attention, founded on a correct know-ledge of the subject, may be formed collectively to have any human character. And although these compounds, like all the other works of nature, possess endless varieties, yet they partake of that plastic quality, which, by perseverence under judicious management, may be ultimately moulded into the very image of rational wishes and desires.'[2]

His doctrine of the nature of education is stated as clearly as

[1] *Second Essay*.   [2] Ibid.

anywhere in an after-dinner speech at a dinner given to Joseph Lancaster in Glasgow in 1812. Education 'will be found to be, *so far at least as depends our operations,* the primary source of all the good and evil, misery and happiness, which exist in the world'. 'Man becomes a wild ferocious savage, a cannibal, or highly civilized and benevolent being, according to the circumstances in which he may be placed from his birth.' 'There are in this city and suburbs many thousand children, who, from their situation, must generally be trained to vicious habits and to poverty, unless you, gentlemen, and our fellow citizens step forth to prevent the evil.' 'Give but a rational education, now easily to be accomplished, to all those in the lower walks of life, and the character of the whole community will rise many degrees; and while none can suffer by this measure, all must be essentially benefited.'

The passages just quoted illustrate the essential features of Owen's belief about education—his missionary zeal to bring help and illumination to thousands of fellow creatures suffering misery and degradation through no fault of their own; his absolute certainty that human society could be remade by the appropriate manipulation of environmental conditions; and his naïve confidence that the benevolent revolution could be accomplished easily and quickly.

One of Owen's wisest insights into the nature of education was his grasp of the truth that education has to do with the whole of life and the whole of a human being and not only with intellectual processes. No activity is too humble and none is too lofty to be the concern of the educator. Speaking of the workpeople of New Lanark, for whom the first stage of reform consisted in the 'withdrawing some of those circumstances which tended to generate, continue or increase early bad habits' he goes on to say that little had yet been done for them positively. 'They had not been taught the most valuable domestic and social habits; such as the most economical method of preparing food; how to arrange their dwellings with neatness, and to keep them always clean and in order; but, what was of infinitely more importance, they had not been instructed how to train their children to form into valuable members of the community, or to know that principles existed, which, when properly applied to practice from infancy, would ensure from man to man, without chance of failure, a just, open, sincere, and benevolent conduct.'

Not only was education in Owen's view something which concerns the whole of a person, but he believed that the educational process could be fully satisfactory only if it was the work of the whole community. Right education in fact was the result of living in the right kind of society. It followed therefore that educational reform was inseparable from the reconstruction of society and Owen quite logically stood committed to an attempt to reform the world. The task proved more difficult than he expected.

For sixteen years at New Lanark Owen was occupied with the first step in dealing with a corrupted society—the removal of bad environmental influences. Housing and drainage were improved, and the people subjected, in the factory and in the general life of the village, to a kindly but inescapable discipline of moral persuasion. The hearts of the villagers were won when, during the American cotton embargo of 1806, Owen continued to pay their wages at a cost to himself of £7,000. No more workhouse children were received after 1809; working hours were reduced to ten and a half, and the minimum working age reduced to ten at a time when children commonly worked at the age of six for fourteen hours a day.

During these years Owen was hampered by the opposition of his partners to his improving the conditions of the workers. The quarrel with his partners in 1812, however, led to a dramatic auction sale in which Owen, backed by new partners among whom were Jeremy Bentham and some Quakers, bought out the previous owners to their great annoyance. Under the new partnership Owen had much more freedom to push ahead with his plans, until a quarrel with William Allen in 1825 over the teaching of religion virtually brought Owen's interest in New Lanark to an end.

The New View of Society had been published in 1813. The Institution for the Formation of Character was opened in 1816; and between 1815 and 1825 20,000 people signed the visitors' book. The educational system included full-time schools for children ranging from one to ten years of age (some in fact stayed till twelve); evening schools (1½ hours a day) for children over ten; and, for adults, lectures and dancing, together with

74

ROBERT OWEN

facilities for reading, writing, and sewing. Owen thus, in G. D. H. Cole's words, 'became . . . the first really creative force for adult education among the workers'. In 1816 there were some 280 children in full-time attendance, and nearly 450 between the ages of ten and twenty attending evening schools. A few continued to attend the evening schools up to the age of twenty-five, but out of forty such, all but one were girls.

No books were used in the infants' school. And it is notable that Owen, himself a voracious reader from an early age, thought that books ought not to be needed in the education of children under the age of ten. Instead of books there were pictures, models, flowers and other natural objects; and, for the older children, maps and charts. In place of formal studies there was plenty of bodily activity, including dancing; and Owen believed as fervently as Pestolozzi that, for young children, play is in itself an educative activity. There were no prizes or punishments; but all subjects were made as interesting as possible by conversation, pictures, and natural objects. Great care was given to the choice of suitable reading material. Geography, which in Owen's view was specially valuable in demonstrating the influence of environment, was taught with frequent description of places and people. The happiness and good behaviour of the children, and their kindness to one another, were remarked upon by many visitors. Apparently no provision was made in the curriculum for drawing, modelling, or other constructive work.

In every enterprise promoted by Owen education was an essential element. The schools were the best features of New Harmony and Queenwood. The Owenite societies had a strong interest in education; and, of the sixty-five branches of the Society of Rational Religionists at least fifty had educational activities at one time or another, whether classes for adults only or schools for children as well as adult classes.[1]

There is little doubt that Owen's ideas were his own. Although the chronology of his autobiography is unreliable, it is certain that *The New View* was written before he met Pestalozzi, Fellenberg, and Oberlin. He may have known something of Fellenberg in 1813, when an account of his work was published in William Allen's periodical, *The Philanthropist*. But

[1] Cf. T. E. Brassington, *Robert Owen and his Followers*.

75

it is very unlikely that Owen consciously borrowed anything from the continental reformers, and still less likely that he caught their spirit in the atmosphere of England. When he did meet the continental reformers he was specially taken with Fellenberg, and sent his two elder sons to Hofwyl. The efficient of Fellenberg's settlement no doubt appealed to Owen, and both men believed in education as an instrument for changing society.

What is perhaps more remarkable than Owen's independence of thought is the rapidity with which, outdistancing his contemporaries, he drove through to the logical conclusion that the objective must be nothing less than a reconstruction of society as a whole.

The extravagancies and absurdities of Owen's later years have obscured the wisdom of his insight into the nature of education. He appreciated the educational value of play and all kinds of practical activity; and he was preaching and practising the education of the whole child long before that modern slogan had been invented. If his doctrine of the potency of environment was dubious philosophy it embodied a needful and salutary educational truth. He grasped, as few reformers have, the organic relation between education and social change; and he realized that, ideally, education is nothing less than the whole community in action. At a time when the monitorial system was exciting public admiration, Owen would have nothing to do with education on the cheap. Finally, and most important of all virtues in an educator, Owen loved children. 'Probably the only people who would have had a really good time in Owen's model communities,' says G. D. H. Cole, 'would have been the children'.[1]

It is interesting to set against this brief catalogue of Owen's merits as an educational reformer the criticism which he provoked from William Maclure, who was mainly responsible for the educational work at New Harmony and with whom Owen irrevocably quarrelled. Maclure opposed Owen on two grounds. First, that Owen was unrealistic in his belief that adults could be reformed by education. Maclure came to the bitter conclusion that educational efforts were worth while only with orphans; in 1827 he opened a school for orphans, which

[1] *Robert Owen*, p. 110.

flourished for twenty years. The second ground of objection
was that Owen did not appreciate the meaning of intellectual
discipline. 'Like certain present-day advocates of "progressive
education" he acted as though he believed that facility in
newer techniques of instruction was an adequate substitute, in
a teacher's qualification, for the intellectual stimulus that comes
from actual participation in the advancement of knowledge.
Owen wanted to adapt the curriculum to modern life by
emphasizing the sciences, but he regarded the entertaining
presentation of a body of ascertained results as the equivalent
of a laborious and painful discipline in scientific thinking.'[1]

It was largely the comprehensive nature of Owen's vision
which ensured the failure of his plans. His logic was un-
exceptionable but his schemes were too grandiose for practical
achievement. Yet, while all his efforts for the reform of society
foundered and left no lasting mark on our national institutions,
he nevertheless was in a real sense the pioneer of a number of
important movements. He was the first systematic exponent of
modern socialism although he was never interested in political
action. The Owenite societies gave an impetus to modern
rationalism. He played his part in promoting factory reform
and his American adventure had some influence (through the
colony at Nashoba) on the anti-slavery movement. He could
fairly claim to have initiated the co-operative movement in this
country, although from its second birth at the time of the
Rochdale pioneers it followed a very different course from what
Owen had envisaged. It was Owen who made the first serious
attempt after the Combination Acts of 1799 to organize labour
for powerful action; here again the movement had to change
its whole character in order to succeed, and the Amalgamated
Society of Engineers was almost everything that the Grand
National Consolidated Trades Union was not.

In the field of education, and especially adult education,
Owen's influence on later history was mainly indirect and in-
tangible, though none the less real for that. It is true that the
first infant school in England, established by James Mill,
Brougham, and others, was intended to be a replica of the
school at New Lanark. But it turned out very unlike its prototype. Owen's real contribution was his unshakable faith in

[1] Bestor: *Backwoods Utopias*, p. 192.

education as the power for building a better world. His tomb bears a bronze plaque showing Robert Owen holding out his hand to a procession of workers, bowed with toil. The character of the English working-class movement probably owes a good deal to the fact that its acknowledged leader at a critical point in its history appealed to something more generous than class hatred and held up an ideal that embraced the fulfilment of the human spirit as well as the satisfaction of bodily needs.

IV

As a person Owen is difficult to estimate and remains somewhat baffling and paradoxical. He changed greatly as he grew older. The failure of his schemes, instead of making him pay more careful attention to practical detail, made him more grandiose in imagination and more apocalyptic in utterance, until the efficient manager of business had become a seer living more and more in a world of fantasy, increasingly portentous and reiterative.

Yet even when full allowance is made for the change that came over him, Owen remains somewhat incomprehensible. There is no doubt of his efficiency at New Lanark or of his shrewdness in his younger days. The story of how he kept his mouth shut on being appointed, at the age of eighteen, manager over five hundred workmen is often told, but is worth telling again.[1] 'I looked grave, inspected everything very minutely, examined the drawings and calculations of the machinery. . . . I continued this silent inspection and superintendence day by day for six weeks, saying merely yes or no to the questions of what was to be done or otherwise, and during that period I did not give one direct order about anything. But at the end of that time I felt myself so much master of my position as to be ready to give directions in every department.' Yet he showed such incompetence at New Harmony, when he was only fifty-three and ought to have been still at the height of his powers, that his blunders were the despair of his two sons. The contrast between the efficiency of New Lanark and the débâcle of New Harmony can harely be attributed to the unfamiliarity of the geographical and social conditions in America; for Owen's basic mistakes at

[1] *Life*, p. 29.

New Harmony would have been elementary errors anywhere —the failure to apply any principle of selection to the settlers, the failure to define their status (whether partners, tenants, or employees) and the failure to appreciate the fact that the settlement was consuming more than it produced.

Owen's personal defects are only too obvious. He had no sense of humour—though he was invariably good humoured; which, however, is not the same thing. His curiously rigid and literal mind rendered him incapable of making allowances at the level of theoretical planning for the contrary imperfections of human nature. Anyone for whom the doctrine of original sin is not a self-evident truth must be lacking in humour and one would like to be able to place Owen, with his extraordinary doctrine of the formation of character and the perfectibility of human society, face to face with someone like G. K. Chesterton and listen to the conversation that ensued. If he had possessed a sense of humour, how much more he could have relished the retrospect of his own life. Yet he had been capable of seeing life as a joke, he would have lived it very differently.

He was a poor judge of men and of the effects of his actions upon public opinion. His son Robert once wrote to him[1]: 'His weak point always was to believe in everybody and everything that favoured, or professed to favour, his peculiar views.' Owen's power of believing whatever he wished to believe and of ignoring whatever he did not wish to see can scarcely ever have been exceeded. Harriet Martineau, who got Owen to promise to read the Four Gospels in return for her promise to read Hamlet as a lesson in necessitarianism, commented: 'Robert Owen is not the man to think differently of a book for having read it, and that from no want of candour, but simply from more than the usual incapability to see more than what he has made up his mind to see.'[2]

Intellectually naïve, Owen's explanation of human problems (his 'one idea') was far too simple. And like many self-educated men he had an exaggerated opinion of the power of knowledge and ideas. His theory of education was for him a flaming sword with a few strokes of which he believed he could destroy the forces of darkness. Owen's great mistake was that he believed

[1] Letter to M. P. Trist, quoted by Bestor, op. cit., p. 187, n. 94.
[2] *Autobiography*, quoted Podmore, *Robert Owen* (1906), ii, 634.

that it was necessary only to behold truth in order to pursue it—
that, as Plato thought, virtue is a function of knowledge. 'These
principles require only to be known in order to establish themselves.' Owen never achieved the deeper insight revealed in the
collect for the first Sunday after Epiphany which recognizes
that it is one thing 'to perceive and know what things we ought
to do' and quite another thing to 'have grace and power faithfully to fulfil the same'. Making no allowance in his estimate of
human nature for what the theologians call original sin, he fell
into the Promethian illusion that man can perfect himself by his
own reason and ingenuity. Mr. G. D. H. Cole somewhere says
of Owen that, despite his rejection of orthodox religion he was
deeply religious by nature. The truth would rather seem to be
that he was profoundly ethical by nature; for the assumption
that man is self-perfectible is fundamentally irreligious. As to his
rejection of religion, his natural lack of humour perhaps helped
to betray him. If he had not started with the solemn and absurd
assumption that man is a rational being he would not have
evolved the argument that the acrimonious warfare between
religious sects proved that no religion was true; rather he
would have realized that the fiercer the controversy the more
likely there is to be some truth worth fighting about.

Owen was intensely sure that he was right, and was only
saved from gross arrogance by his kindliness and personal
modesty. The adulation which he received from some of his
disciples was enough to turn anyone's head. Of his denunciation
of religion in 1817[1] he wrote: 'The deed was done. Truth had
escaped, as it were by a miracle.' And he bought 30,000 copies
of *The Times* containing his address and sent them to leading
people all over the country. He believed that the effect of that
day had begun at once, and would continue ever afterwards.
That is to say, he took to himself the credit for having set
religion on its decline in the modern world.

He was indefatigable in expounding the truth as he saw it.
One cannot but pity his fellow travellers who had no escape
from him during the five weeks voyage to New York in 1824.
He became more and more prosy as he grew older, and his un-
deviating and long-winded insistence that humanity will
become virtuous if it can be got to see the truth made him one

[1] *Life*, p. 163.

of the greatest bores of his time. With Owen genius very nearly
was an infinite capacity for taking pains; and this capacity can
become very tedious.

He had a passion for important people and loved to send
copies of his writings to crowned heads and ministers of state.
In his later years he became an incorrigible tuft-hunter, and not
even death could remove the great out of the range of his hob-
nobbing; H.R.H. the Duke of Kent continued to oblige with
communications from beyond the veil. Yet Owen when young
was popular wherever he went; he had friends who were faithful to him all through life, and many people testified to his
personal charm and persuasive eloquence. This doctrinaire,
humourless, long-winded, irrepressible, obstinate man must
have had great virtues to compensate for these heavy liabilities.

He was an original. Naïve in its general conception, yet
ingenious in its elaboration, his thought was never second-
hand. It is always refreshing to meet someone who is free from
the intellectual parasitism so common in the academic world.
Owen at least did his own thinking.

He was without guile and without malice. His utter and un-
affected simplicity of mind and heart endeared him to his
friends and disarmed his enemies.

He loved his fellow men. It is comparatively easy to love
humanity as a kind of academic gesture. But Owen did more.
He liked people; and the simple truth is that people like to be
liked. Anthony Trollope's mother wrote in 1829 of Owen's
gentleness, kindliness, and genuine affection for his fellow
human beings.

He never argued. It is a fact that argument annoys people
more than assertion. Argument leaves the victim no escape; he
must argue back or accept defeat. Assertion strikes a blow but
leaves the victim a free man. Owen endlessly asserted. But he
waited quite politely for people to agree with him. And many
found themselves drawn unaccountably in his direction.

Finally, he had invincible courage and unlimited zest for
life. He was never dispirited by defeat or embittered by failure.
First in school in the morning (even at the cost of scalding his
stomach with porridge) and first in the race home—from those
early days at Newton to his last battle with death, he was game.
One day in 1857 he travelled in great pain to Liverpool to

address the National Association for the Promotion of Social Sciences. He was hoisted to the platform by four policemen and introduced by his old friend Lord Brougham. Owen was unable to deliver more than a few sentences, though these he uttered 'in his grand manner', proclaiming 'his ancient message of science, competence, and goodwill to the world'. Brougham then tactfully intervened, clapping his hands and saying: 'Capital, very good, can't be better, Mr. Owen! There, that will do.' There could be worse epitaphs.

4

BENTHAM AND THE UTILITARIANS

*

N. HANS

A lecture delivered at King's College on 30 January 1951;
Sir Fred Clarke in the chair.

Jeremy Bentham and the Utilitarians are considered abroad as typically English. Bentham's 'felicific calculus' or merchant's account of profit and loss, as the basis of moral philosophy, was accepted as the expression of English national character. Napoleon even called Englishmen 'the nation of shopkeepers'. It is true that utilitarian motives were always present in the works of English-speaking philosophers. Bacon, Hobbes, Locke, Hume, Paley, Priestley could all be called utilitarians even before the school was firmly established by Bentham. But it would be a misconception to identify utilitarianism with the English national tradition. Taken in its narrow, Benthamite, meaning, utilitarianism does not reflect the complexity and fulness of the English way of life and thought. The builders of the English cultural heritage invariably coupled utilitarian motives with spiritual ideals that surpass the narrow mercenary appeal. Whether we mention Wycliffe or Sir Thomas More, Jerard Winstanley or Archbishop Cranmer, they all believed in absolute spiritual ideals based on the Christian tradition. The founder of English philosophy, Francis Bacon, wanted to build a Solomon's House to promote the knowledge of secret motions of things and the enlarging of the bounds of human empire to the effecting of all things possible. . . . It is dedicated to the study of the works and creatures of God.[1] Here we see clearly expressed three motives for scientific research: a religious motive to understand the Divine purpose in the world, an intellectual motive to study the secrets of nature, and the utilitarian motive to improve man's estate. Behind the astonishing growth of science and inventions engendered by the Royal Society and the English pioneers of the seventeenth and eighteenth centuries all three motives are founded in combination. Robert Boyle, Isaac Newton, John Locke, Bishop Berkeley, Joseph Priestley, Richard Price, all these Englishmen and a host of lesser lights were believing Christians. Their interpretation of Christianity was often unorthodox and ran counter to the traditional attitude of the High Church party, but no one doubts that they believed in God and in absolute values. They looked indeed upon science as a further justification of Christian revelation. The Comenian idea of *propagatio fidei per scientia* was the moving force of their scientific activities. Thus up to the very end of the eighteenth century the three reasons for progress in science in England were united. Only in their unity do they represent the fullness of the English tradition. Separated from each other they become narrow and distort the national heritage. The religious attitude divorced from the intellectual and utilitarian aspects has ever been apt to take the shape of denominational fanaticism and intolerance. The utilitarian approach when it ignores spiritual values degenerates into a narrow hedonistic calculation of pain and pleasure.

Scientific discoveries led to new inventions applied in industry and agriculture. The industrial revolution enlarged men's faith in machinery and mass production. Numerous articles, pamphlets, and even books exalted 'useful knowledge' and the application of science 'to arts and crafts'. Mechanical improvements they held to be the main spring of human progress. Religion, literature, the fine arts, and even pure science were contemptuously brushed aside to make place for utilitarian mechanical inventions. As a contemporary versifier expressed it (1774):

> *'Tis great, 'tis wonderful, sublime,*
> *No doubt to build the lofty rime!*

[1] *New Atlantis, Works,* edited J. Spedding, iii. 145.

But deaf to what the poet sings
Tho' charm his muse the ears of kings,
The 'patriot' sees more wit and good in
Th' invention of a marrow pudding!

This preference for marrow puddings, however, did not bring with it a greater standard of life for the lower classes. The economic and social consequences of the industrial revolution have been too frequently described to be repeated again. The unity of English society, although based on a hierarchy of status, was disrupted. The closely knit rural community receded before the new slums. The growing conflict between two opposed classes of capitalists and proletarians, afforded a classical example for Karl Marx in his *Capital*. Economic cleavages were growing ominously when Jeremy Bentham started his crusade.

The famous formula, 'the greatest happiness of the greatest number', accepted by Bentham as the main principle of his moral philosophy, was not invented by him. He found it in the works of Beccaria, Helvetius, and Priestley; and he himself stated that he took it from Priestley. None of these writers, however, nor any English utilitarian before Bentham, had based his moral philosophy exclusively on the 'felicific calculus' of pain and pleasure. It was Bentham who accepted it as the governing principle of moral behaviour. 'Nature' says Bentham 'has placed mankind under the governance of two sovereign masters, *pain* and *pleasure*. It is for them alone to point out what we ought to do, as well as to determine what we shall do.'[1] Rules of moral behaviour whether individual or social, according to Bentham, are logically deduced from this statement and calculated by what I called the merchant's account of profit and loss. In his definitions Bentham did not distinguish morality from legality, for him what is legal is *ipso facto* moral. Kant wrote his books in vain: Bentham did not study them. Although it is obvious to an average uneducated man, that prostitution, for instance, though not a crime yet is immoral, this distinction was not recognized by Bentham. To what lengths his lack of moral sense, and I would add his lack of taste, could lead him is shown by his defence of infanticide and

[1] *An Introduction to the Principles of Morals and Legislation* (Chap. i, opening sentence).

homosexuality. Impressed by the Malthusian arguments on the surplus of population and the resulting misery, Bentham openly advocated homosexuality as the best substitute for birth control.[1]

It is evident that his attitude towards religious tradition was openly hostile and irreverent. He devoted a whole volume to an attack on the Church of England, and his biassed and un-historical approach led him to make sweeping generalizations. Religion is always 'perverted', is always a system full of hypo-crisy, foolish superstititions, and deliberate lies. 'Religion', says Bentham 'not only in the Church of England form, but in every form, is seen hanging on a thread . . . which is in continual danger of being cut; while, without the support of their arm, the powers of the Almighty is in constant danger of being over-borne, his intentions defeated, his promises violated. To these to whom the promises of their God afford not any sufficient assurance, it were not to be expected that any firmer assurance should be afforded by any human promises.'[2] In a book en-titled *An Analysis of the Influence of the Natural Religion on the Temporal Happiness of Mankind*, published in 1822 by George Grote from the papers of Bentham, the utilitarian point of view on religion is clearly expressed. 'Whether the doctrines be true or false, is a point on which I do not intend to touch. If false, they may be useful: if true, they might be dangerous. The question, therefore, is, throughout, only as to comparative magnitude, number, and proportion of bad and good effects produced.' It is usual for historians of education to blame the High Church party for the atmosphere of denominational in-tolerance and resulting 'religious difficulty' in education. It seems that the blame should be shared by Bentham and his followers. By their negative attitude towards religion they alienated their nonconformist allies and gave an excuse for the defensive position taken by the High Church party. The 'religious difficulty' of England was a very mild conflict in comparison with the struggle between Catholicism and secularism in Latin countries. It is just because Bentham failed to win the support of the majority of English intellectuals that England was spared the internecine wars of France, Spain, and other Latin countries. And it is not astonishing that Bentham was hailed as a prophet in the Catholic-secular countries of

[1] In appendix to *The Theory of Legislation*.　　　[2] *Works* xiv. 42.

Europe and America and in Orthodox-secular Russia, whilst his influence upon social attitudes in Protestant countries was slight.

We are not now discussing the utilitarian philosophy of Bentham, but his contribution to educational theory and practice. His moral philosophy is untenable, logically inconsistent, and psychologically unsound. When John Stuart Mill in his loyalty to his father's friend attempted to vindicate Bentham's principles, he unintentionally refuted them. Admittedly, however, Bentham's moral theory serves as a necessary background for the study of his schemes of educational reform. Many sound ideas found in his educational writings were vitiated by his narrow utilitarian approach. In the field of legal and social action, where the utilitarian point of view is legitimate, Bentham was undoubtedly an outstanding pioneer. He greatly influenced legal and social reform in all the English-speaking countries, in Spain, Russia, India, and Latin America. But if we are to call him a pioneer in the field of education we must make substantial reservations. Here his influence was mostly indirect and not always of a positive character. Before I turn to the main theme of this chapter I would like to dwell for a moment on what I call 'the Russian episode' in Bentham's career.

When Bentham went to Russia in 1786 to spend a year and a half with his brother Samuel at Krichev, near Mogilev in White Russia, Catherine II was firmly established on the throne and as recently as 1782 she had reformed the state system of education founded by Peter the Great in 1701. Peter the Great was, perhaps, the greatest utilitarian of the eighteenth century. In his educational measures he followed utilitarian principles faithfully and ruthlessly. His first institution was the 'School of navigation and mathematics' in Moscow and it served as the centre of the whole subsequent system of schools. It was modelled on the Royal Mathematical School at Christ's Hospital, and the first teachers were two English alumni of Christ's Hospital.[1] All the schools founded by Peter were utilitarian based on 'real' scientific knowledge and mathematics. There was no place for the traditional classical subjects

---

[1] N. Hans, 'The Moscow School of Mathematics and Navigation (1701)', *Slavonic Review*, vol. xxix, no. 73, 1951.

whether of Western Latin or East European Greek-Slavonic origin. The schools trained craftsmen, engineers, soldiers, sailors, teachers, and civil servants. Religion, literature, and the fine arts were conspicuous by their absence. When Catherine undertook a general reform of the educational system she did not change its secular and utilitarian character established by Peter. In her secondary schools only five hours a week were devoted to religion and nine hours to Russian, whilst twelve hours were allotted to modern languages, twenty-seven hours to geography and history, twenty-seven hours to sciences and mathematics, and eighteen hours to drawing. It was a modern or a 'real' school in the full sense of the term. There were, however, two important innovations. First the school system was intended for the whole population and not only for those who would be professional specialists, and, secondly, it was co-educational, open to both sexes on equal terms.

It was known at that time in England that Peter's schools were based on English models. When Samuel Bentham went to Russia in 1780 he had a letter of introduction to Sir James Harris, the British Ambassador, which said: 'It is a great triumph for the memory of Peter the Great that an Englishman should go to learn shipbuilding in Russia'.[1] That Jeremy Bentham also knew about Peter's reforms and admired him is evident from several allusions to Peter in his works. That he was cognisant of the nature of Catherine's school reforms may be presumed from the following facts. When Samuel settled at Krichev to build ships and train personnel for the navy, he could find only a few men who were able to assist him in this task. One of his assistants was a teacher of mathematics in Kremenchug secondary school. He happened to be a native of Strasburg and spoke French. Thus when Jeremy Bentham arrived at Krichev in February, 1786, he was able to speak French with this Alsatian; and during the long winter evenings when Samuel was absent for weeks on end, Bentham[2] doubtless met the teacher and heard about the Catherinian secondary

[1] Letter by Sir Gilbert Elliot of 14th July 1779, quoted by S. M. Bentham in her biography of Samuel Bentham.

[2] In his letter to Alexander I of Russia of May 1814 (*Works*, vol. ii, ed. J. Bowring) Bentham says: 'of the particularities of Russia I am not altogether without experience. Two of the most observant years of my life were passed within her limits.'

schools. Thus Bentham came into contact with the new school system, maintained by the state, secular in character, utilitarian, modern in curriculum, and co-educational. All these features reappear in his scheme of Chrestomathic schools. Another point is of interest. Samuel Bentham, as colonel of a Siberian regiment, opened in 1789 a school for his soldiers and their children, where he introduced the method of mutual instruction by pupils. Jeremy Bentham certainly knew about that experiment before he heard of Dr. Bell's Madras system. The most important result of the Russian episode was the invention of the panopticon. According to Jeremy Bentham's own statement[1] the idea was his brother's but the name was supplied by him. Samuel Bentham had thousands of soldiers and workers under his control at Krichev, and for better supervision he devised a circular building with wings radiating from the centre, all of which were within the chief officers' constant view. The name panopticon described the purpose of the building. Jeremy took up the idea and, with Samuel's assistance, prepared plans for such buildings suitable both for prisons and schools. The story of his unsuccessful attempt at prison reform is well-known. The failure of King George III and his aristocratic government to fulfil their promises to Bentham drove him into republicanism. In this mood it was easy for James Mill to convert him to democracy. That Bentham was not a democrat by conviction is evident from his relations with autocratic monarchs and his hopes of reform through the medium of enlightened despots. He enjoined his brother Samuel to use all means of finding favour with Catherine in order to promote his ideas of legal reforms. He calls her 'our dear Kitty' and says in his letter 'she is well-worth a little trouble'.[2] Bentham was well aware of the methods of promotion employed by Catherine and his innuendo is unmistakable in the letter. As it happened, Samuel fell in love with a Russian girl of aristocratic family, and after an unsuccessful wooing he retired to Krichev. Even after his disappointment in George III and his conversion to republicanism we still find Bentham putting his faith in enlightened despots like Alexander I. The panopticon is the

[1] J. Bentham, *Works*, xi. 97.
[2] Letter to Samuel of 28th December 1779, quoted by Halévy, *Growth of Philosophic Radicalism*, p. 86.

embodiment of the idea of enlightened absolutism. Whether in prison or in schools the all-powerful autocrat controls every movement of prisoners or pupils with a complicated system of rewards and punishments and with unremitting supervision of their work and behaviour. It is interesting to note that Russian prisons during the Tsarist period and the Russian concentration camps during the Soviet regime were built and organized according to the panopticon model. Bentham even advocated placing a swivel gun in the central circle on an elevation to control the whole prison in case of revolt. The machine-gun in a central tower controlling the concentration camp is only a modern adaptation of the same idea. His Chrestomathic school in a panopticon building was the educational equivalent of his prison.

Chrestomathia means useful learning and was known in the eighteenth century as a term for a collection of articles of useful knowledge. The word was used in Russia in that sense and has become a part of ordinary Russian speech. Yet it has not been accepted for general use in western Europe.[1] Under this title, in 1815–7, Bentham published his famous contribution to educational theory and practice. There was little which could be described as new and original in the views expressed in this book. We may discuss them under three headings: the organization of the school, the curriculum, and the general principles.

As we have seen the school building was to be designed on the panopticon model with one school-room for 600 pupils. 'The above number is understood to be generally regarded as the greatest number, that, in one and the same *school-room*, can be taught under the constant inspection of one and the same Master.'[2] Apart from the panopticon principle, the whole organization of school work was modelled on the Bell-Lancaster monitorial system, which is too well-known to need recounting here. Bentham thus describes the advantages of the monitorial system which results in the 'maximisation' of effort. (1) *Saving in money*. Every professional teacher would need to be paid; no such scholar-teacher needs to be, or is paid. (2) *Saving in time*.

[1] Basedow published his *Chrestomathia* in 1776 in Latin and it seems that Bentham alluded to it when he stated that the term had been used before.
[2] *Chrestomathia*, p. 73.

Under the inspection of one professional general master, the whole number of scholars may be cast into as many classes as there are different branches of instruction . . . the instruction of all these classes going on at the same time. (3). *Increase in relative aptitude.* The grown-up professional teacher has only one motive for his work—the fear of being dismissed. 'In it he can find neither instruction, amusement, nor, except that fear, any other cause of interest.' The scholar-teacher, on the contrary, acquires honour and power as a reward. Whilst a grown-up under-master is liable to have an opinion of his own, and with that a will of his own, contrary to that of his superior and employer', the juvenile monitor will be 'a completely subject teacher'. At the same time 'by teaching others he is teaching himself'. 'The application of this principle,' says Bentham, 'is an essential feature operating to the complete and purposed exclusion of all such naturally reluctant and untractable (grown-up) subordinates.' It is the same principle of utilitarian despotism which was to be applied in prison reform. The prestige of Bentham's name made the Bell-Lancaster system universally accepted and thus the spiritual vigour of English education was vitiated for many decades. That mutual instruction within limits could be used with advantage cannot be denied. Pillans adapted monitorial methods in his Edinburgh High School with great success; but he did not abolish separate class lessons, nor did he dismiss his professional assistants. It was this prepossession with the greatest numbers and the bookkeeper's calculus of expenses which made the system so vicious. Industrial methods of mass production with their total disregard for the human factor were simply transferred into the schools. Even after Bentham's death this principle haunted English education in the utilitarian system of 'payment by results'.

In the matter of the curriculum, Bentham was more original and more progressive. His curriculum is entirely modern or 'real' and is divided into six stages according to age-groups. The whole course lasts seven years from seven to fourteen. The preparatory stage is devoted to the three R's. *Stage I* includes natural history, geometry, and drawing. *Stage II*—all parts of physics and chemistry, geometry, geography, history, drawing, and comparative grammar. *Stage III*—application of sciences to industry and agriculture, geography, geometry, history, drawing, and grammar. *Stage IV*—all branches of medical science, geometry, geography, history, grammar, and drawing. *Stage V*—mathematics, astronomy, history, drawing, grammar, technology, book-keeping, and commercial subjects. The fine arts, physical training and sports, religion and literature are specifically omitted. There is little originality in his curriculum. Modern schools existed in the eighteenth century in Russia, France, and Germany, and were known to Bentham. His contacts with Russia have already been mentioned; his contacts with France were extensive and personal. Brissot and Condorcet were his friends and correspondents, and he certainly knew the educational schemes of the revolutionary period, and in particular Condorcet's project of a modern and technological curriculum and the *écoles centrales* of the Convention. But it was not necessary to cross the channel to find an example of a modern school. The Royal Mathematical School at Christ's Hospital was founded in 1672 and private academies with scientific technological curriculum abounded in England in the eighteenth century.[1] At the turn of the century about two hundred academies were spread over England. Moreover Bentham had personal knowledge of these institutions. In one of his letters he mentioned Elphinstone, master of Kensington Academy, and said that he had dined with him in his school. Bentham very often visited Bath. In the beginning of the nineteenth century there was a well-known academy, kept by Florian, which had a curriculum almost identical with the Chrestomathic School. But in addition to all the subjects mentioned by Bentham, Florian included the fine arts, literature, and physical exercise. Bentham was also well acquainted with the famous school at Hazelwood, kept by Sir Rowland Hill, and he advised Rivadavia, the Argentine leader, to send his two sons to it. Rivadavia was so much impressed by its modern curriculum that he sent six other Argentine boys to Hazelwood. Bentham himself sent two Greek boys there and paid for their maintenance. Thus there is no lack of evidence that Bentham was well aware of the 'academy' practice in England. His curriculum was no original invention but a repetition of existing examples with the utilitarian omission of literature, the fine

[1] N. Hans, *New Trends in Education in the Eighteenth Century* (Kegan Paul, 1951), chap. iii, iv, and v.

arts, and physical exercise, and that was surely no improvement.[1]

In his general ideas on educational aims and principles
Bentham is as narrowly utilitarian as on organization and
curriculum. The aim of education is thus defined by him:
'Education is a series of conduct directed to an end; before any
directions can properly be given for the education of any
person, the end of education must be settled. The common end
of every person's education is Happiness.' We must always
remember that it is not the happiness of each individual human
being that matters, but the happiness of the greatest number.
Bentham himself is conscious that his harsh discipline of unremitting supervision in a panopticon school could hardly
produce what Kant would call autonomous persons. Bentham
asks these questions: 'Whether the liberal spirit and energy of
a free citizen would not be exchanged for the mechanical
discipline of a soldier or the austerity of a monk?' And—
'Whether the result of this high-wrought contrivance might
not be constructing a set of *machines* under the similitude of
men? To give a satisfactory answer to all these queries . . . it
would be necessary to recur at once to the end of education.
Would *happiness* be most likely to be increased or diminished
by this discipline? Call them soldiers, call them monks, call them
machines; so they were but happy ones, I should not care.'[2]
If we were to apply Bentham's 'felicific calculus' to measure
the amount of pleasure and pain produced by the application
of the monitorial organization of Bell and Lancaster among the
pupils and teachers I am rather doubtful as to the outcome on
the balance-sheet. The general views of Bentham on education
are neither original nor very striking. When he says that 'observation and experiment compose the basis of all knowledge',
he repeats Bacon, Comenius, Locke, Rousseau, Priestley, and
Pestalozzi, and most of the practical masters of the eighteenth
century. When he advocates the common education of both
sexes he follows the practice of the Russian state system of 1782.
Florian of Bath Academy advocated co-education before Ben-

[1] Although I cannot find any reference in Bentham's writing to the
educational ideas and practice of David Williams it is certain that Bentham
knew of him through their personal mutual friend Brissot. Williams received
French citizenship at the same time as Bentham.

[2] *Panopticon Schools. Works*, iv, 64.

tham and Mrs. Florian conducted an academy for girls on the same modern-scientific lines as her husband's boys' school. From all this evidence, it appears that Bentham has not contributed anything original to the theory and practice of education in the sense of offering novelties. He was not an educationist and we should not expect a lawyer to be an expert in education. His greatness lies in another field, in the domain of legislation and state action. From this broader point of view and in a somewhat indirect fashion he can justly claim a place among the pioneers of English education. Professor Francis Cavenagh pointed out in his article on the centenary of Bentham's death,[1] that Bentham's insistence on State intervention was his most important contribution towards English education. 'Education' said Bentham, 'is only government acting by means of the domestic magistrate.'[2] In preventing crime, the State has, through education, to help the family. 'In regarding education as an indirect mode of 'preventing offences, it requires an essential reform,' wrote Bentham in 1802. 'The most neglected class must become the principal object of care. The less parents are able to discharge this duty, the more necessary it is for the government to fulfil it. It ought not only to watch over orphans left in indigence, but also over the children whose parents no longer deserve the confidence of the law with regard to this important charge.' In his *Tracts on Poor Laws and Pauper Management*, he again insisted on state intervention in education. 'The multitude included under the denomination of the poor, compose the bulk of the community. . . . If, in point of real importance the education of the rich can bear any comparison with that of the poor, it can only be in respect of the influence which the conduct of the former class has over the latter. . . . Yet these are the classes whose case is so generally overlooked by the writers on education: partly as not being worthy of their notice; partly as not lying within their reach.'[3]

His plan of education for the House of Industry (1797) was the starting point for factory legislation with its recognition of the principle of compulsory attendance. The activities of Sir Edwin Chadwick, Bentham's secretary, in this field are the direct result of Bentham's influence. In connection with his

[1] Drittes Heft, *International Education Review*, 1932–3.
[2] *Principles of Penal Laws, Works*, ii, 589.   [3] *Works*, viii, 395.

industry schools, Bentham proposed to establish a National Charity Company for the collection of relative data to augment useful knowledge. 'The institution of the proposed Company would afford the first opportunity ever presented to mankind, enriching the treasury of useful knowledge by contributions furnished on a national scale, and on a regular and self-embracing plan.'[1] 'It was the same desire for exact data,' says Cavenagh, 'that led him to secure the official recognition of births, deaths, and vital statistics.' 'Indeed,' adds Cavenagh, 'this collateral application of the proposed industry house-system has proved more important than the scheme itself.'[2] We should also mention Bentham's suggestions for the recruit-ment of the civil service as another indirect contribution to the cause of education. Thus Bentham's influence was greatest in the field of state action and national planning. Here the activities of a whole band of his followers, the Benthamites or the 'education-mad party' made a direct contribution to education, which the hermit of Queen's Square Place was unable to make himself.

But before we discuss their work we have to pay special attention to the greatest of them, Bentham's friend and colla-borator, James Mill. Mill himself denied being Bentham's disciple 'though he was drawn to Mr. Bentham by the sympathy of common opinions, and by the respect due to a man who had done more than anybody else to illustrate and recommend doctrines, which were of first-class importance to the happiness of mankind'.[3] Whether Mill was a disciple of Bentham is debatable, but that he influenced Bentham in his turn and was instrumental in bringing the latter into the camp of democracy is firmly established. As Halévy sums it up: 'Mill rendered Bentham as much service as Bentham rendered Mill. Bentham gave Mill a doctrine, and Mill gave Bentham a school.'[4] James Mill is as much a utilitarian as Bentham in accepting 'the greatest happiness of the greatest number' as the final touchstone of moral behaviour. However, Mill is very cautious in his definition of happiness and leaves it 'undetermined'. He even considers the possibility of intellectual as well as moral

[1] *Works*, viii, 424.   [2] Drittes Heft, *Intern. Ed. Review*, 1932–3.
[3] *Fragment on Mackintosh*, p. 124.
[4] *The Growth of Philosophic Radicalism*, p. 291.

forms 'which can by no means be resolved into the grosser elements of the senses'.[1] Thus he approaches much closer the ideal of morality and draws the distinction between moral and legal behaviour. He also considers calculation as necessary for good behaviour. 'Morality is an attribute of intention', says Mill, 'and an intention is then only good when the act intended has in sum of its ascertainable consequences a superiority of good over evil'.[2] But as men live in society they provide each other with motives for doing moral actions and abstaining from immoral ones. Here Mill almost abandons the calculation of pain and pleasure in favour of unselfish altruistic actions, because it is important for other men that each man should act without a personal interest in the results of his action. Mill is still reluctant to quit the firm foundation of pain and pleasure, but by his acceptance of spiritual pleasures valued as superior to sensual ones, he anticipates the argument of his son John Stuart Mill. This is no longer Bentham's 'felicific calculus' consisting of simple addition and subtraction of quantities of pain and pleasure.

According to the testimony of John Stuart Mill in his *Autobiography*, James Mill 'deemed very few of pleasures worth the price which must be paid for them. The greater number of miscarriages in life, he considered, to be attributable to the over-valuing of pleasures.' The puritanical Scottish upbringing made itself felt and it showed through the verbal acceptance of Bentham's principles. In his religious views, James Mill was an agnostic. 'This is the only correct statement of his opinions,' says John Stuart Mill. 'For dogmatic atheism he looked upon as absurd. . . . My father's rejection of all that is called "religious belief" was not primarily a matter of logic and evidence: the grounds of it were moral still more than intellectual.' And he continues, 'of unbelievers, as well as of believers, there are many species, including almost every variety of moral type. But the best among them . . . are more genuinely religious, in the best sense of the word, religion, than those who exclusively arrogate to themselves the title.'

If James Mill attacked Christian creeds and Christian churches it was primarily because in his opinion they deviated from the high spiritual ideal announced by the founder of

[1] *On Education*, section iii.   [2] *Fragment on Mackintosh*, p. 164.

Christianity.[1] Allying himself with utilitarians and with atheists like Francis Place in a common campaign against the monopoly of the Church of England, James Mill was in fact much nearer to the Protestant dissenters than he knew. In his educational views he was more consistent and lucid than Bentham; and his article on education even now can be read with profit, whereas the unreadable *Chrestomathia* is of interest only as a historical document. Mill's educational theory stands on three legs: first his emphasis on the psychological approach and the doctrine of association of ideas; secondly his belief in the progress of humanity and the perfectibility of human nature; thirdly, his sincere adherence to a democratic theory of government, with popular universal education as a necessary prerequisite. Mill himself states that his doctrine of association of ideas is taken from the writings of Locke, Hume, Condillac and Hartley. He applies the doctrine to education and maintains that 'the business is . . . to put the knowledge which we possess respecting the human mind, into that order and form, which is most advantageous for drawing from it the practical rules of education.[2]

If the modern psychologist rejects the associationist doctrine of Mill as out-dated by more recent research, his main principle holds good in all times. The belief in the perfectibility of human nature was taken by Mill from Condorcet: it led to the same conclusion about the omnipotence of education. Mill is conscious of the influence of heredity and innate individual differences, but the social differences between the classes were, it seems to him, due entirely to environment and education. 'This much at any rate is ascertained', says Mill, 'that all the difference which exists, or can ever be made to exist, between one class of men and another, is wholly owing to education.' He here repeats in his own words the well-known statement of Robert Owen that 'any character . . . may be given to *any community*'. Thus education is conceived as a means of social reform to produce a truly democratic society.

In his optimism Mill overestimated both the simple structure

[1] In 1812 Mill published *Schools for all, not Schools for Churchmen only*. Here he advocated undenominational schools accepting Christian tradition as a common basis.
[2] *On Education*, section i.

of our mind and the power of education for our social regeneration. The article *On Education* begins in the approved utilitarian manner: 'The end of education is to render the individual . . . an instrument of happiness, first to himself, and next to other beings.' To attain this end Mill enumerates 'the qualities of mind, to the production of which the business of education should be directed'. The first quality is *intelligence*. 'But mere knowledge is not enough; a mere magazine of remembered facts is a useless treasure. The ingredients of intelligence are two, knowledge and sagacity. This union, then of copiousness and energy; this possession of numerous ideas, with the masterly command of them' is one of the ends of education.

A second quality necessary for happiness is 'a perfect command over man's appetites and desires. This is what the ancient philosophers called *temperance*'. To these two individual qualities Mill adds two social ones necessary for the happiness of other men—*justice* and *generosity*. 'It thus appears,' says Mill, 'that the science of Ethics, as well as the science of intellectuals, must be carried to perfection, before the best foundation is obtained for the science of Education.' Mill's conclusion that psychology and ethics form the bases of education transcends the narrow utilitarian approach of Bentham. When he comes to the application of these principles, Mill quite rightly includes in education the physical and social environments from the earliest age and extends education after the formal school training to the adult stage.

Following Rousseau and Helvetius, Mill emphasizes the importance of proper nurture in infancy and of pre-school training. Using this broader meaning of education, Mill divides it into four branches. Under *domestic* education he 'denotes all the child hears and sees, more especially all that it is made to suffer or enjoy at the hands of others, and all that it is allowed or constrained to do' in the parental house. It is most important because the 'primary habits form the fundamental character of the man'. The second branch he calls *technical* education. This includes general basic education and vocational training.

'There are certain qualities, the possession of which is desirable in all classes. There are certain qualities, the possession of which is desirable in some, not in others. As far as those qualities extend which ought to be common to all, there ought to be a correspondent training for all. It is only in respect to those qualities which are not desirable in all, that a difference in the mode of training is required.'

The qualities of intelligence, temperance, and benevolence, are desirable for all and should be the main business of education. Technical education, however, is having chiefly to do with intelligence.

'Till recently, it was denied, that intelligence was a desirable quality in the great body of the people; and as intelligence is power, such is an unavoidable opinion in the breasts of those who think that the human race ought to consist of two classes —one that of the oppressors, another that of the oppressed. . . The question whether the people should be educated, is the same with the question, whether they should be happy or miserable. The question whether they should have more or less of intelligence is merely the question, whether they should have more or less of misery, when happiness might be given in its stead. . . . As we strive for an equal degree of justice, an equal degree of temperance, an equal degree of veracity, in the poor as in the rich, so ought we to strive for an equal degree of intelligence. . . . Besides the knowledge of faculties, which all classes should possess in common, there are branches of knowledge and art, which they cannot all acquire, and in respect to which, education must undergo a corresponding variety.'

The next two branches Mill calls *social* and *political* education. 'These two branches' says Mill, 'operate upon the whole period of life, but more directly and powerfully after the technical education is at an end; and the youth is launched into the world under his own control! Whilst domestic and technical education largely depends upon the structure of society and social education imparted by it, so the social education depends on the political education. The political education is like the keystone of the arch; the strength of the whole depends upon it.' Even 'the most important part of the physical (that which operates with greatest force upon the greatest number, the state of aliment and labour of the lower classes), is, in the long run, determined by the action of the political machine. . . . When the political machine is such, that the grand objects of desire are seen to be the natural prizes of great and virtuous conduct —of high services to mankind, and of the generous and amiable sentiments from which great endeavours in the services of mankind naturally proceed—it is natural to see diffused among mankind a generous ardour in the acquisition of all those admirable qualities which prepare a man for admirable actions; great intelligence, perfect self-command, and over-ruling benevolence'.

Without over-straining the imagination we may read in Mill's article on education a blue-print or at least a pre-view of the ideas, of the Education Act, 1944. The insistence on infant education; the demand for universal basic education for all classes with differentiation in due time according to abilities and future functions, and irrespective of origin and financial means; the importance of adult education and its social and political training; these are all features which made the Act 1944 the Magna Carta of education. If Mill went wrong in his psychology and in his belief in mass methods of the monitorial system, we can forgive him as in our own time we witnessed the rise of behaviourist psychology and totalitaran mass indoctrination. If we strip his ideas of the terminology of Bentham we see in them a deep moral purpose akin to religious inspiration.

Comparing Mill with Bentham, we observe but a superficial similarity. Whilst Bentham subordinated both the intellectual search of truth and the moral inspiration of religion to narrow utilitarian ends, Mill deeply respected the power of reasoning and attacked existing forms of organized religion mainly because they deviated from high moral ideals. In this respect Mill was true to the totality of the English tradition, of which I spoke in my opening remarks. Although it is a fact that both Bentham and Mill were secularists, we must recognize that there are two varieties of secularism. One is hostile to any religious tradition, bitterly opposed to any participation of the Church in the system of national education, and is in fact intent on mass indoctrination of the rising generation with its own doctrinaire creed. Bentham belongs to this school. Another form of secularism rests on a deep conviction concerning democratic choice, on both the collective and individual plane. It believes in the freedom of choice between the acceptance of traditional faith and its rejection, and it objects to Church intervention in so far as it obstructs this freedom. This is where James Mill took his stand. His son John Stuart Mill developed these views, following his father and moving away from Bentham.

It remains for me to make brief reference to the participation of James Mill and other utilitarians in the educational movement of their time. The story is well-known. There were four movements at that time in which the utilitarians took an active part. First we note the infant-school movement started by Robert Owen in his New Lanark institution. Both Bentham and James Mill assisted Owen, and Mill even started an infant school in London. Secondly, the Lancasterian movement had its Benthamite wing. Here the utilitarians appeared as allies of the Protestant dissenters, and in due course they came to blows about the reading of the Bible and Sunday religious services. After a protracted struggle the former had to retreat from the purely secular position and to accept undenominational Christianity as the basis of moral instruction. Thirdly, the utilitarians actively participated in the foundation of the un-denominational University of London in alliance with Catholics, Jews, Protestant dissenters, and Liberal Whigs. Here again after a struggle the utilitarians had to give way before the stronger influences of Brougham and the Christian dissenters and to abandon their plans of an aggressive secularist institution. Francis Place was excluded from the inner councils precisely because of his atheism.

Fourthly, the utilitarians took part in the activities of the Society for the Diffusion of Useful Knowledge, a movement launched and sustained by Brougham. In Parliament the utilitarians were represented by Hume and Roebuck. Brougham was a half-hearted Benthamite and was often in disagreement with the utilitarians. Joseph Hume, however, was a follower of Bentham and became prominent in his fight for the abolition of taxes on knowledge, and for his advocacy of national system of education.

In 1833 another pupil of Bentham took the leading part in the House of Commons. This was the Anglo-Indian, Arthur Roebuck, who represented the younger utilitarians centred around John Stuart Mill. His scheme of national education reflected the views of James Mill. He advocated compulsory, non-sectarian, and state-aided education and the establishment of teachers' training colleges. Backed only by the other two utilitarians in the House, Hume and Grote, Roebuck was compelled to withdraw his Bill. They failed because they were alone. It is remarkable that whenever the utilitarians ventured into the field alone without seeking aliance with one or other of the religious groups, their projects ended in failure. Bentham's panopticon, his project of a chrestomatic school, the West London Lancasterian Association of James Mill and Francis Place—none of these led to any practical results. And whenever the narrow utilitarian principles were accepted in educational policy they brought with them periods of educational stagnation. Witness the monitorial mass production and in due course the system of 'payment by results'; although to do them justice, they were not directly responsible for the latter. Only later in the more liberal interpretation of doctrine as provided by John Stuart Mill did utilitarianism become a positive force in English education. In its initial stage, dominated by Bentham utilitarianism served as a corrosive acid eating away the imperfections of the metal, but incapable of creating anything new. To change the metaphor, the utilitarians cut away the brushwood of superstition, abuse and intolerance; yet they themselves did not succeed in showing or spreading tolerance. The churches have learned their lesson and have accepted in some measure the English tradition of tolerance of heterodox opinions; but the modern secularists, the spiritual descendants of Bentham, have still to learn to tolerate the traditional spiritual heritage of past ages in whatever form it has survived their attacks.

*   *   *   *   *

How far can we align the doctrines of freemasonry with utilitarianism? There are interesting links in the sphere of educational reform. From the time of the foundation of the Grand Lodge of England in 1717, the masonry of all countries took an active part in the promotion of the diffusion of knowledge among the people. This particular expression, 'diffusion of knowledge' was used by Comenius and after him by all the masonic reformers of education in all lands. That utilitarianism, as formulated by Bentham was accepted by masonic groups as their creed is a proposition which cannot be adopted without reserve. The English masonry was true to the unity of the religious, the intellectual, and the utilitarian aspects of culture: it was neither anti-religous, nor anti-clerical. The Continental and Latin American masonry, on the contrary, was aggressively anti-Catholic and even anti-religious. Voltaire's call *ecrasez l'infame* was to them a battle cry.

Now it is well-established that Bentham's foreign friends and admirers were masons. Rivadavia of Argentina, Miranda, the famous Spanish adventurer and revolutionary, Brissot and Condorcet, the French Girondins, Prince Adam Czartoryiski, the Polish leader, and Alexander's foreign minister, the famous Russian statesman, Speransky, were all masons and Bentham's friends. It was Miranda indeed who converted James Mill to secularism.

Many of Bentham's English friends were masons; Brougham, indeed, was an active member of the society. The English masons did not accept Bentham's militant anti-clericalism and quarrelled with him about it. Yet they did take part in all educational movements of that time led by Henry Brougham. The Lodge of Antiquity, for instance, lent the mallet which Wren had used in laying the foundation of Saint Paul's for the foundation ceremony of the University of London, The foundation dinner took place at the Freemason's Tavern. The Society for the Diffusion of Useful Knowledge was masonic in origin. Thus it cannot be denied that there was a certain affinity or alliance between masons and utilitarians. Whether Bentham himself was a mason is questionable. At the end of the eighteenth century a certain J. Bentham is known to have been accepted in one of the London Lodges. Nothing more is heard about him. Whether he was Jeremy Bentham is uncertain. It is probable that the young Jeremy Bentham joined the masonry, and that he very soon discontinued attending the lodge because his opinions did not agree with the ritual and the creed of masonic constitutions. Neither James Mill nor Francis Place, according to evidence, was a mason; but the radical anticlerical Richard Carlile seems to have been one. It is to be noted that when Carlile was imprisoned he was helped both by Bentham and by Mill.

5

JAMES KAY-SHUTTLEWORTH, PIONEER OF NATIONAL EDUCATION

*

A. V. JUDGES

A lecture delivered at King's College on 5 February 1951;
Professor R. H. Tawney in the chair.

James Phillips Kay was born at Rochdale in 1804. He died
as Sir James Kay-Shuttleworth Bt. in London in 1877.
He became the first secretary of the committee of the privy
council, set up in 1839 to deal with educational grants from
parliament. He retired in 1849 when this office had already
become a department of education in miniature.

His remaining activities, which were numerous and covered
the whole mid-Victorian period, were nearly all performed in a
private capacity, though he did to be sure serve as high sheriff
of Lancashire (1863–4), and he was on the royal commission
on scientific instruction (1870–5).

It has more than once been remarked by historians as somewhat odd that he, the foremost authority of his day on popular
schooling, was not appointed in 1858 to the important Newcastle Commission charged with the task of reporting on 'what
measures, if any, are required for the extension of cheap and
sound elementary education.' That the government chose to
abstain from his advice in this connection is not difficult to
explain. It was after all the system which Kay-Shuttleworth
had founded which was on trial before the Newcastle commission; and it did not escape criticism. He lived on to see and
to protest with indignation against radical changes in its charac-

ter of that system made (partly as a result of the commission's findings) during Robert Lowe's vice-presidency of the council. Kay-Shuttleworth did not outlive the era of payment by results; but the vindication of his own point of view presented in the *Memorandum on Popular Education* (1868), one of his ablest essays, helped to bring about the legalized association—one can hardly call it a partnership—of 1870 between local-government initiative and the churches. He was still lively enough in his seventies to play an influential part as financial adviser in the early work of the Girls' Public Day School Company.[1]

It has fallen to me to deal in this series with one who was famous, though not perhaps so famous as he deserved to be, as an administrator; of one who was, in the management of unwilling men and refractory institutions, a constructive genius. As a politician he was a partial failure. As an educational philosopher, though active and persuasive in thought, he had nothing very original to say. His quality showed itself in the practical application of ideas, in his appreciation of their feasibility, and, as I see it, they were nearly always good ideas.

Eighty-one years ago this month the House of Commons sat down to the first-reading debate on the Elementary Education Bill of Mr. Gladstone's government. In presenting the measure Forster made but one reference to the reforms of Kay-Shuttleworth—'a man to whom probably more than any other we owe national education in England'—and this was to remark that he, Forster, proposed now to do away with the denominational inspectorate. 'There are denominational inspectors all through the kingdom, crossing one another continually in the most curious manner.' It was a very odd state of affairs, and it had a history. Each of the main divisions of the inspectoral services had in fact been responsible for visiting a separate set of schools. 'Sir James Kay-Shuttleworth established those concordats with the different denominations, and he did so because he found it almost impossible to help it.'[2]

Here then was Forster addressing the House on his own matured plans: a historic occasion. 'I may say at once,' he had

---

[1] He was first chairman of the company's council. See Laurie Magnus, *The Jubilee Book of the G.P.D.S.T.* (1923), chapters ii and iii.

[2] *Verbatim report of the debate in parliament ... Elementary Education Bill,* 1870, (National Educational Union), p. 9 (17 February 1870).

declared in opening, 'that the government has not brought forward this measure with any notion of compromise.'[1] Whether the patent untruth of this remark provoked interruptions is not on record. If there were none, Forster must have felt that he could get away with anything; and in the event he very nearly did. The episode in Kay-Shuttleworth's official career to which allusion has been made was, I suppose, the most adroit piece of educational compromise secured in the Victorian period. The words too, *denominational, inspectorate*, if any painstaking research student were to undertake a count, would prove perhaps to be the most freely used polysyllabic words in Kay-Shuttleworth's writings and speeches. So that Forster, though he only referred to an obscure episode in an already distant past, yet found a matter of significance.

I must now quote Kay-Shuttleworth himself, a few weeks later, after Forster had already begun to make concessions to his nonconformist and secularist critics. The former writes to Forster as an old hand at the game:

'You will carry your Bill in all essential features as it stands if you are simply resolute and calm; but of course not without the price which every statesman has to pay in serving his country. You will have to do what I have done over and over again in this cause—you will have to disappoint some of your friends in order that the education of the people may not be indefinitely postponed.'[2]

I have chosen this debate as a starting point for two reasons: first, because it forms a link between two ages—we are after all too far away now from Kay-Shuttleworth to take stock of his work in the terminology or idiom of our own time; secondly because that reference of Forster's to the concordats with the archbishops and the other secretarian interests really does lead back another thirty years to what now seems in retrospect to be an important turning point in Kay-Shuttleworth's career. It was at that moment, when he had to concede the right of nominating an inspector of grant-aided church schools to the Church of England, that it became clear to him that he had been harbouring inflated, perhaps unduly grandiose, ideas of of what he could bring about on his own initiative as a social

[1] Ibid., p. 6 (17th February 1870).
[2] T. Wemyss Reid, *Life of W. E. Forster* (1895 ed.), p. 273.

reformer. Thereafter he had to jettison many plans and constructive ideas because, as we have already noted in Forster's words, 'he found it almost impossible to help it'.

We must suppose the full realization that he, the ex-Independent-church Sunday-school master, the now steady-going broad Churchman, the warm believer in religious teaching and moral instruction, was in a sense up against the forces of institutional religion, came to him then as something of a surprise. Could he previously, even in his wildest imaginings, have dreamed that a large part of his further life work would be an attempt to assuage and reconcile the opposing forces in religious politics, the most savage arena which could be found in a period of hard-hitting controversy?

II

Let us first consider the man as a personality. His style of writing, clear, sometimes vigorous and forceful, but not infrequently laden with heavy metaphor and commonplace, tells us a little about him, but not a great deal. We learn from his family record that he was regarded as a good raconteur; but, like other excellent story-tellers, he liked to hear himself talking; he was assured; he valued his own opinions. And, though his mind was always penetrating, one suspects that his associates may sometimes have found him a bore. If so, he was—it is undeniable—one of those indispensable bores who are the salt of the earth.

We have numerous tributes in general terms from contemporaries to his breadth of vision and soundness of judgment. For a man much in the public eye it is surprising that the character sketches are so infrequent and so meagre. Two candid appreciations are however on record. The first I take in part from Dr. Frank Smith's *Life* of Kay-Shuttleworth, based on the family papers.[1] Haworth parsonage is perhaps sixteen miles or so over the moors from Gawthorpe Place, in which James Phillips Kay settled when he married the young heiress bride whose family name he assumed in 1842. From Haworth Charlotte Brontë visited the family once or twice in the early

[1] Published in 1923. The quotation is on p. 225. May I say how heavily I am indebted to this book, one of the few really good biographies of great Victorians?

'fifties, and again after her own marriage, and it was at the
Kay-Shuttleworth's house at Brierly Close in the Lake District
that she met Mr. Gaskell. In her letters she has described her
impressions of the youngish clear-headed and (to her rustic
eyes) polished, northern squire with his sensitive nerves and
observant ways. His proneness to criticize her unorthodox
tendencies and the artist temperament in her produced a sense
of irritation, as also did the manifest desire of the Kay-Shuttle-
worths to launch her into London society as their literary
protegée. However, she grew to like him better. 'In manner he
can be gracious and dignified; his tastes and feelings are capable
of elevation; frank he is not, but, on the contrary, politic. . . .
Courtly and affable in some points of view, he is strict and
rigorous in others.'

Matthew Arnold was equally revealing, though there was not
agreement in all points with Charlotte Brontë. Arnold of course
became H.M.I. a little too late to have Kay-Shuttleworth for a
master, but he knew him fairly well before that at country-house
parties and on other social occasions. To this observer he seemed
a most remarkable person.

'He was not a man of high cultivation and he was not a good
writer. I am told that he might easily have become a powerful
speaker, and I can well believe it. . . . As an administrator,
when he had become Secretary to the Committee of Council
on Education, he did not attract by person and manner. His
temper was not smooth or genial, and he left on many persons
the impression of a man managing and designing, if not an
intriguer. But the faith in public education which animated
him was no intriguer's passion. It was heroic, it was a gift
planted by nature, and truly and honestly followed, cultivated
and obeyed. By no other means than those adopted by him
could a system of public education have been introduced in
this country. . . . He was too a religious man, though both
Church and Dissent distrusted him. . . . He believed as firmly
as Butler, that of education what is called *information* is really the
least part. . . . He did not attract . . . he had faults; . . . both
the clergy and the sects disliked and distrusted him. The general
public was indifferent. It needed a statesman to see his value.'[1]

[1] Matthew Arnold's contribution to T. Humphry Ward's book, *The
Reign of Queen Victoria* (1887), ii, 239–40.

III

Kay-Shuttleworth had four separate careers—as a successful physician, as a poor-law administrator in the field, as civil servant at Whitehall, and as the elder statesman. And the astonishing thing is that he had already achieved, or been forced into, this final position of semi-retirement at the age of forty-five. He lived none the less to the age of seventy-two. Born before the Lancaster and Bell systems had overrun the country, and when the two rival pioneers were indeed still on visiting terms, Kay-Shuttleworth lived to cast a friendly if critical eye on the early exploits of the school boards and to write an article about them.

James Phillips Kay belonged to one of the numerous families named Kay which had for generations been engaged in cotton spinning and manufacture in east Lancashire. His first interests were in and around Rochdale, Manchester, and Salford. He left school early, went into an uncle's bank, and then, at the age of twenty, escaped to Edinburgh to become a medical student. He made a considerable impression by his intellectual quickness, earnestness, and his hard work in the infirmary and among the closely packed families in the wynds of the Canon-gate. Back he came to Lancashire after his M.D. with the evident intention of making medicine his career. He was already an authority on pulmonary disorders; but the fact that he accepted election to the post of senior physician to one of the recently created public dispensaries in the outer fringes of Manchester seems to suggest that Kay's real concern was with what we should now call social medicine.

Kay is remembered in south-east Lancashire for three things: (1) for his work in identifying cholera and coping with it as a disease of foul conditions in the great pestilence of 1832; (2) for the leading part he played in creating the Manchester Statistical Society; and (3) for his contribution to the organiza-tion of cotton-famine relief in the early 'sixties. He is not so well-remembered in his county for his work a few years earlier, in the Burnley neighbourhood, in federating and revivifying the languid and almost moribund mechanics' institutes—inci-dentally one of the more stimulating episodes in the history of adult education. For Kay-Shuttleworth was one of the most skilled diagnosticians in the maladies of social institutions we have ever had; and, in this case, as usual, he saw what was wrong and he knew the right remedy. But this we must pass by.

It was the first activity, already referred to, which imposed the earliest strain on his physique and compelled a change; it was the second which provided him with a reputation as a social investigator.

In 1832 Manchester had yet to become a corporate borough; its recent growth, which was rapid, had followed the whims of factory proprietors and speculative builders; it had experienced the progress of urbanization without knowing urbanity; it was not the worst place in England, if we can attempt to grade the anarchy and material disorder of the new wens, but conditions were undeniably bad. Moreover most of its new population owed no loyalty to local traditions. It had been 'swollen', as Kay remarked, with the Irish specially in mind, 'by the immigration of a large mass of semi-barbarous colonists'.[1] These immigrants, in the undrained Manchester slums, which had to be seen and smelt to be believed, were not of course primitive people with settled manners and customs whom an anthropologist might hope to study and understand. With their miscellaneous origin and lack of cohesion they had virtually no cultural patterns at all and of course no sense of citizenship; and thus they presented a much more difficult social problem. Indeed I think it would not be too much to say that Kay at this point was faced with and came to understand, as few of his contemporaries did, the problem *par excellence* of the industrial revolution, *viz.*, the proper treatment of what I would call the social degradation of the new townsmen, that spiritual depression of the lower element in Disraeli's 'two nations' which persisted as a function of the other half's moral irresponsibility.

The dispensary work in Ardwick and Ancoats brought Kay into contact with a mixed world of vigorous industrial wage earners, of improvident labourers and their neglected offspring, of prostitutes and back-alley thugs, and all the woes and miseries of gin shops, insanitary houses, cellar life, long hours of work and child-labour in the mills. The children were far

[1] Kay-Shuttleworth, *Four Periods of Public Education* (1862), p. 176.

from clean and neat.[1] No-one has ever described that world more
precisely or more effectively than Kay himself in one of the
earliest and most accurate accounts we possess of the sanitary
conditions of the new industrial towns after the rapid spread of
new suburbs which followed the Napoleonic wars; and his work
became a source book for publicists and reformers. Many
people who know nothing of his personal account of clinical
work in the hideous swamp settlement by the banks of the Irk
near Ducie Bridge and the rookery known as Little Ireland,
are quite familiar with its blackest sections, taken over with but
perfunctory acknowledgment in the classic story of the condition
of England in 1844 which was told by Engels twelve years
later.[2]

Shaken by the physical impact of these horrors, Kay asked
what was the remedy. Was it in political action?

We should like to know more of Kay the radical agitator.
John Bright[3] later spoke of how in 1832, during the crisis of
the Reform Bill, he listened with emotion to the young doctor
standing up in the market place in Rochdale and quoting
Shelley to the crowd—the last stanza which the poet had
written into the *Mask of Anarchy* when the news of the Peterloo
massacre reached him in Italy:

> *Rise like Lions after slumber*
> *In unvanquishable number—*
> *Shake your chains to earth, like dew*
> *Which in sleep had fallen on you—*
> *Ye are many—they are few.*

Medical neglect and malnutrition—Kay studied these as
explanations; and moved on to reflections on sanitary ignorance
and incompetence. He handed the missionary work of town

[1] Between 1821 and 1831 the population of the township of Manchester,
not yet a corporate town, increased by 45 per cent, from 129,035 to 187,022
—'a rate of growth probably never before, and certainly never since
equalled.' T. S. Ashton, *Economic and Social Investigations in Manchester,
1833–1933* (1934). A full account of Manchester's struggle with the sanitation and slum tenement problems in the period of Engels' book is given
in A. Redford, *The History of Local Government in Manchester* (1939), vol. ii,
ch. xix.
[2] Frederick Engels, *The Condition of the Working Classes in England* (1892),
ch. ii.
[3] G. M. Trevelyan, *Life of John Bright* (1925), p. 20.

drainage over to Edwin Chadwick in due course; then he
grasped at the real remedy as he now sensed it, the use of
education to create self-respect and to accomplish the reform
of morals. Machine-breaking and industrial unrest were the
results of ignorance. Trade-union agitation in its worst features
could be quelled by knowledge. Kay, to be sure, had not much
use for the Owenite trade union, though I feel sure he would
have thrived in the atmosphere of joint industrial councils
today, where bricks are seldom thrown, though not infrequently dropped. 'If they [the working class] are to have
knowledge, surely it is the part of a wise and virtuous Government to do all in its power to secure to them useful knowledge,
and to guard them against pernicious opinions.'[1] 'Barbarism
and the School are at war,' he said in 1862, looking back on
those days. 'In this warfare the School will be the victor; but
time is an indispensable element of success.'[2]

Study of the facts, he might have added, was another element.
The foundation in 1833 of the Manchester Statistical Society,
of whose early history Professor Ashton has reconstructed enough
to convince us of its devotion to practical human needs rather
than to the advancement of the science of statistics, was the real
beginning of applied social science in this country; and in
respect of its high significance it does not seem to me to be
fantastic to compare the event with the birth of the Royal
Society nearly two centuries earlier. The banker William
Langton and Kay, who were both honorary officers of the
Manchester and Salford District Provident Society, discussed
the need for some agency for collecting social data. During a
tour of Derbyshire undertaken by Kay with some friends the
project took practical shape. The personnel of the provident
society came in as the nucleus of the new statistical society.
Within a few months Kay, who was treasurer, had addressed
the latter body on the condition of the Derbyshire miners; on
difficulties in the construction of dispensaries; on public
swimming baths; on a discussion he had had with the vice-
president of the board of trade concerning a suitable programme

---

[1] Written in explanation of the measures of 1839. *Four Periods*, p. 232.
The radicalism has already evaporated, and his political theory is becoming
set.
[2] *Four Periods*, p. 177.

for statistical investigation; and on the means existing for the
religious instruction of the working classes in large towns.[1]

IV

The formation of the poor law board in 1834, with his friend
Chadwick as its disobedient secretary, led to an offer of one of
the assistant commissionerships of the board, which Kay
accepted and held for five years. He set about devising schemes
for transferring pauper migrants from the south into the cotton
areas; and incidentally he was bitterly attacked for adding to
the population of the slum settlements he had so recently condemned.[2] He was put in charge of the poor-law administration
of the eastern counties under the new and most unpopular Act.
All that I can say about that important formative part of his
career, during which he learned the art of public administration,
must be strictly compressed. His medical skill was but little used
by his employers, though they gave him a fairly free hand. It
was depressing work. The human material that became his
everyday concern seemed to be more lacking in independence
and human spirit than the lustier people he had lived with in
the north. Much of his best work was given to devising ways of
securing, with the aid of rate-payers' money, proper schooling
for the young paupers, whose parents' destitution or in-
difference had brought them as public charges into the deplor-
able mixed workhouses on the countryside. There certainly were
a great many children coming under the new poor law as
victims (if that is the word) of the indoor and outdoor relief
policies.

The campaign for proper schools for destitute children outside the workhouse compound was no negligible part of Kay's
whole programme for the country. He believed in national
intervention: he believed that the nation's prime concern in
the educational field was to rescue from squalor and vice the
poor and neglected child, a task which was as much concerned
with the formation of character as with classroom exercises.
He learnt during his poor-law experiments that the country's
great misfortune was the lack of competent and self-respecting

---

[1] T. S. Ashton, *loc. cit.*
[2] A. Redford, *Labour Migration in England* (1926), pp. 95-6.

teachers in all schools used by the lower orders; and he found, almost by accident, an inexpensive way of training his own teachers within the four corners of the little world he controlled. His first discovery in East Anglia was the pupil teacher—the story of the enterprising boy 'master' William Rush at Gressenhall workhouse is, I think, well-known; his second discovery, under the influence of Stow and Wood, was a practical alternative in schoolroom management to the monitorial method; his third, on being summoned by the commissioners to a post in London, was the manner in which picked pupil teachers might be given a finishing course. The experiment in this last case was carried out in the establishment of a contractor of a large child farm run by the guardians in Norwood. In a very real sense this was the prototype of our present local education authority training college.

The account left to us by Kay-Shuttleworth of the ways in which he contrived, with the help of Scottish-trained senior teachers and the use of the still novel 'gallery', to turn young monitors into promising apprentices and to convert the dismal regimentation of the 'mutual' class organization into a scheme of simultaneous learning is well-worth reading.[1] It gives us a fair notion of the practical originality of his approach and enables us to see him putting into institutional shape the conclusions on which he had reported from his office in Norwich to the poor law commissioners in 1838, in a memorandum which significantly contains the following words.

'A systematic avoidance of the stimulus of inferior motives, such as the fear of punishment, the hope of reward, and the often unworthy rivalry for personal distinction on account of proficiency, which is accompanied with mutual heartburnings and jealousies, will enable the teacher to substitute in their place other motives of a superior nature. . . . The teacher should strive to invest knowledge with its own natural attractions. If he is skilful, he will not need any more powerful incentive to induce the children to learn than the natural craving after truth, when it is presented in simplicity and with the force of novelty.'[2]

[1] 'Report on the Norwood School of Industry' (1st May 1839) in *Reports on the Training of Pauper Children* (1841), pp. 102–26.

[2] 'Report on the Training of Pauper Children and on District Schools', *Ibid.*, pp. 19–76.

It was in this period that Kay made two continental tours in the company of colleagues. They discovered a pupil teacher system already in operation in the Netherlands, and that example was later cried up to give support to Kay's own ideas about training. From Fellenberg's Spartan agricultural school for peasant children near Berne and Wehrli's school at Constance Kay brought back ideas of economical management and hard living. On these he modelled the régime in the private training school which he was soon to set up, with the help of his friend Carleton Tufnell, at Battersea, virtually under his own management, with his own money and with himself as lecturer in education.

Kay never became entirely free from the rather dour preconceptions which he brought into Whitehall from his poor-law days, nor from the idea that national education, using public funds, was a sort of enlightened extension of the original operations of the Bashaws of Somerset House. He never lost his enthusiasm for the district poor-law school, one of the earliest examples of nationalized education in this country; and 'as late as 1848', after he had secured the diversion of part of the parliamentary grant to the support of schools of industry, 'he was privately discouraging the attendance of indoor pauper children at the elementary day schools [under the care of his own department], as offering markedly fewer advantages than the Separate Poor-Law Schools that he advocated.'[1]

It could not unreasonably be claimed that he was the chief begetter of the idea of the district school for poor-law children— i.e., a combined school for the needs of several unions, established outside the precincts of the workhouse—and the instrument of its adoption by the State; though if he had had his way it would have been open free to all the children of the neighbourhood. We have forgotten how numerous were the children on poor-relief throughout the nineteenth century, and how important was the part in educational administration the guardians played, or at any rate might have played, if this design for betterment had had a less chequered career. Mr. Alexander Ross, who is now making a thorough investigation of the neglected subject of workhouse schools, tells me that in that long debate Tufnell was still, in 1874, using Kay-

[1] S. and B. Webb, *English Poor Law History*, ii, 270n.

Shuttleworth's arguments in refuting Mrs. Nassau Senior, and that a generation later still the controversialists who favoured the district school in the fierce discussions raised by the report of the departmental committee of 1894–6 could find little to add to the case Kay-Shuttleworth had made in the 'thirties.

I find it impossible to classify Kay-Shuttleworth. In moral outlook he was allied to the evangelical party; yet he came to dislike them for their pusillanimity in not supporting him in face of high-church aggression. In the educational plans for the poor, as in his belief in the efficacy of poor-law reform, he was a follower of Bentham, surprisingly close indeed in some of his views to the old sage himself. But his allegiance was in general to the 'interference' wing of Benthamism. As statisticians and as disciples of 'thorough' he and Edwin Chadwick, together with Southwood Smith, worked for a time close together; though Chadwick, who, unlike the gentler and more supple Kay-Shuttleworth, had nerves of iron and a heart of millstone grit, was little use at politics and became the administrative planner *par excellence*. Of political radicalism Kay-Shuttleworth was cured by finding himself on the official side in the period of the new-poor-law agitation, by his contempt for Chartist indiscretions, and by the fear which he shared with many others of his day that working-class reformism might topple over into revolutionary anarchy.

In the history of educational policy it is a mistake to be indifferent to changes in the climate of ruling-class opinion. We should do well to remember that when Kay-Shuttleworth became secretary to the committee on education in 1839 the times were anxious and the sky threatening. The period 1837 to 1842 was one of high corn prices, industrial depression, severe unemployment, continuous pressure on real wages, due in part I have no doubt to the competition of child labour which is apt to be at a premium in the labour market in bad times. Dr. Rostow's 'social-tension' chart, with which he attempts a correlation of social attitudes with economic fluctuations, shows in these years a peak, or rather an elevated plateau, of no mean dimensions.[1] The industrial north was alive with a score of separate agitations. The country's settled government seemed to be on the edge of the abyss. Thus, for Kay-Shuttleworth,

---

[1] W. W. Rostow, *British Economy in the Nineteenth Century* (1948), ch. v.

with his sensitiveness to opinion on both sides of the Pennines, educational policy was a branch of social reform and a shield against revolutionary violence.

He was of course only too well aware of the appallingly low state of the existing elementary schools. Yet it is surprising to find how few were the people of that day who shared his views. For a thoroughly objective criticism of the prevailing state of things we have to go to a foreign observer like Horace Mann, the gifted and dynamic secretary of the Massachusetts board of education, whose career offers itself for much close comparison with that of Kay-Shuttleworth. Mann visited the leading countries in Europe in 1843; but whereas he found much to inspire him elsewhere, and was indeed quite impressed by the intellectual activity in Scottish schools, he could find nothing good to say of English elementary teaching. Men of the highest capacities and most extensive attainments in England seemed to falter and grope their way around notions of educational statecraft which in other countries were commonplace.[1] Apart from the poor quality of the instruction, even in the schools sponsored by the two great educational societies—the National and the British—there was the further difficulty of the lack of provision of any schools at all for a large part of the child population of the country.

V

The year 1839 marks the first beginnings of our present Ministry of Education. When Kay-Shuttleworth was summoned to be the executive officer of the privy council's new committee on education, the decision of the government to bring in new administrative machinery, through which it was to try somehow or other to direct educational policy, was already a matter of anxiety to ministers and was under fire. Kay-Shuttleworth was warned by the lord president to look narrowly at the offer of a new post,[2] since the outlook was uncertain. That he was not at once released by the poor law commissioners, but carried on with both offices together, shows how experimental the new

[1] Horace Mann, *Report of an Educational Tour in Germany*, (*etc*. 4th ed. 1857), pp. 32, 44, etc.

[2] F. Smith, *Life*, it 'might prove a precarious, and would certainly be an obnoxious position', pp. 61–2.

departure was conceived to be. In the circumstances the first plans which were put up in committee looked reasonably ambitious. Kay-Shuttleworth asked at once for a government normal school, formed on reformed teaching methods, with practising schools attached, *i.e.*, a state institution. This was the development scheme he pulled out of his pocket on arrival. I think there can be no doubt that the thought of this school as a pilot model was in his head, and that he had a vision of a whole system of normal schools under State management which would be produced in due course.

But the scheme foundered, and the education committee itself was nearly shipwrecked before it had left port. The scheme itself was destroyed by the animosity of sectarian critics in parliament; for, in conformity with ideas which Kay-Shuttleworth never forsook, it was necessary to introduce religious instruction into the plan of the State school, and the education committee actually proposed to decide what part of instruction was appropriate to the Church of England chaplain and what was not, and also to bring in dissenting ministers on a contingent basis, *i.e.*, as required. The Anglicans were the most hostile element; but neither were the dissenters happy.

So powerful was the ill-feeling, which quickly descended to personal attacks on the new secretary, that the children were lost to view in the dispute, as was to happen only too often in nineteenth-century education debates. It is not for the historian looking back on these quarrels to speak with contempt of the motives of the different parties, but rather to try to understand why well-intentioned people behaved with utter disregard to what I was going to say we should all agree with Kay-Shuttleworth were the vital issues, but that would be to forget that these old controversies still stir uneasily amongst us.

We must recognize that the high church party, fortified by the Oxford movement and by conscious rectitude in having accomplished measures of internal reform, felt itself to be in the ascendant, the more keenly since only a few years earlier the very existence of the establishment had appeared to be in peril under radical assaults. Surely no more unfavourable moment could have been chosen by the Whig ministers for asserting what they called 'the civil influence in education'. The forces of dissent were, it is true, for the moment divided and weak,

but the bishops and much of their following had recovered their
sense of obligation and duty towards a national flock and were
in the mood to conduct a divine mission within the authorized
limits of the reformation settlement, and perhaps well beyond
it. The small quarrel over the planning of religious teaching in
a projected training college raised the old stormy issues of
imperium versus sacerdotium. How dare the laymen in Whitehall
presume to say what were the proper limits of religious instruction, or seek to introduce dissenting ministers into a state
institution! Urged on by the bishops, a body of peers took the
unusual step of visiting the queen on behalf of the Lords' house
to complain of unconstitutional action. Lord Brougham, the
political spearhead of the earlier movement for the reform of
elementary education, and now a politician without a job, was
so much impressed by the violence of the Church's reaction,
that he advised his old colleagues to throw in their hand.

This was a lamentable beginning. Unfortunately the
'religious question' had now come into vigorous existence and
was not to be subdued. 'It is the characteristic of such controversies,' said Kay-Shuttleworth rather bitterly, 'that the
interests of the common people are sacrificed to those of the
middle classes: the well-being of the State is postponed to
promote the triumph of a party'.[1] The troubles multiplied and
continued. Kay-Shuttleworth, writing later about this period,
said that logically the first step was the creation of a system of
school inspection, and that the (as it turned out) abortive training system came second.[2] The historical sequence however was
the reverse of this, though very little time separated the two
attempts. I need not stress the importance of the foundation of
her majesty's inspectorate: it not only provided for a certain
continuity of policy and outlook through thick and thin, but
also, by the nature of its development, made possible the evolution of the peculiar English relationship between the centre and
periphery in our State system. The right to inspect and the use
of inspectors to improve standards were fundamental notions in
the new scheme of things. Kay-Shuttleworth picked his inspectors well, in spite of difficulties, and left to his successor a small

[1] Kay-Shuttleworth, *The School in its relations to the State, the Church, and
the Congregation* (1847), p. 15.
[2] *Ibid.*, p. 10.

body of experienced men of culture and wide human interest who in large measure shared his views about the social and moral purposes of the elementary schools, and could show a turn of independence, not to say of insubordinate criticism of their masters' policy, which severely shook Robert Lowe when his excessive economic dogmatism began to disturb values just achieving stability, and would indeed dismay a permanent secretary today.

VI

Kay-Shuttleworth got his inspectorate established, but only after making substantial concessions to religious interests. The first tussle with the Church perhaps gave him an exaggerated conception of its power and influence in the land. He could not risk a continuing quarrel; and he began to revise his views as to the scope of possible action. He gave in very largely on the power of nomination and on the duties of the inspectorate of Church schools. When the Tories came in in 1841 he momentarily lost the initiative: the unsuccessful educational measure for which Peel's government is remembered, namely Graham's factory bill of 1843, was managed by the Home Secretary. The bill was actually *promoted* by enlightened factory inspectors. Had it been carried in something like its original form, with its educational clauses intact, it would have established new official schools in the factory areas, each supported by a poor rate, to receive the children who were now to be excluded from employment; and this system could have been expected to spread outward into the non-industrial areas. Kay-Shuttleworth's individual role in regard to the bill was to advise on the question of religious diplomacy, this time the government being much more friendly to the Church. As I read the evidence, Kay-Shuttleworth, critical as he was of parts of Graham's bill, was the real go-between with the bishops. There can be no doubt that the management of the new schools, if this agreed measure had gone through, as expected, would have put the control of school management and curricula in the factory districts into the hands of the parish clergy and their friends. What had not this time been foreseen was the strength and shrewdness of nonconformist leadership. The outcry from this quarter was immediate, and furious. Dissenters were now drawn together by a rallying cry and became, as never before since the Great Rebellion, a political force.

Though the non-educational clauses of Graham's bill found their way on to the statute book as the Factory Act of 1844—itself a serious achievement on behalf of the children's educational welfare—the lesson to parliamentary draftsmen had been a bitter one, and it was not until 1870 that Her Majesty's government were again in the mood to fight a broad educational reform measure through to the finish.

Kay-Shuttleworth was comforted by the return of the Whigs in 1846. To his own way of thinking they were broader-minded than Graham and his colleagues; and they seem to have been prepared, in spite of recent events, for moderate advances in the direction he indicated. It was at this point that the secretary of the committee of council appears to have come firmly to the conclusion that his earlier vision of a national system with a new sort of schools was utopian. As we should say nowadays, he became a 'realist', in a world of politicians and sectaries, and he was henceforward not above using politicians and sectaries as he found them.

Later on, in evidence to the Newcastle commission, he referred to this crisis in our national history. 'The decision then arrived at amounted to the abandonment of the idea of a common school, and to the adoption as, in the main, the only practicable mode of procedure, of the denominational system.'[1] From this time onwards he used the technique of employing the parliamentary grant to stimulate, encourage, and maintain voluntary effort. This meant accepting and using the types of schools already in existence, and others like them which would be built by religious bodies, but trying none the less to better them by extending the methods already adopted in respect of school erection, *viz.*, augmenting with state grants the funds voluntarily raised by charitable societies. He worked out a scheme for allocating the department's slender financial resources with supreme skill; persuading the managing proprietors of schools to build houses for their teachers and to adopt improved methods of instruction; making it worth their while to appoint experienced teachers at a living wage; coaxing them

[1] Newcastle Commission *Report* (1861), vi, 308.

121

into his plan for raising a new generation of young teachers by apprenticeship in the classroom; helping on the new denominational training schools which had been brought quickly into existence by the religious bodies after their scare when the state normal project had been pointed at them in 1839; and even finding room within the exiguous accounting system for a pension fund for the new-model certificated teacher when he or she would have to retire.

Thus from the encouragement of new school building Kay-Shuttleworth turned in 1846 to the production of skilled personnel; and we cannot doubt that, with his mean little budget allowance, his concentration on teacher-training was good housekeeping. More than that, it was inspired statecraft of the highest order; for the pupil teacher system was his own invention. Seen against later practice of course it may look a poor thing, and we are apt to give less than its due to a plan, later outmoded, which condemned the elementary schools to feed consistently upon their own talent, a circle, we might think, nearly as vicious as that in which 'the Eton boy passed as a scholar to the other foundation of Henry VI, King's College, Cambridge, there automatically attained his fellowship and his degree, and in due course by seniority returned to Eton as a master.'[1]

It is difficult now to appreciate how great were the moral effects of the minutes of 1846; how they provided the minimum conditions for the growth of a worthy profession, and not only produced good teachers, well-grounded, with a sense of vocation and a great devotion to duty, but also set for the first time the standards of good teaching; all this at a time when there was no provision of post-primary schools from which a *corps d'élite* could be drawn. Where else indeed but in his own wretched elementary schools could Kay-Shuttleworth look for his youthful teachers or his state-supported recruits to the training colleges?

It would have been useful for us to consider the social effects of the institution of the pupil teacher system, which, as a piece of well-contrived policy, was Kay-Shuttleworth's great contribution to our educational institutions. What an interesting light on obscure reaches of Victorian life a full-scale investigation of the careers and social milieux of the pupil teachers might

[1] J. W. Adamson, *English Education, 1789–1902* (1930), p. 236.

cast! The new system created one of the broadest ladders up into the white-collared ranges for keen and ambitious boys and girls which that age was to possess. Not the least of its claims upon our attention is that it gave parents a new interest in the schools.[1]

The final period of Kay-Shuttleworth's official career was occupied with the stabilizing of the grant-earning denominational school system; and when at the beginning of 1849 he fell seriously ill under the strain of overwork and of relentless criticism, he left the government firmly committed to a policy beneath the shadow of which we are still bringing up our young.

I do not wish to disparage the work of the voluntary societies: they did their best, or very nearly. Members of the established church, both inside and outside the National Society, put in a vast amount of devoted work. The Methodist record for the period is an honourable one. The Roman Catholics put up schools, largely financed from their own resources, at a considerable rate. And the British Society helped to educate progressive opinion as well as the children themselves. Whilst with a stationary society the voluntary bodies might have got within reach of success in school provision, the plain fact is that the population outstripped them all: they could never catch up.

Kay-Shuttleworth had from the start been in favour of local taxation as the substantial basis for the public provision of cheap education. With it ought to go a wide measure of control by the local community; and this notion of democratic initiative flits in and out of his published writings. That it did not take the form of more concrete proposals at a time when he was in a position of power is attributable to the fact that no network of local government institutions had yet come into existence. The most suitable collecting agency would then have been the poor-law guardians—a sobering thought. The best he could do was to insist in 1847 on school management clauses which would admit lay subscribers as well as ministers of religion into governing committees; and the final controversy which this policy opened up continued on into a discussion about the release of individual pupils from denominational teaching.

[1] Kay-Shuttleworth, *The School in its relations to the State, the Church, and the Congregation* (1847), p. 49.

The natural corollary of the official rule 'no grant aid without religious teaching', which Kay-Shuttleworth so stoutly upheld, was the so-called conscience clause for the shielding of protesting minorities from unacceptable indoctrination. It seems illogical that a clause designed to permit children to be withdrawn by their parents from religious teaching—an escape clause if ever there was one—could be accepted by confessions which based their resistance to any government proposal for undenominational schooling on their assertion that secular and religious instruction are but separate facets of an indivisible whole. But most managers did accept it, though we know of course that official policy in this sphere encountered a good deal of local resistance which had hardly yet died out in 1870.

VII

The question as to precisely what Kay-Shuttleworth himself wanted in religious teaching is an important one in view of his great influence; but it remains something of a mystery. He was capable, we know, of choosing his words to suit his listeners: he talked loosely about both 'comprehensive' and 'combined' systems. Dr. Frank Smith has wrestled manfully with the contradictions in these utterances, but he does not satisfy me that Kay-Shuttleworth ever achieved perfect candour. Perhaps the clearest thing that can be said is that his ideal school would probably have had a Cowper-Temple type of syllabus—excluding the teaching of distinctive creeds—though in the real world for which he had to work he seemed to be vigorously recommending doctrinal teaching; with a conscience clause; and moreover with rate aid.[1]

As I hope my remarks have indicated, in this and other matters Kay-Shuttleworth did not only anticipate later endeavours to secure harmony or compromise, he actually started and gave vigour to certain traditions which have clung to our elementary system throughout its later history. The very fact that I now speak of an elementary system—though since 1944 I have no business to do so—is part of my inherited response to one tradition, in this case perhaps a malign tradition.

[1] *Ibid.*, p. 73. This and the following pages get us nearest to a clear statement.

Kay-Shuttleworth's task was to reconcile the current doctrine of self-help with the realization that the pauper population had no social momentum: it was necessary to prime the pump of culture. There was no question of every citizen's right to educational opportunity; no question, in South Britain, of a common school. Freedom of access to the primary school must remain the mark of poverty until poverty itself had lost its familiar characteristics. After his early retreats, the initiative in the expansion of popular education was left by Kay-Shuttleworth to the religious bodies; the functions of the central government were now limited to the stimulation of voluntary effort, the provision of an intelligence service and the raising of standards. The machinery of central government was left in so untidy a state that Kay-Shuttleworth's successors in office indeed looked primarily to their own reform scheme, their Revised Code, which made nonsense of his principles, as a measure of *relief* from an intolerable strain. But, in noting that, we should not forget that Kay-Shuttleworth left his administrative plans unfinished. Had he remained physically vigorous and in office I do not think his imaginative, constructive powers would have failed him. Nor do I think the main characteristics of his system would have undergone essential change.

The tract which he published in 1847, under a faint pretence of anonymity, in explanation of the council's minutes of the previous year, was in some sense an account of his stewardship, attempting as it did to put the chief acts of government in an order of importance, and assessing, with no mean skill in the use of irony, the strength of the criticism which in its various forms had been directed from high-church and dissenting quarters against the council's motives. It had been a period of barely eight years since he came into office, and yet, what seems to me to be of extraordinary interest, Kay-Shuttleworth believed that his work for public education, slight though its action might have been upon the quality of the schools currently teaching the children of the labouring poor, had greatly altered *opinion* about the need for the schooling of citizens. At the beginning of his period of office 'a considerable portion of the clergy and laity ... confidently held the conviction that the inevitable tendency of an elevated secular education was to unsettle

the mind of the working classes, . . . and if such instruction
were general it was feared that it would prepare an universal
insurrection of the poor against the rich, . . . of a race which
appeared to exist only to labour and to die'.

Now, some eight years later, as Kay-Shuttleworth reviews
his mission, something of great significance seems to have
happened. 'The best condition of the working classes . . . was
no longer considered to be one of unenterprising contentment,
uninstructed reverence, and unrepining submission.' Public
opinion was ready, he believed, for 'a system of national education by which the labouring classes might be made the intelligent supporters of order, and might adopt a faith not without
knowledge'.[1] Was this view justified?

The nation had moved from severe depression through 'the
hungry forties' to relative prosperity. Physical-force Chartism
had collapsed, at least for the time being, perhaps for good.
The forces which Kay-Shuttleworth had been playing so
adroitly were now held momentarily in balance. But for
sectarian jumpiness the State could even have assumed the
initiative in education and opened a chapter of constructive
planning.

Yet we may well regard Kay-Shuttleworth as over-com-
placent about the future. He could hardly have foreseen that
another twenty years must pass before the voluntaryists, his
most hostile critics, represented by Edward Baines of Leeds,
would throw in their hand and their depleted stakes; or before
the Church would yield its ancient claim to monopoly, or the
secularists begin to understand the language of their adversaries.
Kay-Shuttleworth was all this while compelled to stand idly by,
watching the authorities play for time and his own contemporaries one by one despair of action.

I should have liked to round off this account with some mention of Kay-Shuttleworth's work in other spheres—his work for
adult education for example, and his patient attention in his
later days to the reconstruction problems of the northern public
schools. Whatever he touched, whether it was the handling of
delinquent boys, the proper design of an industrial training
syllabus, or the shaping of local government finance, he introduced always some suggestion of practical value within the

[1] *Ibid.*, pp. 59, 60, 72.

limits of the problem set to him; limits which admittedly could on occasion be stretched to accommodate principles not too readily grasped by others; as when, in administering funds collected in New South Wales in aid of cotton-famine relief, he diverted a substantial part of the remittances his committee had received to the purposes of adult education, and told the indignant subscribers that their money had been 'eminently useful in maintaining order, in promoting cheerfulness, and in preventing the contraction of evil habits during a period of unwonted laziness'.[1]

His work as a national figure has to be assessed of course within the sphere of elementary education. Was it more than a coincidence that in the year of Kay-Shuttleworth's appointment to the privy council office, Carlyle was calling down the wind, in that already familiar voice of half-coherent prophecy for *a man*, or at least 'some fit official person', to make Britain tolerably literate—while leaving a final religious settlement to another day? 'To impart the gift of thinking,' said he, 'to those who cannot think, and yet who could in that case think: this, one would imagine, was the first function a government had to set about discharging.'[2] This at any rate was the prime function in the Kay-Shuttleworth design—odd though some of the features must seem to us of this singular progeny of his, conceived in the public dispensary, put out to nurse in the workhouse, breeched in the privy council office, chastised in the vestry, and beaten up in a Leeds newspaper office. As for the later experiences of this long-suffering but fundamentally tough little brat, I leave them to some of the lecturers who follow.

[1] W. O. Henderson, *The Lancashire Cotton Famine* (1934), p. 82.
[2] Thomas Carlyle, *Chartism* (1839), ch. x.

6

JOHN HENRY NEWMAN

*

A. C. F. BEALES

*A lecture delivered at King's College on 13 February 1951;
Professor G. Temple in the chair.*

> If this is a noble testimony to a great Christian life, it is as
> noble a proof of the justice, equity and uprightness of the English
> people. In venerating John Henry Newman it has unconsciously
> honoured itself. CARDINAL MANNING, in his *Panegyric* on Newman,
> 1890.

Just a hundred and twenty years ago, the Bishop of London
preached a remarkable sermon, on the relation of religion
to education. He made three points. First, the great value
of a knowledge of the universe; secondly, that such knowledge
relates to processes and secondary causes, but never to first
causes and ultimate realities; finally—and here are his words—
'Every system of education (therefore) which does not
embrace instruction in the doctrines and duties of our holy
religion, is defective in that which alone can impart to human
knowledge the principle of salubrity and life.'

The event is uniquely important for us here tonight. Not only
for its theme. Not only because this is the very theme of all that
John Henry Newman wrote on education in his long life of
ninety years. But because that sermon was preached by Bishop
Blomfield upstairs here in our chapel, on the occasion of the
opening of this College. In so far, then, as this College has held

fast to its title-deeds, there could be few fitter places for what is, in a sense, a centenary lecture on Newman's *Idea of a University*.[1]

I

But Newman's revelance to our current problems is indeed timeless. He was (as Lewis May has said) doubly an anachronism; for he stretched back to Athanasius and he anticipated Darwin. The other thinkers in this series of lectures were preoccupied with two of the three spiritual problems that fretted Victorian thought: how to make a man politically free yet law-abiding, how to make him morally free yet dutiful. The third Victorian dilemma—how to make a man intellectually free, yet religious—is Newman's pre-eminent field. To it he devoted his life.

Certain parts of his teaching have become the stock-in-trade of all discussions on the universities since, from Sir John Seeley and the royal commission to Sir Richard Livingstone and Sir Walter Moberly today. We have today that wistful stress on the magic of university 'residence', in *Redbrick*. We have a repudiaton of Newman's Anglo-Saxon view of a university as primarily a teaching and not a research institution, in Flexner. We have the warnings against rash specialization, re-echoed in F. R. Leavis. We have the clash between the 'spectator' and the 'ambulance' and the 'participant' views of the university, in Arnold Nash. We have a dull dismay, articulated by Spencer Leeson, at 'the training of experts for ends unspecified'. And we have the discovery of the late Archbishop of Canterbury, that the principles integrating our higher-studies curriculum are 'simultaneity and juxtaposition'.[2]

[1] See F. J. C. Hearnshaw, *Centenary History of King's College, London* (1929), p. 95. Newman doubted how far King's College *had* held fast. In commenting on the *entente* between Gower Street and the Strand, after the grant of the Charter, he tilted at the declared hope for harmonious *purpose* between 'two bodies, the latter of which was born and lives for no other purpose than to nullify the operations of the former'. (Article in Dublin *University Gazette*, 3rd May 1855, reprinted in *My Campaign in Ireland* (1896), pp. 325.*ff.*)

[2] Bruce Truscot, *Redbrick* (1943), and *Redbrick and These Vital Days* (1945); A. Flexner, *Universities: British, German, and American* (1931); F. R. Leavis, *Education and the Universities* (1943); Arnold Nash, *The University and the Modern World* (1945); Spencer Leeson, *Christian Education* (1947). Cf. also recent *German* criticism of the continental view, e.g., C. H. Becker and Max Scheler.

Other parts of Newman's message, on the contrary, have been undervalued and neglected: for example his subtle analysis of the psychological function of the different subjects in the curriculum, in those *Discourses on University Subjects* which seem no longer to be reprinted as part of *The Idea.*[1] In other parts, again, Newman himself had little to say on a problem that has become urgent since: the sociological aspect of education. The gentleman amateur who was Newman's ideal type is no longer considered an adequate type of upper-class training in a society that expects the 'enlightened expert'.[2] But on the question of sociological rights and duties, Newman's thought has been completed by Jacques Maritain, just as Froebel socialized Pestalozzi's *Anschauung.* The passage is beyond price:

'Social life . . . subordinates the individual to the common good, but always in order that the common good flow back upon the individuals, and that they enjoy that freedom of expansion or independence which is insured by the economic guarantees of labour and ownership, political rights, civil virtues, and the cultivation of the mind. . . . The man and the group are intermingled with each other, and they surpass each other in different respects. Man finds himself by subordinating himself to the group, and the group attains its goal only by serving man and by realizing that man has secrets which escape the group and a vocation which is not included in the group.'[3]

That passage epitomises Catholic social and educational teaching today. Newman did not write it, but it could not have been written from any standpoint but that of the transcendental Christian Humanism of which Newman was England's outstanding nineteenth-century exponent. It completes his thought.

As Mandell Creighton once said, however, a man is best judged less by what he did than by what he chose to do. What Newman chose to do was to remind his generation of *ends*, already lost sight of in the pursuit of means and machinery. That is the perspective of his work, too, which can help us most today; for our British view has continued to contract. We have achieved at last an educational planning based on contradiction.

[1] Cf. F. Charmot, *L'Humanisme et l'humain* (1934), and J. Castiello, *A Humane Psychology of Education* (1937), p. 234.
[2] Nash, *loc. cit.,* pp. 171ff.
[3] Maritain, *Education at the Crossroads* (1943), pp. 14–15, 98.

The leading work on our curriculum today declares impeccably
that 'the question of a curriculum does not arise until the prior
questions of why society exists at all, and what functions its
schools are to fulfil, have been settled first'. But the dust-jacket
of that *Report* announces that, having already decided the
length of school-life and the kinds of school, we must now plan
their content.[1]

II

In Newman's long life of achievement (always the same age as
the century), there were some remarkable near-misses. Trinity
College at Oxford, which brought him to tears of joy in his old
age by making him an honorary fellow in 1879, might never
have had him at all as a young student, had not his father asked
an Oxford friend for advice as to 'which university?' when the
cab was already at the door and the young John Henry's
luggage already aloft. Or again, his great hope in becoming a
cardinal was that he might now at last urge, at the Pope's side
and as one of his advisers, the schemes for educational reform
among laity and clergy for which he had so long striven. How
much he could have done, we shall never know; for his journey
to Rome on all this in 1880 was prevented by a fall which broke
two of his ribs. Or again, the red hat itself might not in the end
have been conferred, had not the Duke of Norfolk written post-
haste to warn Manning (who had incontinently notified
Newman's 'refusal' of it to *The Times*) that Newman was not
refusing it but only wanted the Pope to know, before ratifying
the honour, that he did not wish to have to go and live in
Rome: he preferred to live in Birmingham.[2]

So too were there paradoxes. The cardinal of 1879 was
the man who had helped to unseat Peel for favouring Catholic
Emancipation. He was the champion of Papal supremacy, yet
(according to Frederick Denison Maurice) he disliked Luther
less for his anti-Popery than for his revolt from Aristotle and
Aquinas. His range of intimate friends was a whole cross-
section of several nations; yet so remote was he from politics that
his letters from Rome in 1848 (of all years) record no unusual

[1] *Report on Curriculum Reform* ('The Content of Education'), 1945.
[2] Wilfrid Ward, *Life of Newman*, i, 32, ii, 440–6, ii, 476,

events; and so remote was he from popular literature that once when he read a novel that deeply appealed to him he gravely regretted that it had no index. His mind and spirit were of an unearthly serenity; yet I have found no recorded occasion when anyone heard him laugh outright. When his *Apologia* appeared in 1864, it was the scholastics that it upset, not the scientists; Sir Charles Lyell was fascinated by Newman's argument on probable evidence as the basis of ordinary certitude; the scholastics misunderstood it, till he paraphrased it for them in a simile that a child could understand. Above all, the educationist who taught in the tradition of Aquinas, Sadoleto, Cardinal Antoniano, the Jesuits, Joseph Calasanctius, and John Baptist De la Salle, got his message not so much from them as from Oxford and Oscott.[1] He is beyond all doubt the greatest English Catholic educationist since the Reformation; yet, whereas his writings have formed whole generations since, and inspired those Newman Societies which form the graduate-wing of so many of the University Catholic Federations throughout the world, the two practical attempts he made in his lifetime to actualize the higher education he conceived became total failures.

There is not often a career more happy in things eternal and at the same time more sad in things temporal. Newman could never fit, as Manning fitted so neatly, 'into the machine'. The contrast between the Richmond drawing of him, in the Oriel days to which he ever looked back so wistfully, and the several photographs of his Catholic decades, is arresting. And the contrast again, between those photographs and the portraits of his serenity after 1879, when his fear had gone 'forever' that his dedicated life was misunderstood by even the highest in the Church Militant, is poignant in the extreme. The motto he chose for his cardinal's shield, and for his pall—*Cor ad cor loquitur*—typifies Newman's immortal soul. But his mortal temperament is revealed in a typical sentence he wrote to Pusey in 1866, before his second abortive attempt to create a Catholic College at Oxford: 'I look forward to it (he said) with great distress.' His intimate correspondents might well have called those words, had they known the expression, Dr. Newman's signature-tune.

[1] *Life*, i, 193, ii, 43; F. Maurice, *Life of F. D. Maurice*, ii, 615.

So much of his life is indeed epitomized in those words. Compared with the swashbucking distrust of Kingsley (to whom we have to be grateful, for he produced the *Apologia*), the distrust of his own friends and superiors seared his soul. Compared with the insensate hostility of Mgr. Talbot in Rome, who once went so far as to say that 'Dr. Newman is the most dangerous man in England' (but later set his own assessment on his own judgment by dying in a mad-house), the hostility of Manning and W. G. Ward, who shared Newman's profoundest aims in education and loved him while they fought him in the public press, came near at times to breaking his heart. Because he could identify himself with so much in all parties, in each of the public questions of the day from the Thirty-Nine Articles in 1833 to the definition of Papal Infallibility in 1870, Newman could never be wholeheartedly acclaimed by any party on any subject: and this was torture to him. On so many of the issues the passage of time has proved him more right than even he knew. Consider them. He had preached the need for an intellectual apostolate, in an age that was coming to regard the case for Christianity as simply not intellectually reputable. He had urged the place of an educated laity in realms of *initiative* in which the Catholic Church has rarely been altogether happy to visualize them. He had taught the simple impossibility of any clash between theological dogma and natural science. He had said what makes the world go round is less perhaps the logic of what men believe than the psychology of why they believe (the whole essence of his *Grammar of Assent*). He had tilted at the paradox of a clergy rooted in the people they served yet trained in the disembodied atmosphere that most seminaries then had. He had thundered out the great value of the Established Church of England as a co-bulwark against infidelity (at a time when his fellow-Catholics were prone to rejoice at each fresh Anglican reverse). And he stood for a revitalized humanism in the universities such as they had known in the first period of the Renaissance, the period of Erasmus and Saint Thomas More. But, in all these matters, the storms he had to encounter, from friend and foe alike, were such that they would be more understandable (humanly speaking) if it had really been some inscrutable design of Providence, having brought him into the Catholic Church, to drive him out again.

133

Perhaps he was *inevitably* unhappy. For his deepest convictions, says his biographer, 'were so compatible with a keen sense of all that told against them'.[1] Thrice only did he strike out as men expected him to: in his *Present Position of Catholics*, just after the outcry caused by the restoration of the hierarchy in 1850; in his *Apologia* defending his own honour and that of the Church in 1864 against Kingsley; and late in life, in *My Campaign in Ireland*. For the rest, he combined a human flair for incisive criticism of constituted authority, with a superhuman flair, when authority spoke within its sphere, for what his Superiors must sometimes have felt was a most implacable submissiveness. All parties looked to him, so wide was his understanding of their several facets of the truth, and his faith in their motives. He has been compared to Pascal, and Fénelon, and Bossuet, as defender in his own day against the erosions of faith they had resisted in theirs. But while he cheered Montalembert, he was not a liberal Catholic of the school of Lord Acton; and while he cheered Dupanloup over Papal Infallibility, he was no Gallican. He was fundamentally ultramontane, but it was the ultramontanism of doctrine and never in the least of politics: of Lacordaire, not of Manning or Cardinal Cullen. And while he wrote on universities (for the few), it was at heart because he treasured so deeply the destinies of the many.

Hence W. G. Ward could denounce him as a liberal, and James Anthony Froude could caricature him as an obscurantist, and both remain his friends. Hence also, the latest editions of his university lectures in this country can blithely omit the three Discourses which alone give the others any ultimate meaning at all. (It is only just to add that his latest Irish editor does the same.)

There is a whole century and more of testimony to his personal charm and magnetism. Those who detested his Catholic ideas, but had met him, loved his person and his voice.[2] Several hundreds made up the total of Oxford Movement converts who followed (even preceded) him in seceding to Rome. His influence on the Young England Party of Lord John Manners—like that of his fellow-Oratorian, Faber—was

[1] *Life*, i, 14.
[2] J. A. Froude, *Short Studies*, i, 154, for a sustained description.

ROCANV

profound.[1] 'There are four people', wrote Matthew Arnold to Newman in 1872, 'from whom I am conscious of having learnt' —and Newman was one of them.[2] Mark Pattison wrote of him late in life as 'my dear master'.[3] At the other extreme, no one's enmity to him came within miles of being personal. 'I think', Newman himself said to young Wilfred Ward in 1885, recalling the elder Ward's opposition to him over the Oxford Oratory schemes and the *Rambler* quarterly, 'I think his theory was that I was all the more dangerous because I was so attractive—that I was a sort of syren of whose fascination all should beware'. There was no hint of arrogance in this, however. On the contrary, he once expressed himself 'relieved' to hear that an original idea he had conceived was not original after all; 'I feared', he said, 'that if none *had* thought of it, it was not very probable it could be sound.'[4]

III

His own intellectual formation was built up from a body of imaginative literature which, curiously enough, shows its influence in his own style rarely, outside the *Lyra Heroica* and the *Dream of Gerontius*. In particular he owed much to Milman's *Church History* and to the novels of Sir Walter Scott, from which he drew two fixed principles: 'Holiness before peace', and 'Growth the only evidence of life'.[5] Here are the germs of his *Essay on the Development of Doctrine*, and the reason why all that he said and wrote on philosophy and education was subordinate to (and to him meaningless without) religious duty. Academically, while cutting his teeth on Gibbon and Locke, he came upon Joseph Butler's *Analogy of Religion*, yet another book written to arrest a tide of latitudinarian infidelity. Butler's illuminating insistence that 'probability is the guide of life', in matters small and great, Newman matured into the distinction between a man's *certitude* on a matter and the reasons that he could *give*

[1] C. Whibley, *Lord John Manners and his Friends*, i, 70–2; Monypenny, *Disraeli*, ii, 164.
[2] W. F. Connell, *Matthew Arnold*, p. 33.
[3] *Life*, ii, 481.   [4] *Ibid.*, 494, 496.
[5] For a full analysis of the background of Newman's thought see S. P. Juergens, *Newman and the Psychology of Faith in the Individual* (1928), ch. v; and F. McGrath, *Newman's University: Idea and Reality* (1951).

for his certitude; a distinction that dominates the *Grammar of Assent*.

Butler, and Paley's *Evidences*, were the books on which, at fifteen, he had begun to erect his religious position, starting from a certitude of only two things—God's existence, and his own.[1] It is a meagre initial equipment perhaps, but only the minority today seem to have as much.

It was at Oriel, where he spent the only carefree years of his whole career, that the Provost (Hawkins) and Whateley taught him 'to think correctly', and to venerate tradition, with dogma as the touchstone of tradition: the kernel of his work on *The Arians of the Fourth Century*. What he affectionately called the Oriel *clique*, of Copleston, Davison, Whateley, Hawkins, and Arnold, influenced his mind for all time. It was from Hurrell Froude that he derived by 'moral contagion' his lifelong equation of liberalism with latitudinarianism, and saw in it the sapping of any ultimate faith in humanity. And it was from Blanco White, a Catholic-turned-rationalist, that he grasped how the educated mind could so 'naturally' find pause, though not permanent rest, in indifferentism.[2]

With his theological development we are not here concerned, from the moment when he became a High Churchman in 1828 on a diet of the early Fathers, down through the years of the *Tracts for the Times*, with his anticipation of Darwin by fourteen years, and his ultimate secession and departure from Littlemore. Few pilgrimages in modern history have been more widely or more touchingly reconstructed by the historians. Our concern is with his educational ideas. And to that there are two sides.

In his war on continental liberalism we have the negative side. In his three great educational books we have the positive side. His practical schemes at Oxford and in Ireland are the bridge between.

He planned his course while an Anglican, he put it into action when he became a Catholic. The seeds of nineteenth-century unbelief were already being sown around him in the agnosticism of Matthew Arnold, J. A. Froude and Thomas Huxley. All

[1] *Apologia*, p. 198.
[2] Newman's *Letters*, i, 105–7; i, 114; R. H. Hutton, *Newman*, pp. 21, 36; *Life*, i, 38.

these men he was to know with increasing intimacy. Even before his conversion he saw the Catholic Church as the one educational institution certain to ride the coming storm. But while he saw her as a living power, endowed with all the vitality and recurrent freshness that had ennobled some of Macaulay's prose about her, and sustained by supernatural strength, still he saw her crippled and enervated, first by the decay of theological schools after the French Revolution, and then by the onset of a centralizing movement—Lammenais and De Maistre and the predecessor of Pius IX—unsympathetic to intellectual experiments or to popular education at large. In such circumstances he looked on the tactic of Wiseman and Manning and W. G. Ward and Talbot—to withdraw within the citadel and do battle with the modern mind from the ramparts—as fatuous and suicidal.

What is important here in Newman is that he identified liberalism with latitudinarianism, and both with that supreme contribution of the Renaissance—individualism: 'the view that it is not at all important what doctrine a man holds, so long as [like Hitler] he acts up conscientiously to whatever doctrine he does honestly hold'. As a view of Revelation, and as a guide for education, Newman pronounced this view to be absurd. But it was in the ascendant; and (as Whitehead has said) 'the notion that every action is at once a private experience *and* a public utility, had to be born again', what time the twin doctrines of individualism and competition were producing not the vaunted harmony but industrial slavery.[1]

To Newman the matter was terribly urgent. The intellectual outlook of the century was apt to become set in the groove of John Locke—that *moral* certitude, on anything, was invalid and impossible: especially as the Christian school of Paley had seemed to accept this principle, while the Evangelicals on the other hand were championing no intellectual grounds for faith at all.[2] The work to be done, accordingly, was precisely what the Oxford Movement had set itself to do: to 'impart intellectual depth to . . . traditional theology and spiritual life to its institutions'.[3] Here the universities were the key-position.

[1] Hutton, p. 92; A. N. Whitehead, *Adventures of Ideas*, p. 36.
[2] Juergens, p. 4.
[3] *Life*, i, 105 and note.

IV

So urgent was it all, that from the moment of his reception into the Church of Rome Newman saw his mission as one of action. In his first year, at Maryvale, he contemplated founding a divinity school, and then abandoned it for the wider mission of preaching to all and sundry, as soon typified in the Birmingham and London Oratories of Saint Philip Neri (1848–9), which are today his ecclesiastical monuments. He chose the Oratorian life, from among the other Orders, for its rule and its range. To him the unacknowledged legislator of the world was not the poet but the dedicated man. From the start he saw his Oratory as including 'the function of a Mechanics' Institute' and an ecclesiastical training college. Such a notion was perhaps impossible amid the prevailing outlook of the professors in Rome, so little aware that 'theologians unfamiliar with the minds of unbelievers might be ineffective in polemic'.[1] In any event, Newman's practical genius, ever drawn to help the lay world *direct*, concentrated henceforth on the two projects that have made his public career as a teacher—the Irish university scheme and the plan for Catholic undergraduates at Oxford and Cambridge.

There can be no doubt whatever that, in setting up three inter-denominational colleges in 1846, at Galway and Cork and Belfast, Sir Robert Peel had made an iraenic gesture towards the Catholic majority in Ireland, debarred by their consciences from Trinity College in Dublin and lacking any alternative university education. It is equally certain that the Archbishop of Dublin, Dr. Murray, was in favour of Peel's scheme. For while in theory the new Queen's Colleges would be inter-denominational, they would he thought become overwhelmingly Catholic in fact; at all events that was what had happened already in the Government's inter-denominational primary schools. But in taking a realistic view on this question of 'mixed education' Dr. Murray was almost alone among the Catholic Irish. The fall of Peel, and the known views of the late Pope, and the new Pope (Pius IX), fortified the Irish Hierarchy in

[1] Lewis May, *Newman*, p. 82; *Life*, i, 123, 149, 24, 247, and letters in ch. iv–vi; Hutton, p. 120.

banning the three Colleges, at the Synod of Thurles in 1850. They decided to establish instead, for themselves, a Catholic University of Ireland. This was to be the answer of Dr. Paul Cullen (later Archbishop of Armagh) to the dangers latent in the new liberal-scientific education, which had already transformed Oxford itself in the space of ten years, as Mark Pattison records.

So far Newman agreed. But Newman feared equally the tendency of denominational education to become obscurantist. When therefore the Bishops invited him in April 1851, at Wiseman's instigation, to become Rector of their new university, it was in that spirit of *via media* that he accepted: a middle way between the Queen's Colleges which excluded theology and the Cullen idea which would exclude science. To that extent the initial situation can be seen to predetermine the line of argument he was to take in his lectures on *The Idea of a University*, building on what he had already preached in Saint Mary's.

He looked, for a precedent, not to medieval Paris or Oxford, for times had changed. Scholasticism had long since fallen from its thirteenth-century peak; the conduct of inquiry had by now long been set in a direction empirical rather than deductive; all higher education had now to be accommodated to industrialism and proletarianism. Newman's Irish University, the *forum* in which he delivered the lectures on the *Idea*, was based on the precedent of modern Belgium, where the Catholic University of Louvain had been set up, with Papal approval, in 1834, carrying five faculties, maintained from the private contributions of the Catholic part of the population, and led by a Rector (Dr. Franz de Ram) whom Newman had consulted diligently.[1]

But the initial situation presaged equally the entire failure of the enterprise. When Newman went to Ireland, it was 'as if a Persian cat of royal lineage had strayed by accident into some

---

[1] *Life*, i, 314–15; L. van der Essen, *L'Université de Louvain, 1425–1940* (1945). Louvain is one of the climaxes in the survey of *The Rise and Progress of Universities* in which, for the Dublin *University Gazette*, Newman traced the flowering of university life from Athens onwards, through medieval Paris and Oxford, to the reform movements he had himself shared in, and the collateral developments in the U.S.A. at Yale (published as vol. iii of his *Historical Sketches*).

great, draughty, dilapidated house, where the pets, a miscellaneous rabble of hard-bitten, wire-haired terriers, were suffered
to roam at will. Some of the terriers growled . . . others
glowered . . . while some (but they were very few) frolicked
and gambolled'.[1] Not only so. The College was to be in Dublin
—Dublin was in Dr. Murray's diocese—and Dr. Murray was
against it. Newman stipulated for a free hand in the appointment of professors, but Dr. Cullen contrived to outwit this by
the massive simplicity of not answering letters for two whole
years, and meanwhile making the appointments himself.[2]
Cullen, we are told, was 'a conscientious administrator with
with the intellectual outlook of a sacristan'.[3] Newman's
determined efforts to recruit professors from England, to supply
the university background which Irish scholarship lacked,
came to grief from two directions: the English dons could not
come, and the Irish bishops would suffer neither Englishmen
nor Young Irelanders.

'It is very wonderful', wrote Newman early on; 'Keble,
Pusey, Maurice, Sewell, who have been able to do little against
Liberalism at Oxford, will be renewing the fight, although not
in their persons, in Ireland'. But disillusionment came quickly.
'These Bishops are so accustomed to be absolute', he found,
'that they usurp the rights of others and ride roughshod over
their wishes and their plans, quite innocently, without meaning
it, and are astonished, not at finding out the fact, but at its
being impossible to these others'. He seemed to be carrying out
'not a great Council's resolve but a hobby of my own!'[4]

The educated Irish laity were known to be in favour of mixed
education. The cannier among the Bishops realized that the
Catholic University would therefore wilt (twelve of them
petitioned Rome against it!) and that Newman's dream of
Dublin's central position attracting scholarship from both
England and the United States was a chimera. Wise priests
warned him (over their ubiquitous cold mutton) that the class
of student needed did not exist in Ireland. The middle-class was
too poor, the rich went to Trinity or to Oxford, and the chance
of any thriving 'evening population, answering to the day-

---

[1] Lewis May, p. 136.   [2] Professorial list in *Life*, i, 359 and note.
[3] Lewis May, p. 129.
[4] To Mrs. W. Froude, October 1851, *Life*, i, 312; also i, 323, 327.

pupils of King's College, London', was negligible.[1] In any case, argued Dr. Doyle, 'how can separate education be carried on completely? When people are mixed, and society is mixed, education must be mixed'. But it was to need a further forty years before this view could prevail, even among the Catholics of England.

Newman was bound to fail: even had he secured a royal charter for the university. Not that the Irish knew the whole of his plan. 'One special idea I have', he wrote to Healy Thompson in 1853, 'of course all this is secret, to try to get an influence over the principal schools and Colleges in Ireland. . . .'[2] How would the bishops of the Synod of Thurles have reacted to that! But they knew enough to grasp that the higher education of Catholic Ireland was to be handed over to an Englishman, and a very recent convert-gentleman at that. Q.E.D.

Nevertheless he left behind him, after the four unhappy years, some brilliant mosaic-pieces, for those who came after him to integrate if they would. There are the University Church, the *University Gazette*, the Medical Schools, the Engineering Schools, and the cult of Celtic literature under O'Curry. But the enduring monument is his *Discourses*.[3]

In the failure of his Oxford scheme in the next decade there is far more true irony. For this foundered on the rock of liberalism itself. His adversaries in the Church were able to persuade Rome (such was Newman's fairmindedness in every question he touched) that he was tainted with the very latitudinarianism he was withstanding; and worse still, that he was encouraging the laity in a like perdition.

The charge was superficially plausible enough. When the *Rambler*, edited by Capes and Simpson and Acton, lampooned the ultramontanes in France and England, Newman could not but sympathize, even while he feared, as any Roman, the dabbling of these young intellectuals with the utilitarian ideas of John Stuart Mill, which would make them what he once called 'a bad imitation of polished ungodliness'.[4] From a

---

[1] Cf. Fr. Curtis, the S. J. Provincial, in *Life*, i, 333.

[2] *Healy Thompson Mss.*, custody of Catholic Record Society.

[3] For the post-Newman history of the Irish University, see the bibliography at pp. 165–6 of R. J. McHugh's (1944) edition of Newman's *Idea*, and McGrath, ch. xx.

[4] *Sermons to Mixed Congregations* (No. 6), 1849.

critical attitude to their faith, in the crisis of the century, the balance would undoubtedly be gain and not loss; 'conservatism in essentials . . . (but) new replies to new difficulties'. It was in just that way that the educated Christian apologetic had reacted at the two peak-points in the past, in the patristic and the scholastic ages. 'There is no greater mistake', Newman declared, 'than to suppose that revealed Truth precludes originality in the treatment of it'. But the bishops were too busy, and the aristocracy were 'left without leaders'. All honour, then, to Acton and the *Rambler*—provided they tempered moderation with tact.[1]

But that was the last thing the *Rambler* was disposed to do They had only themselves to blame, accordingly, when, acclaiming certain parts of the liberal tenets in Europe that only a bigot would have resisted, political and scientific freedom as preached by Montalembert in France and Döllinger in Germany, they allowed the Old Guard of Ultramontane watchdogs (Manning and Ward) to infer that they were adopting the liberal programme *in toto* (Pius IX and the *Syllabus Errorum* in due time notwithstanding). Acton brought the liberal-ultramontane controversy to England hot from Germany, where he had been reared in it. These were the elements that produced the world-shaking climax of the Munich Congress of 1863, when Acton and Döllinger together were censured by Rome.

On the principle, then, that he who touches pitch is defiled, Newman's *own* orthodoxy came inevitably into question when, in 1859, with a characteristically Newman gesture, he intervened to save these young pioneers from their own headstrong zeal by taking over the editorship of the *Rambler* himself. Once again he was seeking a *via media*, this time between Ward and Acton. Once again he got the worst of both worlds.

The ironies in all this are colossal. We have Ward confiding to Newman that 'the Cardinal [Wiseman] is an omnipresent supreme inquisitor . . . abounding in most admirable instincts but not a reasonable being in any shape', and yet a few years later refusing Newman space in the *Dublin Review* to clear his name, lest Dr. Newman *become* (save the mark!) the leader of a school of thought. Wiseman meanwhile had passed from irritation (at what the *Rambler* said of his own views on the

[1] Cf. *Life*, i, 433, 436.

Newcastle Commission of Education) to fury (at H. N. Oxen-
ham's jaunty criticisms of the whole system of *clerical* education
—based on quotations torn, without Newman's permission,
from Newman's own works). When the *Rambler* finally elected
to pontificate about the Temporal Power of the Papacy (in
Garibaldi's year 1861, of all years), it was finished. And though
Newman easily cleared his name among the bishops and the
laity at large, he failed to allay the suspicions of Manning and
Ward. Since, then, it was they who held the ear of Rome,
through Mgr. Talbot, Newman's Oxford scheme was doomed
from the start.[1]

This Oxford scheme was to Newman a second-best, a
Catholic University having failed and there being no likelihood
that Prior Park or Oscott could become one. To Newman, as
indeed to Wiseman at first, there was a happy omen in the
fact that the religious tests which excluded Catholics and
Nonconformists from Oxford and Cambridge degrees were
removed in 1854. But to Manning and Ward the 'trickle' of
boys to the ancient universities that at once began was matter
for alarm. And the rumour in 1864 that Newman was buying a
plot of land in Oxford, on which to build an Oratory, was
baleful indeed.

There is no doubt that Newman did actually envisage a
Catholic permeation of Oxford, whereby the University could
do for future generations what Oriel had done for him. 'Can
the Oratory', he wrote to Hope-Scott at the outset, 'that is,
[can] I, when once set up, without saying a word to anyone,
make the Oratory a Hall?'[2] As to dangers of faith, he argued
that there would now be a Catholic return to Oxford in any
case; and that the wise course for the bishops was 'to preside
at that return and minimize its dangers'. This is the line (and
almost the words) taken by Cardinal Vaughan in settling the
matter—thirty years later. Nor was it the idea to infiltrate a
controversial advance-guard. Newman saw the problem as
that of Catholics *and* Anglicans fulfilling their responsibility, as
'creative minorities', at a time of growing intellectual crisis.
He went ahead, bought his land, and issued his circular.[3]

[1] *Life*, i, 439, 501, 526; and *Healy Thompson Mss.*
[2] *Life*, ii, 51; Hope-Scott *Memoirs*; and cf. *Life*, ii, 126.
[3] *Ibid.*, 44–5, 57, and ii, 486 for his tribute on this, in a letter to Pusey in
1882.

But to Ward and Manning this return of Newman to Oxford, at the very moment when his *Apologia* had endeared him anew to the whole nation, would be 'like Napoleon landing in France after his escape from Elba—and no Waterloo in sight'. The prospect of Newman attracting Catholic youth to Oxford, in the insidious intellectual climate of a secular university, was too awful to contemplate. Hence the feverish correspondence between Manning and Ward in London and Talbot in Rome, which has been so often retailed in all its disedifying richness, whereby in the end the bishops (except Newman's own Ordinary, Ullathorne) issued their *non placets*, fortified by the approval of Roman authorities little in touch with the English scene, as they have sometimes been since.

Anything like an objective approach to the matter, such as Wiseman had professed to secure by circulating to a number of distinguished converts (though not to Newman) a questionnaire, was vitiated by the terms of the questionnaire itself. Maisie Ward has summed up its purport: 'Do you think Catholics should be prohibited from attending the Universities, or are you an enemy of God and man?'[1]

The biographer of Bishop Grant of Southwark, writing some ten years later, before the atmosphere had changed, records with incredible unconcern that 'it remained to pacify the irritation provoked by what some ambitious and worldly-minded Catholics were pleased to consider an arbitrary and narrow-minded ban'. They must have been very pleased to call it that.[2]

From this Oxford episode there emerge, in revolutionary quality, two themes, both of them significant for the altered picture of the same fundamental problem in our own century. These are: Newman's trust in and championship of the laity, and his sense of the surviving strength of the Church of England.

Lay initiative, to him, was an acid test of health in the Church. He never forgot what had been achieved by the un-

[1] Maisie Ward, *The Wilfrid Wards and the Transition* (1934), p. 265.
[2] The second phase of this enterprise, when Ullathorne again offered Newman the Oxford Mission, in 1866-7, is given in detail in *Life*, ii, ch. 24. For the later history of the Catholic return to Oxford (after 1895), following Manning's abortive attempt at a Kensington College, see *sources* in the letters printed in the biographies of the principal persons concerned, and *outline* by H. O. Evennett in *The English Catholics, 1850-1950* (1950), ch. 10.

official adventurers of the Oxford Movement itself. A long letter to Capes, as early as 1851, came near to a veritable *programme* for an intellectual lay apostolate. So did the *Rambler* article which roused such a storm against him in 1859, on 'Consulting the Faithful in Matters of Doctrine'—a function he traced historically through those critical moments at which, as at the Council of Nicea, the laity had guarded the tradition against even unorthodox bishops. Mgr. Talbot felt that Newman wished 'to govern the Church in England by public opinion'. 'Are they not doing the Holy See a grave disservice,' cried Newman, 'who will not let a zealous man defend it *in his own way*, but insist on his doing it in their way or not at all?'[1]

And by the same token he cherished the Establishment. He would not weaken it, least of all in Oxford. Once and once only did he attack the Church of England—and then as counter-attack for the outcry on the restoration of the hierarchy. 'I don't', he said of his permanent position, 'I don't look on the Church of England as important in contrast to Dissent, but as a bulwark against infidelity which Dissent cannot be. . . . The various denominations exist under the shadow of the Establishment, out of which they sprang, and did it go would go too. . . . Infidelity would take possession of the bulk . . .'. 'The Anglican Church', he said in 1863, 'upholds far more truth in England than any other form of religion would, and than the Catholic Roman Church could.'[2]

In this attitude he has been followed most closely by the Thomist school in Maritain, Gilson and Christopher Dawson. 'There does exist, indeed', said Maritain to the Americans during the War,

'. . . among the divers great metaphysical outlooks, if they recognise the dignity of the spirit, and among the diverse forms of Christian creeds, or even of religious creeds in general, if they recognise the divine destiny of man, a community of analogy as concerns practical attitudes and the realm of action, which makes possible a genuine human co-operation.'[3]

Neither policy—the lay formation, and the alignment of all the Christian forces—was absent from anything Newman subsequently wrote. 'When I see a thoughtful young man', he

[1] Cf. Newman's letters, in *Life*, i, 262*f*, 502*f*; ii, 69, 147, 208.
[2] Cf. *Life*, i, 232*f*, 259; i, 651.　　[3] *Education at the Crossroads*, p. 7.

wrote late in life, 'I feel a kind of awe and even terror. . . . How will he be able to stand against the intellectual flood that is setting in against Christianity?' The watchwords must be: full discussion, and specialized research. It was thus an intense delight when Leo XIII's Encyclical honoured the Thomist philosophy in 1879. For in Aquinas lay that fulness of conception as to education which had been the positive side of Newman's work: to which we now turn.[1]

V

While it is true that the discourses long since known to the world as *The Idea of a University*, which Walter Pater called 'the perfect handling of a theory', give the core of Newman's teaching on education, they cannot be considered alone. For the *University Sketches*, the *Apologia*, the *Grammar of Assent*, and many of his collections of sermons and historical sketches are integral parts of the same *corpus*. To read Newman piecemeal, as was once said of the writing of history, is to tear a seamless robe.

Hutton saw in all Newman's writing 'the most unhesitating confidence that difficulties will vanish utterly away when viewed in the full light of the Christian Revelation'. Certainly Newman himself roundly explained that ten thousand difficulties do not necessarily make one single doubt. It is there perhaps, that we find the secret of that profound insight into the difficulties of others, which was the basis of his gift as a teacher in handling them, in that limpid style modelled consciously on only one man—Cicero: a style untouched by the famous newman 'irony' till he was past fifty, a style 'always aiming at effect and never missing it'.[2]

Nor is it fitting to read any of his three major educational works as classics issuing from a don's study. They were thrown into the world's arena. That is the very atmosphere they breathe: of a strategist thankful that he is fighting on interior lines, since he may be struck from the back as well as from the front. The practical reforms for Oxford University that show through his letters as an Anglican are buttressed by the philo-

[1] *Life*, ii, 473*f*, 497*f*.
[2] Hutton, p. 7; Augustine Birrell, *Essays*, p. 185; and cf. Sir A. Quiller-Couch, *Art of Writing*, p. 31.

sophical position he expounded as a Catholic. The age of mass-production which was literally cheapening factual knowledge terrified him, lest it should make the cry of Utility irresistible to the whole of the next generation. For these were the marvellous decades of railways, the telegraph, photography, and the submarine cable. Wherefore he lectured on the essence, and the limitations, of true knowledge.

From each negative element in the prevailing background he draws a positive. The Queen's Colleges were inadequate—because religion must be central to education. A university would be worth the effort involved to establish it—because of a fundamental purpose in the *idea*. And above all, the paradox, about the function of a university being intellectual and not moral, so misunderstood by his contemporaries: that a liberal education means knowledge for its own sake precisely because knowledge has *no* 'own' sake, but serves the transcendental purposes for which man was created.

All this was said for the benefit of those who looked back, to the reforms at Oxford under Copleston and Davison during the attacks of the *Edinburgh Review*, and of those who looked forward, to 'integral' action on the report of the Royal Commission on Oxford which was sitting as he prepared the lectures.[1] For the benefit of all the protagonists he took the discussion far beyond the narrow limits of hitherto, of a university as a classical institution (half clerical seminary and half race-course, said Huxley), and argued in terms of an almost limitless curriculum, focussed in the four historic Faculties of Arts, Law, Medicine, and Theology'. And here as elsewhere his argument is the same for the older universities and the provincial universities, which at the time were dimly heralded in the new College at Liverpool, the same for the old classicism of the public schools and the new 'utility' and 'smatterings' of the mechanics' institutes; the same for the believer and the agnostic. He was lecturing in a Catholic university, but the foundation of his argument was the Natural Law of the natural man.

[1] For the university reforms, see C. E. Mallet, *Hist. Univ. Oxford* (1927), vol. iii; D. A. Winstanley, *Later Victorian Cambridge* (1947); T. L. Humberstone, *University Reform in London* (1926); and A. I. Tillyard, *History of University Reform* (1913). And see Newman's memorandum to the Irish Bishops in November, 1851, in *My Campaign in Ireland*, pp. 77–8.

The range of curriculum he envisaged has been challenged in our own day by Bruce Truscot, not only on the ground that *studium generale* originally meant the people rather than the subjects of study (which is a point Newman himself made clear), but because Newman intended *universal* knowledge at all. But we must not forget the limiting qualities in Newman's use of both 'knowledge' and (still more) 'liberal education'. What he canvassed was that, while different specializations might well be as varied a feature in the future as in the past, 'all branches of knowledge are pre-supposed or implied, and *none omitted on principle*'.[1] Universal knowledge was to be a negative sanction: a criterion of non-exclusion. And no doubt many of those who do disagree with him (that it is the business of a university to teach all branches of knowledge), face to face with the fragmentation of knowledge due to that same specialization, feel a trifle wistful. With Newman, *un*related study is dangerous to true humanism; specialization therefore can be evil; but specialization is necessary in the modern world; it must therefore be saved, by liberal education, from disintegration—just as the specialist don is saved by continuous contact with his fellow specialists. Historically the upshot of this has been curious. For while Jowett at Oxford took the Newman view (of a 'teaching' university) too far, the modern universities have set too little store on it, but tended instead to research begun too soon on an insufficient background of general education.[2]

Nor was the 'idea' a matter of *dillettanti* studies pursued by a privileged minority of cultivated 'gentlemen', as (again) some of the best-quoted passages have been glossed. The Introductory Discourse is devoted largely to making plain that the author's argument is for *all* comers, on a basis of simple 'human reason and wisdom', and concerned with practical questions. And 'if a practical end must be assigned to a University course', he says towards the end, 'I say it is that of training good members of society. Its art is the art of social life, and its end is fitness for the world'.[3]

[1] Cf. *Redbrick*, pp. 46–7; *Idea*, Appendix to the (rare) first edition of 1852, and pp. 20, 378 of standard (Longmans) edition.
[2] Cf. W. R. Halliday, in *Schools of England* (edited by J. Dover Wilson), (1928), pp. 244–5.
[3] *Idea*, p. 177.

'I have laid down,' he says, summing up the burden of the nine Discourses (originally ten),

'that all branches of knowledge are, at least implicitly, the subject-matter of its teaching; that these branches are not isolated and independent one of another, but form together a whole or system; that they run into each other, and complete each other, and that, in proportion to our view of them as a whole, is the exactness and trustworthiness of the knowledge which they separately convey; that the process of imparting knowledge to the intellect in this philosophical way is its true culture; that such culture is good in itself; that the knowledge which is both its instrument and result is called Liberal Knowledge; that such culture, together with the knowledge which effects it, may fitly be sought for its own sake; that it is, however, in addition, of great secular utility, as constituting the best and highest formation of the intellect for political and social life; and lastly, that, considered in its religious aspect, it concurs with Christianity a certain way, and then diverges from it; and consequently proves in the event, sometimes its serviceable ally, sometimes, from its very resemblance to it, an insidious and dangerous foe.'[1]

In the light of that passage the incidental affirmations which have since caught the public imagination fall into place. The supreme educational problem was then what it still is: how the traditional Christian heritage could be upheld 'and yet be fully alive to the changed outlook wrought by science in a new age; how Faith was to be definite, yet compatible with breadth of view'.[2]

Newman's resolution of this dilemma is his central contribution. Theology must not be excluded: not only because theology is a part of knowledge and therefore necessary, but more vividly because of the inevitable bearing of subject upon subject. Not only, that is, because it was imperative to answer Brougham and Maltby, but since, as a subject, theology was *servus servorum* to all the others. Omit it, and the result would be an anthropocentric view of all other subjects, intentional or not. One subject, without the others, dare not dogmatize; for each of them explains but a part of the full human personality of man. The omission of any one science prejudices accuracy, in pro-

[1] *Idea*, p. 214.   [2] Wilfrid Ward, in *Life*, i, 390.

portion to the importance of what is omitted. Religious truth in particular, said Newman, is 'not only a portion but a condition of general knowledge'. Any science considered *in vacuo* would be tempted to jump its categories, in ways condemned long before by Bacon and by Aristotle.

The unity of knowledge necessitated an integrated curriculum permeated in all its subjects by a basic philosophy of life. Here no 'conscience clause' could guarantee the religious freedom of the student; while any exemption from the religious instruction would destroy the unity of the curriculum. The argument led thus, logically, in an England of mixed religious allegiance, to the notion of religious dualism in education, with equal maintenance from public funds.

'I wish', said Newman, 'I wish the intellect to range with the utmost freedom, and religion to enjoy an equal freedom. What I am stipulating for is that they should be found in one and the same place, and exemplified in the same persons'—as they had been in the days of Albertus Magnus and Roger Bacon, and as they are today in the public education of Scotland, Holland, and Eire.

Now, *that* is the perspective in which to judge what Newman had to say about 'knowledge its own end', and about 'a liberal education'. Knowledge, he says, can be an end in itself, and its own reward. It may have other advantages, but its 'acquisition' is sufficient satisfaction for the human mind. Liberal education is that which 'stands on its own pretensions and does not minister to something beyond it'. As with Aristotle, useful knowledge is that which bears fruit, liberal knowledge that which tends to enjoyment. As with the men of the Renaissance, it is the purpose of the university to educate rather than to instruct. Learning, as Aquinas had taught, is a discipline and 'habit of mind'. Using the analogy so loved, indeed, by Aquinas, between the teacher and the doctor, 'Health' (says Newman) 'is a good in itself'—even if nothing came of it.

It was perhaps the defiant retort to utilitarianism in all this that has caused these passages to be so warmly misconstrued ever since, by those who would take the *Discourses* apart from the *Grammar of Assent*, and both apart from the historical context which demanded of the author certain overtones for certain immediate purposes. The antithesis between the liberal and the useful is *not* sharp. One of Newman's major concerns was to convince the devotees of Edgeworth and Locke, and of Bentham and the Mills, that it was not sharp for them either. The real point about health being a good in itself though (in theory) nothing came of it, is that in practice something certainly *will* come of it; that the liberal *approach* to learning *contains* the instructional and utilitarian approach, but goes *beyond* it, in not seeking knowledge merely 'for its matter', and 'expelling the excitements of sense by the introduction of those of the intellect'.[1]

The passage about the university training 'good members of society' is the climax to that analysis. It is best read as a twin passage to his inimitable description of the 'gentleman' as the product of that philosophical education he is describing. But it must never be forgotten that Newman's university, in these Discourses, like More's polity in the *Utopia*, is built not upon Revelation but upon the Natural Law. While the pagan reader, then, may be dismayed at the high standards of personal excellence set by Newman's gentleman, he may take comfort in the reflection that the Christian reader, conscious that all this can be achieved by the life of nature, short of that life of grace for which he knows the channels are open to himself, has grounds for vastly greater chastening still.

Newman's answer to the Victorian problem, then, of how to make a man intellectual and yet religious, is the burden of *The Idea*, so far as education goes. His philosophical answer to it is the burden of his contemporary letters, buttressing the case for a full and open *forum* for all scholarship. In a word, a collision between the natural science of the visible world and the theological science of the invisible world was impossible. They are 'incommensurable'; they need 'only to be connected—never to be reconciled'; science and dogma, as parts of the same Divine Truth, cannot conflict.[2] In the long run,

'If anything seems to be proved . . . in contradiction to the

---

[1] *Idea*, especially Discourse VII; and cf. Maritain's argument, that if you educate to 'make a *man*', you will also (incidentally) have produced the good citizen (*Education at the Crossroads*, 15). Cf. also A. N. Whitehead, 'The notion of *mere* knowledge is a high abstraction which we should dismiss from our minds. Knowledge is always accompanied with accessories of emotion and purpose' (*Adventures of Ideas*, p. 12). Also Tardivel, p. 101*f*.

[2] 'Christianity and Physical Science' (*Idea*, p. 431).

dogmas of faith, the point will eventually turn out, first, *not* to be proved, or secondly, not *contradictory*, or thirdly, not contradictory to anything *really revealed*, but to something which has been confused with Revelation.'[1]

Apparent temporary antagonism must be tolerated; premature syntheses must be allowed their run; men of science must learn humility—from the reminder that Bacon also denied Copernicus; theologians must learn humility—from the recollection that the Church at the height of her temporal power was the Church of the schoolmen of Paris and Oxford, of Aquinas and Bonaventure. 'Unless he is at liberty to investigate on the basis . . . of his science, he cannot investigate at all.' 'Great minds need elbow-room.'[2]

There is his *Magna Carta* of scholarship. The danger in his own day, of infidelity through drift, was as real to him as the resultant danger, of infidelity through totalitarian indoctrination, is to us today, when 'against our present materialized spirituality the active materialism of atheism and paganism has the game in its hands'.[3] Yet, paradoxically enough, the Newman who led the onslaught on the ideas that produced our new paganism would be the last today to ban Marxist teachers.

There is, however, one root-and-branch criticism that would sweep away the whole argument of the Discourses, as a beautiful delusion: the criticism which frankly denies the premises, and regards Truth as *not* ascertainable, or alternatively as confined *in* man, falling back accordingly into subjectivism and a denial of objective value—the last resort, logically, of latitudinarianism. Here we are reaping the whirlwind today. Thomas Huxley commanded a vast following for his dictum that 'education is the instruction of the intellect in the laws of nature, under which name I include not merely things and their forces but men and their ways'; and for his claim that a liberal education so conceived 'not only prepared a man to escape the great evils of disobedience to natural laws, but has trained him to appreciate and seize upon the rewards that nature scatters'.[4] But it was only a step to his later editor, Sir Oliver Lodge,

---

[1] *Idea*, p. 466.
[2] 'Christianity and Scientific Investigation' (*Idea*, p. 474).
[3] Maritain, *True Humanism*, p. xvi.
[4] 'A Liberal Education' (in *Lecture and Lay Sermons*).

equating this with 'seeing life whole', when already the thought
is really locked in the vicious circle of anthropomorphism and
consequent agnosticism. Only a few more steps bring us to that
abandonment of objective value which C. S. Lewis has now
repudiated for us as 'the abolition of man'. What C. S. Lewis
has called the *Tao* is being forsworn: that doctrine, decisive for
education, and common to the Platonist, the Aristotelian, the
Stoic, the Christian, and the Oriental, 'the belief that certain
attitudes are really true, and others really false, to the kind of
thing the universe is and the kind of things we are'.[1]

Newman sensed all this a century ago: before the word
agnostic had been invented. He prophesied that the future of
humanist education would be decided less by the philosophers
than by the psychologists; that the sceptic of the future would
abolish theism not by refuting it but by ignoring it, not by
attacking it but by allowing it to discredit itself through the
antiquated apologetic and tenuous hold on men's hearts to
which its own indifferent example had reduced it,[2] and that
what men needed to understand, rationally, was the nature of
the mental processes that go to the making of *any* kind of view
or opinion, false or true, and therefore to the allegiances and
social codes that follow from such certitudes.

That is why he wrote his *Grammar of Assent* in 1870, the year
of the Education Act. Thomas Huxley himself said of that Act
that, while 'nobody outside the agricultural interest now dares
to say that education is a bad thing', to make people learn to
read and write and cypher (merely) was 'very like making a
child practise the use of a knife and fork and spoon without
giving it a particle of meat'.

Newman's *Grammar of Assent* should be a book with a great
future: if it can be rescued from oblivion. Its burden is that
'moral proofs are grown into, not learnt by heart'. Men act
—and give allegiance—less logically that psychologically.[3]
Newman accordingly psychologizes both the Baconian and the
scholastic method, to draw two illuminating distinctions.

[1] *The Abolition of Man* (Riddell Lectures, 1943), pp. 11–14.
[2] Cf. *Idea*, the Address (in Part Two) on *A Form of Infidelity of the Day*.
[3] One may recall the wry reflection of Aquinas, on the poor lookout 'if
the way of reason were the only road open to a knowledge of God', since so
so vast a majority of mankind would have to remain in total darkness
(*Contra Gentiles*, vol. i; and *Summa*, I, 32, arts, 1, 8).

The first is the distinction between conclusions or convictions on the one hand, attainable by logic, and *assents* on the other hand, which are a matter of the whole personality accepting a proposition on grounds that should include logic but will always go beyond it. The second distinction is between *notional* assents, which, as an intellectual conviction, may never issue in action, and *real* assents, which will. Men can hardly be expected to die for an opinion or even a notional assent; history has been made by real assents. He deals therefore with the whole field of personal grounds of belief, 'implicit', 'subconscious' reasoning, which the educated and the uneducated share, by the operation of that totality of rational influences which he described as the 'illative sense': that 'power of spontaneous action in the human reason whereby it draws its conclusions from premises of which it is only in part conscious, and judges those conclusions to be warranted', and then *acts* on them. The application of this to teaching—and to the teaching of religion in particular—is obvious.[1] So much depends, in arriving at assents, on the antecedent circumstances of each person concerned. 'Men differ from each other not so much in the soundness of their reasoning as in the principles which govern its exercises. . . . These principles are of a personal character.' Men about him were being moved less by arguments from design and order, as in the scholastics and in Paley, than by arguments from conscience, as in the famous lectures of F. D. Maurice then still current; less by Hellenism than by Hebraism. For Newman, then, as for Matthew Arnold, a balance in education had been lost and must be redressed.

That is where one can derive great advantage from reading the *Grammar of Assent* before the *Idea of a University*. Argument whether the function of education is primarily to train the intellect or to train the will can become futile if pressed too far. In moderation it has given us in practice the voluntaryism of the

---

[1] *Grammar of Assent*, ch. 9; and cf. *Life*, ii, 263. 'So often explanations of faith are accepted as religion', says the biographer of Janet Erskine Stuart, of the Sacred Heart Order, 'and yet no trust in God grows in those who are learning. The root of faith is trust, but trust in a person, not in an argument. . . . Arguments and controversy hold an honoured place, but should not be allowed to usurp the field of religious teaching. But neither should "pious practices"; these without solid foundation do not stand the stress of life' (M. Monahan, *Janet Erskine Stuart*, 1922 and 1934, p. 216).

Jesuit schools and the intellectualism of the Thomist Dominican
schools. In urging that the school must *specialize* on the intel-
lectualist side, since the school is the only one amongst a man's
educational agencies equipped to do this for him, Maritain
follows Newman.[1] But at the same time, for both of them, the
key to a man's character is the use he makes of his 'illative
sense'. For conduct is a matter of committing the whole
personality.

The issue raised by James Anthony Froude, on this very
matter, was therefore crucial: that, whatever the overthrow of
Locke's view, of assent as being 'proportional to evidence' and
admitting of degrees, Newman offered no criteria for dis-
crimination between assent to truth and assent to delusion; in
short, though Froude nowhere used the word, that the *Grammar
of Assent* was itself a textbook in subjectivism.[2] But the answer
to this had been given six years earlier. And that is where
advantage comes from reading the *Apologia* first of all. For it is
there that we have the classic vindication of the theology of
objective values, without which an educationist becomes a
charlatan.

That, at last, is where *all* Newman's educational writing comes
to rest. To Newman, for all his tribute to it, *intellectual* excellence
provided *no* guarantee whatever of lofty living, unless the rest
of the character were trained. The will operates on, or rejects,
what the intellect proposes. But there are no sharp distinctions,
for an act of real assent, with its consequent 'commitment', is
an act of the whole personality. The core of Newman's educational teaching is *the complete unpredictability of the 'cultured mind'
as a determinant of character, unless in the service of a religious ideal.*
Education is a matter of 'the interior transformation of the
whole man'. Not all who read the *Idea* have grasped that *that*
is its message: though it still remains that (for Newman) the
University's main task *is* intellectual.[3]

We end, then, with Newman's teaching on Man. It is to be
found *ex professo* in none of his educational works as such. Nor
is it to be grasped from his sermons, as readily as from his
letters. Yet it is the integration of all he said and wrote. By it

[1] *Education at the Crossroads*, pp. 27–8.   [2] *Short Studies*, ii, 102, 125–6.
[3] Cf. on this his *Times* letter on Peel's Tamworth Speech, as early as 1841;
and the discussion in McGrath, pp. 274–86.

he would help us avoid the pitfalls of mistaking means for
ends.

VI

The interdependence of all the sciences, the disinterestedness
with which they must be studied, and their relation to the
conduct which the person liberally educated will have to show
forth, have been described together as 'the development of
humanitas': in which process 'the character is as necessary to
the training as the training to the character'.[1] The touchstone
is a concept of three words—the whole personality.

This is the conception that the long line of Christian theologians had taken from Aristotle, baptised (in the *Summa*), and
had seen come into its own as a determinant of education
during the first period of the Renaissance. To the best educationists of the middle ages, everything in this world had been
'endowed with the spiritual qualities of the next'; education
had been functional, and the *persona humana* unique in being a
little higher than the brutes and a little lower than the angels.
In the later period of the Renaissance the 'total' conception
of personality had begun to go to pieces.

The Christian pedagogical revival today, in looking back to
find any fulness in the doctrine of personality taught by its
predecessors, has to look as far as Comenius: and not all today
who revere Comenius, for the humanism that underlay his
realism, remember that he was a bishop. Today in the West
the Christian humanists whom Newman taught are warning us
how far the disintegration of personality has gone. There are
several keys to personality, of which the economist has one (for
man is what he eats), and the psychologist another (for man is
a creature of psychic urges), and the biologist another (for man
is a response to biological impulses). All these are keys, and the
secret of personality is not to be unlocked without any one of
them. But none of them is *the* key: only all of them together,
and some too that have been lost. This is today at last a commonplace. But it was a lay philosopher and theologian, more than
the professionals, who made it so—by diagnosing the supreme
need today as being re-integration, into

[1] Lewis May, p. 124, quoting Osbert Burdett, *Critical Essays*, p. 177.

'theological man, with his complete nature, body as well as mind, communal as well as personal, infused with spirit, which acknowledges an eternal authority, an intention and object existing outside the course of history as well as within it, and whose values and standards are permanent, however much their expression may change with the changes wrought by time.'[1]

That quotation from Dorothy L. Sayers enshrines, exactly, the fundamental teaching on education offered to Victorian England, amid the distractions of its superficial prosperity, by John Henry Newman.

His 'liberal education' springs from the same clear source as that of Erasmus: the full conception of 'theological man', dehumanized and eventually bestialized if his divinity is lost sight of in his humanity. *Mere* humanitarianism, as fathered on Europe by Rousseau, is the beginning of the end. *Persona humana* may seem to issue, as during the Renaissance, in an exclusive and aristocratic school of leadership. But that is so only if the conception is envisaged quantitatively. Qualitatively it means a kind of leadership—by force of example, by attention to the really fundamental values in conduct—that is the only democracy worth the name.

There are two Humanisms, with a gulf between them. One is the anthropocentric humanism of today, the product of an exaggerated conception of sin (born of the Reformation), and an exaggerated conception of human perfectibility (born of the Renaissance). Its strong points are nowhere more fairly marshalled than in Sir Walter Moberly's *Crisis in the University*. The other is the traditional Christian humanism, theocentric and founded on Revelation.[2] There is no compromise between them, nor between the educational motivation they produce. In the field of education the difference is—at whatever level—the difference between the professional teacher and the dedicated teacher. It is no accident that in an economic blizzard the teaching Orders do not need to attract by higher salaries.

There is no slightest doubt where Newman stood in all this. He would have been the very last to agree that the purpose of his *Discourses* was to discuss universities. His historic position as a humanist pioneer is that, at a point in English and Irish

[1] Dorothy L. Sayers, *Begin Here* (1940), p. 126.
[2] Moberly, pp. 71–93; Maritain, *True Humanism*, pp. 17, 19.

history when to thoughtful minds of all shades the attack on personality could no longer be ignored, he focussed the problem and he gave his answer. The function of a University was intellectual: to give a 'liberal education'. But a liberal education, as such, was morally and religiously neutral. There lay its danger: unless the whole character were meanwhile formed by means of a balanced curriculum, with believing students taught by a real 'team' of (specialist) believing teachers. 'I want', said Newman, 'the religious man to be intellectual, and the intellectual man to be religious.'

AUTHORITIES

NEWMAN'S WORKS

Letters and Correspondence, ed. Anne Mozley (2 vols., 1891).
The Arians of the Fourth Century (1831).
University Sermons (1843).
Essay on the Development of Doctrine (1845).
Sermons on Various Occasions (1859 and 1874).
The Idea of a University (i.e., the ten *Discourses on the Scope and Nature of University Education*, 1852; second edition 1859, omitting Discourse V; standard edition, including the *Discourses on University Subjects*. The text here used is that of 1927, Longmans).
Apologia Pro Vita Sua (1864).
An Essay Towards a Grammar of Assent (1870).
My Campaign in Ireland (1896).

BIOGRAPHIES AND STUDIES OF NEWMAN

Wilfrid Ward, *Life of John Henry Cardinal Newman* (2 vols., 1912).
Others by G. G. Atkins, 1931; William Barry, 1905 and 1927; F. L. Cross, 1933; G. J. Donohue, 1927; R. H. Hutton, 1891; Lewis May, 1929 and 1945; Bernard Newman, 1925; H. J. Jennings, 1890; J. Elliott Ross, 1933; Charles Sarolea, 1908; Henry Tristram, 1933; A. R. Waller and H. G. S. Barrow, 1901; Alex Whyte, 1902.

EDUCATIONAL STUDIES OF NEWMAN

T. Corcoran, *Newman's Theory of Liberal Education* (Dublin, 1929).

T. Hoeffken, *Newman in Liberal Education* (Kirkwood, Miss., 1946).

F. de Hovre, *Catholicism in Education* (Benziger, 1934).

S. P. Juergens, *Newman and the Psychology of Faith in the Individual* (Burns, Oates, 1928).

Fergal McGrath, *Newman's University: Idea and Reality* (Longmans, 1951).

W. F. P. Stockley, *Newman, Education, and Ireland* (Sands, 1933).

F. Tardival, *J. H. Newman, Educateur* (Paris, Beauchesne, 1937).

And editions of *The Idea of a University*, ed. May Yardley (Cambridge University Press, 1931), and R. J. McHugh (Browne and Nolan, 1944); and the *University Sketches*, ed. George Sampson (Walter Scott, 1902).

Note: Apart from his Rectorship of the College in Dublin, Newman did not often go beyond the philosophical foundations of Catholic higher education. For examples of its detailed application, see Janet Erskine Stuart, *The Education of Catholic Girls* (Longmans, 1912), especially chapter iv; and J. J. Ryan, *The Idea of a Catholic College* (New York: Sheed and Ward, 1945).

7

HERBERT SPENCER
AND THE SCIENTIFIC MOVEMENT

*

J. A. LAUWERYS

*A lecture delivered at King's College on 19 February 1951;
Professor C. H. Williams in the chair.*

In 1861, that is some eighteen months after the appearance of Charles Darwin's *Origin of Species*, a short book was published in London under the title of *Education: Intellectual, Moral, and Physical*. It consisted of reprints of four review-articles which had appeared in quarterly journals during the previous six or seven years. Though their author was clearly not a scholar and though he had no specialized expert knowledge of the topics he was discussing, his writings had attracted attention by their boldness and unorthodoxy and, even more, by their vigour and verve. The author, Herbert Spencer, then about forty years of age, had slowly been making a name for himself as a publicist of radical views, with a deep respect for science and none whatever for authority. In his educational views, he displayed large and generous commonsense. He disliked repressive and punitive discipline: he wanted children to be treated in a kindly and humane way. He saw no reason for the subjection of women or for attempting to turn them into pallid 'ladies': he preferred them healthy, rosy, and robust. And he was an apostle of self-help: he realized the importance of acitivity in the classroom and accepted the implications of Locke's dictum that the learner can no more understand through his teacher's understanding than he can see through his teacher's eyes.

In all this there was nothing very original. What *was* new was the philosophical framework in which Spencer sited his discussion, coming back again and again to a general evolutionary and developmental standpoint. Furthermore, he took up firmly and unambiguously a slightly scandalous attitude. Chiefly in his first chapter he urged vigorously the view that there was no justification at all for awarding the paramount role in general education to Latin and Greek, either at the secondary or at the higher levels. He considered that the core of any curriculum should consist of positive knowledge—of Science. He saw little value in the traditional linguistic culture of his day which, she thought, made men conform too easily to established practice and pay to authority unwarranted respect. He himself had become a writer without studying grammar,[1] a thinker without studying formal logic,[2] a master of words without knowing Latin or Greek[3] or, indeed, any foreign language. The knowledge which had real value, in his opinion, was that which might have some application to personal life, to industry, or, better still, which might serve to illuminate the grandest truth of the natural and social worlds —the law of inevitable progress, the doctrine of the evolution and development of the universe and of man through the survival of the fit and the automatic elimination of the unfit.

The success of the book was great and almost immediate.[4] Barely seven years after publication, R. H. Quick included Spencer's name among those of the great reformers whose work and thoughts he described in his justly famous book. A modern historian of education, Birchenough,[5] says that Spencer's influence is such '. . . that it is hardly possible to exaggerate it. Among other things, it inspired the work of the Code Reform Association (1881) and the demand for the reform of the standards and curriculum imposed by the Education Department'.

[1] See preface to *Autobiography*.

[2] Letter to Professor Brough 1895. Quoted in Duncan's *Life and Letters*, p. 418.

[3] *Autobiography*, i, 84, 88, 102.

[4] Between 1878 and 1900, 42,000 copies of the cheap edition (at 2s. 6d.) had been sold. In addition, 7,000 of the ordinary edition at 6s. This apart from the American editions.

[5] *History of Elementary Education*, 2nd ed., 1930, p. 356.

Abroad, the reception was, if anything, even more favourable. Within twenty years the book had been translated into more than fifteen languages—including Modern Greek. 'Anomalous enough (said Spencer). While in England the educational authorities cry "Greek literature rather than Science" in Greece they cry "Science rather than Greek literature!"' For many years—and even now—our continental colleagues consider that England has produced two educational classics, and two only—Locke's *Thoughts* and Spencer's *Education*—and (who knows?) it well may be that these two do in fact exhibit and realize the English genius, so largely compounded of common-sense and practical insight, more characteristically than anything else we have in this field.

For two generations, students in our training colleges and departments of education were brought up on a diet of which Spencer's *Education* was an important ingredient. And this is strange because the very people who prescribed it for study were its harshest critics. They deplored its one-sidedness, its illogicality, its biased argumentation, its lack of scholarly quality—and went on setting it as a special book. It must be admitted, however, that during the last twenty years the vogue shows signs of fading away: both the experts and the students display signs of boredom, perhaps because the problems discussed by Spencer are not the ones now thought important and because the evolutionary framework has now no charm of novelty. Nevertheless, we should remember that an excellent edition, indeed the best available, was produced as lately as 1932.[1] Its editor was Professor Cavenagh, the distinguished holder of the Chair of Education in this College, whose too early death leaves us all with a sense of both personal and professional loss. Cavenagh's Introduction and the notes he appended represent a masterly evaluation of Spencer's contribution—in a sense a final one. I confess that Cavenagh's essay makes the task of anyone following in his footsteps a most ungrateful one.

You will have observed that we have in all this something very like a paradox. Here is a writer with very little experience of schools or schooling—either as pupil, as teacher, as head-

[1] By the Cambridge University Press in the series 'Landmarks in the History of Education'. Cavenagh gives a very useful bibliography.

master, or as administrator. He has no very original ideas to
express nor is he describing, as a Pestalozzi might, thoroughly
tried out educational practices. Chiefly, he attacks existing and
dominant educational ideals. He proposes to replace a one-
sided literary and humanistic bias in secondary and higher
education by an equally—though no worse—one-sided scientific
and factual bias. The impact of his thought and writing is very
great. How does this come about? Where did Spencer get his
ideas? How is it that he had the courage to publish them—
and with such calm assurance of being right? To whom was he
addressing himself? Who were his allies? Why did he arouse so
much and such intense interest? What, in fact, was the nature
of his successes and of his failures?

A brief and preliminary answer is one in terms of Spencer's
own character and temperament. The son of middle-class,
rather lower middle-class, parents; brought up in an intensely
nonconformist dissenting atmosphere; opinionated, argumenta-
tive, always opposed to doing or saying or thinking what everybody else was. 'Won't work, my dear Spencer, won't work' his
friend Potter, father of Mrs. Sidney Webb, said to him when
the professional doubter defiantly proclaimed his practice on
a Sunday morning of deliberately walking against the tide of
church-goers.[1] But it does work, if one's aim is to call attention
to oneself.

A man of unorthodox views, largely self-educated, unbroken
in will by the academic disciplines, appealing always to
commonsense and reason and fact to justify his prejudices—
seldom to the authority of books—sure of himself and original
as are so many autodidacts. A man of immense, amazing self-
confidence—as were so many eminent Victorians—with a sure-
ness of himself his portraits reveal.

'Memory' (says Mrs. Sidney Webb,[2] who as a girl saw
much of him and was deeply influenced by him) 'recalls a
finely sculptured head, prematurely bald, long stiff upper lip
and powerful chin, obstinately compressed mouth, small
sparkling grey eyes, set close together, with a prominent
Roman nose—altogether a remarkable headpiece dominating
a tall, spare, well-articulated figure, tapering off into dimin-
utive and well-formed hands and feet. Always clad in primly

[1] Beatrice Webb, *My Apprenticeship* (London 1926), p. 24. [2] *Ibid.*, p. 25.

163

neat but quaintly unconventional garments, there was distinction, even a certain elegance, in the philosopher's punctilious
and precise and lucid speech. . . . But the sharpest imprint on
my youthful mind was the transformation scene from the
placid beneficence of an unwrinkled brow, an aspect habitual
towards children and all weak things, to an attitude of tremulous
exasperation, angry eyes and voice almost shrewish in its shrill-
ness—when he "opined" that his or anyone else's personal
rights were being infringed.'

An Olympian, yes, but not a placid Olympian. Behind the
outward calm serenity and assurance were the snake-filled pits
of nightmares—let us remember, too, in building up the
picture, the Spencer who dosed himself nightly, year after year,
with morphia and tossed restlessly and sleeplessly on his bed[1]—
for this, too, illustrates an aspect of the Victorian mind.

More than all this—a man of will, determined to impose
himself upon his environment. It is fascinating to observe how,
as he gets older, he gradually transforms his surroundings to
suit himself and his wishes. No reading of tiresome books—in
fact, very little reading, except light novels. No writing—dictation, and not too much of that. No arguments—he claimed the
delicate state of his health forbade him. The company of
friends—yes, he enjoyed that—provided he did not have to
endure the nonsense they were apt to talk; so he had special
ear-plugs made which cut out having to listen. The protective
life of an imaginary invalid—who lived to be eighty-three, and
could still read and write without spectacles when he felt he
would like to prove his capacity,[2] and who seldom feared, up
to the age of fifty or more, long walks across desolate moors;
an invalid who loved good wine and good food. I cannot for-
bear, here, to tell the story of Spencer's chairmanship of the
Special House Committee at the Athenaeum, though his very
much prized membership of that famous club in no way proves
his appreciation of good food! 'A more comically ineffective
Committee than ours I never sat upon', writes Sir Francis
Galton.[3] 'Spencer insisted upon treating the pettiest questions

---

[1] *Autobiography*, ii, pp. 93, 198, 454. Spencer himself is careful to point
out (a) that opium is a good thing, (b) that his dreams were pleasant and
always rational, though he cannot remember much about them! Psychi-
atrists do not accept such explanations.

[2] Duncan, *op. cit.*, p. 459.   [3] Quoted by Duncan, *op. cit.*, p. 509.

as matters of serious import, whose principles had to be fully argued and understood before action should be taken, with the consequence that we made no progress. Many funny scenes took place, one was with the butcher, who had supplied tough meat. Spencer enlarged to us on the subject of toughness in the same elaborate and imposing language with which his writings abound, and when the butcher appeared he severely charged him with supplying meat that contained an undue proportion of connective tissue. The butcher was wholly nonplussed, being unable to understand the charge, and conscious, as I suspect, of some secret misdoing to which the accusation might refer.'

Will, the will to change the environment to his own desires; nonconformity; an unbounded assurance of being the voice of common-sense, truth, reason, and science—these explain much. But the impact of a man on his time is always the result of a compound interaction. Place a piece of sodium into petrol, nothing happens. Put it into water and you get an almost explosive reaction: it is not sodium alone, nor water alone, but the two together that produce the effect. So, too, with Spencer and his age: a hundred years earlier or later and he might have made little impression. But in 1860—was he not the epitome, the condensation, so to speak, of the great nonconformist middle classes whose activities were transforming the face of England and of the world? Was he not expressing in sonorous, eloquent, pompous language the myths of advance, progress, and conquest which, powerfully, were driving them on? Did he not embody their will, their energy, their faith in science and reason—as well as their narrow provincialism, their suspicion of the obscure and the irrational, their discomfort before the manifestations of the Arts? Was he not a quintessential Philistine?

And think of the state of English society. For fifty years or more, and with ever growing impetus, science had been applied to the processes of production of material goods. New discoveries were being made continually, largely as the result of ignoring obstacles and of disdaining the voice of experienced authority. There seemed to be no bounds to the possible and no limits to the increase of national wealth and power.[1] Of course, there was another side. Just as behind Spencer's own calm, assured,

[1] Cf. Matthew Arnold, *Culture and Anarchy*.

majestic countenance there were shadows of nightmare; so, too, behind the facade of prosperity were slums and horrors. For many it was indeed a bleak and melancholy age—but thinkers felt sure that it could and would certainly be warmed and cheered by the progress of science, medicine, hygiene—if only reason and positive knowledge could be applied as successfully to human and social as to technological and industrial problems. For this, clearly, education would have to be transformed.

The new spirit, however, had made little difference to what went on in secondary schools or universities. Philanthropists were struggling desperately with the problem of providing some sort of elementary education for the masses of the industrial towns. On the other hand the leaders of the great public schools were more interested in the best ways of turning Philistines into Barbarians than in teaching science to both. A knowledge of theoretical science was, indeed, spreading among all classes, but chiefly through agencies other than the ordinary schools—through mechanics' institutes and cheap, popular encyclopaedias, for instance. The upper classes got some general knowledge through books and lectures, such as those delivered at the Royal Institution. Attention was indeed beginning to be paid to higher technical instruction. In 1836, a Normal School of Design was established and its control vested in the public office later termed the Board of Trade. In the 40's, following the example given by Liebig in Germany, a College of Chemistry was founded in Oxford Street, and other institutions of a like kind followed. Then came the Great Exhibition of 1851, which focused attention on the need for providing technological and scientific education if the quality of English products and the prosperity of British industry were to be maintained. It led, of course, as is well-known, to the establishment of the Science and Art Department at South Kensington.

At the secondary level, however, little was being done to adjust education to ongoing change. It is true that many private schools included some elementary science or natural philosophy in their courses. But the great fortresses of the established order[1]

---

[1] Matthew Arnold, *Culture and Anarchy*: 'When I go through the country, and see this and that beautiful and imposing seat of theirs crowning the landscape, "There," I say to myself, "is a great fortified post of the Barbarians".'

—the older public schools and universities—stood firmly by the grand old fortifying curricula and made but very grudging concessions to the demand for modern knowledge. They, of course, set the tone for the grammar schools; they represented the dominant tradition. Anyone who, like Spencer, exhibited the unreason of this state of affairs and who, while attacking obvious absurdities of the age, defended those forms of freedom and those myths which had served to advance the well-being of those classes which had no attachment to the older cultural traditions, was assured of a sympathetic audience. His popularity was certain, since he sailed with the wind and the tide.

But let us take a closer look at the development of Spencer's ideas. He was born at Derby in 1820 into a family 'characterized by individuality almost amounting to eccentricity, by pugnacious tenacity in holding to their opinions, by self-assertiveness, and by a disregard for authority'.[1] His father, an intelligent, religiously-minded, excessively conscientious man, usually earned his living as a teacher. He knew little of literature or philosophy but was chiefly interested in science. His ruling idea, which he transmitted to his son, was that of natural causation: nothing happens without a cause and the whole web of events is connected into a system of causality.

Herbert attended a school kept by his uncle William, where he acquired a good deal of miscellaneous information. It was noted that the tendency to set authority at nought was already strong—'the fitful nature of his father's discipline and the gentleness of his mother's sway exerting no efficient check on his self will'. 'As regards the influence, both moral and intellectual, of his uncle and his father, it is hardly possible to overestimate it. Towards current opinions their attitude was invariably critical, their conclusions being reached by reference to underlying principles, not to authority. Rarely were their discussions enlivened by lighter touches of wit or humour. Terribly in earnest, they did not debate for debating's sake or for victory. Literature, history, and fine art concerned them less than scientific, religious, and social questions, which were discussed in the boy's hearing from day to day. Thus early were sown the seeds of that interest in social, political, and religious topics which he retained to the last.'[2]

[1] Duncan, *op. cit.*, p. 4.   [2] Duncan, *op. cit.*

As T. H. Huxley said, on reading about Spencer's boyhood in the *Autobiography* and referring to the family, 'Men of that force of character, if they had been less wise and less self-restrained, would have played havoc with the abnormal chicken hatched among them'.

At thirteen, Herbert Spencer's formal education was complete and he was sent off to another of his uncles, the Reverend Thomas Spencer, who held a living at Hinton Charterhouse. Thomas tried to teach the boy a bit of Latin; so he ran away and walked home—150 miles in three days—but was sent back again. In an informal way he studied a good deal: chiefly mathematics and elementary science. It is fascinating to observe how his later interests and later character traits are already present in embryo at this time. Thus, he pays a great deal of attention to phrenology,[1] and one remembers that later his philosophical outlook always assumes that mental characteristics are closely paralleled by rather obvious physical traits. Or, again, another example: a few weeks after taking up trigonometry he writes to his father 'I believe I am thoroughly master of it, and I could do any question in it'. Quite properly his father replied, 'Your faults arise from too high an opinion of your own attainments'. But this reproof had no effect. Many years later he wrote,[2] after having read three or four pages of the book, 'I remember making acquaintance with Mill's System of Logic . . . and reading his criticism on the syllogism and agreeing with it: perhaps all the more readily because it expressed dissent from an orthodox doctrine'. Or again, in an entirely different field;[3] 'I had been delighted to find in Mr. Ruskin one who dares to express unfavourable opinions about some of Raphael's work. . . . Naturally, therefore, I opened *Stones of Venice* with raised expectations. On looking at the illustrations, however, and reading the adjacent text, I presently found myself called upon to admire a piece of work which

[1] In his youth, Spencer was very interested in phrenology. In his *Autobiography* he gives a reading by a phrenologist which begins: 'Such a head as this ought to be in the Church. The self-esteem is very large.' He was then about twenty-one. Later, he wrote several articles for phrenological journals and, at the age of twenty-six, invented an apparatus for making exact measurements of heads. It is tempting to look for some direct influence from Combe upon Spencer, but I have not been able to trace it. Spencer himself mentions only Spurzheim.

[2] *Autobiography*, i, p. 242.　　　　　　　[3] *Ibid.*, p. 351.

seemed to me sheer barbarism. My faith in Mr. Ruskin's judgment was at once destroyed; and thereafter I paid no further attention to his writings.'

At the age of seventeen, Spencer, having had a little practice of teaching in his uncle William's school, accepted a temporary post in another school run by a Mr. Mather, a friend of his father's. He kept the job for four months only and, in his *Autobiography*, asks himself whether he did wisely in leaving it.[1]

'I think it not improbable that had I been in possession of the needful means, and furnished with a sufficient staff of adequately intelligent assistants, I might have done something towards exemplifying a better system of education. Freed from the executive part of the work, and responsible only for devising methods, superintending the execution of them, and maintaining order, the function would have been one not unsuitable to my nature; and might have been well discharged.'

Under other conditions 'I should, I believe, have failed. In the first place, I dislike mechanical routine; and though rational plans of education would make lessons much less mechanical than they are at present, a considerable part must always remain mechanical. In the second place, I have a great intolerance of monotony; and many, if not all, of a teacher's duties are necessarily monotonous. In the third place, my desire to carry out my own ideas, alike in respect of what constitutes a good education, in respect of the methods used, and in respect to the order followed, would probably have caused frequent differences with parents.'

The immediate objection to teaching, however, was that the work was very badly paid—he had little trouble in finding what was at first a congenial and always a better paid post in connection with the building of railways. Surprising as it seems, we find the boy directing gangs of navvies who were making cuttings, raising embankments, and even building bridges to Spencer's own designs. At this time, too, he never hesitated to tell his superiors, the chief engineers, how they might improve the large bridges they were building. Nor did he hesitate to publish in newspapers mathematical discoveries which were new to him, though not to others.

However, these practical activities gradually became less

[1] *Ibid.*, i, pp. 123, 124.

pleasing. He evidently desired something more general, less routinized. His mind was moving from the concrete to the abstract, from the known to the less known. He wanted to become a writer. At the age of twenty he tells his father 'I was thinking the other day that I should like to make public some of my ideas upon the state of the world and religion, together with a few remarks on education. I think, however, that I may employ my time better at present.' What he did was to leave his employment as an assistant surveyor and to potter about. It was at this time that he wrote a series of thirteen long letters to the *Nonconformist* newspaper, one of which dealt with National Education. In each of his letters he endeavoured to show that 'the function of government is simply to defend the natural rights of men—to protect person and property—to prevent the aggressions of the powerful upon the weak'—and no more. His claim that government should not promote national education was in line with Nonconformist opinion of that time. This was well-illustrated in 1843 'when the nonconformists, in a transport of blind zeal, threw out Sir James Graham's useful Education Clauses'.[1] The letters actually seem to lay the ground plan of Spencer's *Social Statics*, published seven years later, and they express a general point of view which he never abandoned.

Between the ages of twenty-two and twenty-nine Spencer had no regular employment. We find him engaged in radical politics, acting as secretary to a branch of the 'Complete Suffrage Movement' and flirting with the Chartists. He occasionally writes and does some sub-editing. He earns a good deal of money by advising on railway surveys. He invents a metal paper-clip, designs a machine for making it, and earns as much as £70 in one year from it. At one moment, in 1848, he even thinks of opening a school. As he puts it:[2] 'Another thought which arose was that of reverting to the ancestral profession. . . . Might it not be possible for my father and myself to (set up a model school) not, indeed, to carry out the principles of Pestalozzi in particular, but to initiate an advanced form of education? For the linguistic teaching, masters might be employed; while the teaching of the sciences—mathematics, physics, chemistry, astronomy, etc.—we might carry on our-

[1] Matthew Arnold's words.   [2] *Autobiography*, i, p. 322.

selves.' But nothing came of the idea—it seemed too un-promising.

Taking stock, in later years, of this period of his life, Spencer summed up in the following words:[1]

'There had been during those years a varied intercourse with men and things. In surveying and levelling, in making drawings for railway works, and in discharging the functions of secretary and sub-engineer, my first engineering period was passed. After this came a time of scheming and experimenting—mechanical, chemical, electrical; and a time during which there was some artistic cultivation in drawing, modelling, and music, as well as some pursuit of natural history: a time, also, of public political activity, as well as political writing, broken by brief efforts to open for myself a literary career. Then followed a second engineering period, bringing me in closer contact with the preliminary business of railway making, joined with the exercise of some authority, as the regulator of assistants and supervisor of plans. There was thus afforded me, along with increase of technical experience, increased experience of men— a further increase of this last experience being brought by en-tanglements in law suits. Next came the period distinguishable as that of inventions—successful and unsuccessful, but chiefly the latter. This extended somewhat further my physical know-ledge, as well as my knowledge of life, its difficulties and its ups and downs; which last was added to during the subsequent period of suspense. In short, there had been gained a more than usually heterogeneous, though superficial, acquaintance with the world animate and inanimate. And along with the gaining of it had gone a running commentary of speculative thought about the various matters presented. . . .'

'The implications of phenomena were then, as always, more interesting to me than the phenomena themselves. What did they prove? was the question instinctively put. The conscious-ness of causation, to which there was a natural proclivity, and which had been fostered by my father, continually prompted analyses, which of course led me below the surface and made fundamental principles objects of greater attention than the various illustrations of them . . .'

Spencer goes on to quote that he had enjoyed little formal

[1] *Ibid.*, i, p. 335.

education—'artificial culture' he calls it—and had never passed an examination. He thinks this an advantage, because the very conception of training 'implies a bending of the shoots out of their lines of spontaneous growth into conformity with a pattern', and thus formal education stultifies originality, though it 'leaves a liability to mental action unguided by adequate acquaintance with facts'. He quotes approvingly Edison's dictum that 'college-bred men were of no use to him'. Spencer also points out how many distinguished engineers, James Brindley and George Stephenson among them, had received no early instruction at all while Smeaton, Rennie, James Watt, and Sir Benjamin Baker, builder of the Forth Bridge, had received no regular engineering instruction. The general inference drawn 'is that the established systems of education, whatever their matter may be, are fundamentally vicious in their manner. They encourage *submissive receptivity* instead of *independent activity*'.

It will have been noted, in all this, how small a part was played by reading or by formal study in Spencer's intellectual formation. Indeed, it seems very doubtful whether he ever read a book at all seriously, excepting light novels of which he was a voracious consumer. Take, for instance, his study of Kant. This is how he describes it:[1]

'I found in Mr. Wilson's home a copy of a translation of Kant's *Critique of Pure Reason*. This I commenced reading, but did not go far. The doctrine that Time and Space are "nothing but" subjective forms—pertain exclusively to consciousness and have nothing beyond consciousness answering to them— I rejected at once and absolutely; and having done so, went no further. Being then, as always, an impatient reader, even of things which in large measure interest me and meet general acceptance, it has always been out of the question for me to go on reading a book the fundamental principles of which I entirely dissent from.'

Or again—another instance:

'One book I looked into left an impression. This was Coleridge's *Idea of Life*; the substance of which he was said to have borrowed from Schelling. The doctrine of individuation struck me; and as was presently shown, entered as a factor into my thinking.'   [1] *Ibid.*, i, p. 252.

172

Nor did he *think* arduously and continuously. He recounts a curious conversation he had with George Eliot, who—at least many people who knew them both assert it—was in love with him, a fact which Spencer was later most anxious to deny.

'Considering how much thinking I must have done, she was surprised to see no lines on my forehead. "I suppose it is because I am never puzzled", I said. This called forth the exclamation "O! That's the most arrogant thing I ever heard uttered." To which I rejoined—"Not at all, when you know what I mean." And I then proceeded to explain that my mode of thinking did not involve that concentrated effort which is commonly accompanied by wrinkling of the brows.'[1]

If, then, Spencer neither read books nor studied, where did he get his knowledge? Where did he pick up his ideas? Chiefly, I believe, from conversations with friends and acquaintances, from occasional lectures,[2] newspaper articles, and so on—as well as from a superficial glance at books which he was called upon to review. He breathed the intellectual air of his times, he acquired unconsciously a knowledge of what was being said and thought; and what he thus picked up, he gave back again in sonorous language and much amplified—swelled out, so to speak, to cosmic proportions. As an organ pipe, or an empty shell, picks out from the confused and mixed movement of the air a particular note to which it resounds and which it amplifies, so Spencer picked out from the intellectual medley amid which he lived all the facts that supported the idea of the evolution of nature, of man, of society—the doctrine of development and progress from the homogeneous to the heterogeneous, the indefinite to the definite—and all this as the operation of a natural process, an example of absolute causality. Thus, unless man's stupidity interfered too much, things would go on improving. Or so he hoped.

Mrs. Sidney Webb tells[3] how, one day, in conversation with T. H. Huxley, she 'ventured to put forward the idea that Herbert Spencer had worked out the theory of evolution by

[1] *Ibid.*, i, p. 399.
[2] e.g., 'I have taken to the study of bones, which being interpreted, means that I am attending a course of Professor Owen's lectures on Osteology.' A few years later he was telling Owen how to improve his theories.
[3] *My Apprenticeship*, p. 27.

grasping the disjointed theories of his time and welding them into one. "No", said Huxley, "Spencer never knew them: he elaborated his theory from his inner consciousness. He is the most original of thinkers, though he has never invented a new thought. He never reads: merely picks up what will help him to illustrate his theories. He is a great constructor: the form he has given to his gigantic structure is entirely original: not one of the component factors is new, but he has not borrowed them".' This was the opinion of a friend. Jowett, who of course had little use for Spencer, spoke less kindly, calling him 'a very Tupper of philosophy . . . a fellow . . . who knows little of physical science, and gives back to scientific men their own notions in a more general form. Of course they worship him as a god, and instead of being thought an empty sciolist, he is regarded by them as the philosopher of the future'.

Yet, paradoxically, it is just these characteristics that give Herbert Spencer his peculiar importance in philosophy as in education. For he has all the qualities of his defects. Precisely because he did not read, he was free from respect for dead or bookish tradition. Precisely because he carried no academic baggage he was able to express better than anyone the ideas of his age. Just as Kelvin was the supreme Victorian man of science and Tennyson the most representative national poet of his age, so Spencer was its most typical philosopher, who expressed brilliantly what many of the most energetic elements of his country thought about the world. Like those of his contemporary, Wagner, though in another field, his compositions had a limited number of *leif-motifs*—indeed some might say Spencer used but one—the doctrine of evolution. But how magnificently worked out! What virtuosity, what verve, what force! And, above all, what grandeur of view and of conception!

In point of fact, however, there is at least one more *leit-motif* in Spencer's thought and writing—radicalism. Not the trade-union socialism of today which seeks equality above all things, and sees in the State the great protector and the universal provider, but that deep radicalism which considers the greatest good to be the freedom of the individual from external constraint and which looks upon all state activity with deep suspicion. This fear of the State was undoubtedly a family tradition with Spencer. Nevertheless, other influences gave it final shape. Sir Ernest Barker suggests[1] that the chief of these was that of Thomas Hodgskin, who was Spencer's colleague on *The Economist* in 1849. Hodgskin was an anti-Benthamite radical who, like Godwin, 'believed in the natural right of humanity, at which Bentham had scoffed. He extended to politics as well as to economics the doctrine of *laissez-faire* whereas Bentham, leaving economics to the free play of natural forces, had claimed law and politics as the sphere of scientific regulation. . . . The function of government was accordingly negative: it extended only to the securing of a free field for the operation of natural laws; and human laws were as prejudicial as natural laws were the reverse. The ultimate goal . . . was a state of anarchy, in which government had disappeared, and the sentiments of each were automatically adjusted in a spontaneous harmony with those of all.'

Spencer himself, though not in the strict sense a Benthamite, was deeply affected by the ideas of the philosophical radicals.[2] In 1843, indeed, he wrote that 'he had been reading Bentham's works, and meant to attack his principles shortly', but twenty years later he wrote to J. S. Mill that he had been greatly startled to find himself classed with the Anti-utilitarians. 'I have never (he said) regarded myself as an Anti-utilitarian. My dissent from the doctrine of Utility as commonly under-stood, concerns not the object to be reached by men, but the method of reaching it. While I admit that happiness is the ultimate end to be contemplated, I do not admit that it should be the proximate end.'

The different streams flowed together and found expression in Spencer's first book, published in 1850, the full title of which was *Social Statics*: *the conditions essential to human happiness specified and the first of them developed*. He intended this to be a sort of natural-history ethics. He pointed out that among animals the destroying agencies at work continually weed out the sickly, the malformed, and the least fleet or powerful. By this and kindred processes all vitiation of the race through the multiplication of its inferior samples is prevented. Mankind is

---

[1] *Political Thought in England* (London, 1915), pp. 87 sq.

[2] Duncan, *op. cit.*, p. 519, quoting H. Macpherson: 'To the utilitarianism of Bentham and Mill, he has given something like a scientific foundation.' Spencer himself thought that what was chiefly wrong with the Benthamites was an insufficient knowledge of science.

and should be subjected to this same beneficent though severe discipline. Spencer urged that when a Government tries to prevent the misery necessitated by the stress of competition and the consequent struggle for life, it eventually creates far more misery by fostering the incapable. He said of the spurious philanthropists that these 'sigh-wise and groan-foolish people' bequeath to posterity a continually increasing curse.

One of the chapters of the *Social Statics* deals with national education—evidence that his interest in education[1] had by no means been dissipated by his concern with politics and ethics. And four years later, in 1854, he published in the *North British Review*, under the title 'Method in Education' a long article which is reprinted as Chapter II of *Education*. Ostensibly it was a review of five books: Dr. E. Biber's *Life of Pestalozzi* which had appeared in 1831; a book on *Language as a Means of Mental Culture and International Communication* by C. Marcel; Thomas Wyse on *Education Reform* (1836); James Pillan's *Principles of Elementary Teaching* (1828); and John Bell's *Rudimentary Art Instruction* (1852). Spencer's article begins with some general sociological reflections, among which we find it said that methods of teaching reflect the ideals, the practices and the institutions of society, 'while "believe and ask no questions" was the maxim of the Church, it was fitly that of the school. Conversely now that Protestantism has gained for adults a right of private judgment and established the practice of appealing to reason, there is harmony in the change that has made juvenile instruction a process of exposition addressed to the understanding' . . . In this free-trade era, when freedom and lack of government control are accepted as ideals . . . 'modern modes of culture must correspond to our more liberal religion and political institutions'.

And so, Spencer goes on to urge, in a way that would un-

[1] Spencer's educational views are discussed in detail by Gabriel Compayré in *Herbert Spencer and Scientific Education*. This was translated from the French and published in English in 1908. It was the second volume of a series of monographs by Compayré, the first dealing with J. J. Rousseau, the third with Pestalozzi. The French historian remarks in the preface that he is 'acquainted with no more genuine disciple of the author of *Emile* than the writer of the charming essay on *Education* (though)—they, doubtless, differ profoundly in their general views regarding mankind and the universe.' But Spencer took pains to convince Compayré that he had never read the *Emile* and knew nothing about Rousseau.

doubtedly have appealed to Samuel Smiles, self-help as an educational ideal. In doing so, he gives a mass of advice, based no doubt on what he had heard from his father and uncles as well as on the books he was reviewing. He condemns rote-teaching and learning by heart. He recommends teaching from the concrete as well as experimental or heuristic approaches — very sensible and practical advice of the kind given in training colleges. He discusses at some length various maxims of method such as 'proceed from the simple to the complex and from the indefinite to the definite'; 'start from the concrete and end in the abstract'; 'proceed from the empirical to the rational'; 'the education of the child must accord both in mode and arrangement with the education of mankind, considered historically[1]'; 'the process of self-government should be encouraged to the uttermost.'

Critics have pointed out that in stating these principles Spencer indulged in overmuch repetition and that, moreover, they are abstract and difficult to apply in practice. But this is to misconceive Spencer's purpose:[2] though ostensibly writing about educational method his real interest was philosophical. His mind was already moving towards a grandiose conception. He wanted to subsume in one single comprehensive formula all the happenings of nature: from the building of nebulae to the mental functioning of a young child. At this stage, he was concerned with the relations of mind to matter and wanted to show that 'mental development has its place in the theory of development at large'. He was also desirous of exhibiting clearly the connection between education and biology. In his view 'education is a process of perfecting the structure of the organism and making it fit for the business of life' so that not only 'that effect of exercise by which the faculties are fitted for their functions . . . but also the acquirement of knowledge serving for guidance is, from the biological point of view, an adjustment of structure to function'. If teachers could be made to see these truths and would conform to them, they would be basing their work on sound science and psychology and they would understand how to make learning 'a process of self-instruction, and by consequence a process of pleasurable instruction'.

[1] Condillac's principle.
[2] Cf. Emile Thouverez, *Herbert Spencer* (Paris, 1907), pp. 30 sq.

Five years after the publication of this article came a second —this time on 'Moral Education'. It appeared in April 1858 in the *British Quarterly Review*, and it pretended to be a review of Locke's *Thoughts on Education* (1710); of Jean Paul Richter's *Doctrine of Education* (1848); and of articles which had appeared between 1831 and 1835 in the *Quarterly Journal of Education*. It is typical of Spencer's writings: carelessly composed but eminently readable, and as full of commonsense as of quirks and oddities. Listen to this, for example: 'Savageness begets savageness, and gentleness begets gentleness.' 'Be sparing of commands, but whenever you do command, command with decision and consistency'. And then, strangely up-to-date:

'Do not regret the display of considerable self-will on the part of your children. The independent English boy is the father of the independent English man, and you cannot have the last without the first. German teachers say that they had rather manage a dozen German boys than one English one. Shall we, therefore, wish that our boys had the manageableness of German ones, and with it the submissiveness and political serfdom of adult Germans? Or shall we not rather tolerate in our boys those feelings which make them free men, and modify our methods accordingly?'

The general theory he adopts is that of natural consequences: that is, let the young learn what is right and what is wrong by making them see the consequences of their actions—the child who has burnt himself will no longer play with fire. As Cavenagh points out, this approach leads Spencer into all sorts of dilemmas. 'By ruling out extreme cases, he is able to construct practical rules for everyday punishment, which are sensible enough, but in the process he tacitly abandons the doctrine of natural consequences. The watchful parent, who lets the child burn himself just enough to "learn him better" is totally unlike nature; Spencer is driven to admit that "during infancy a considerable amount of absolutism is necessary" and the "self-government" that he wisely advocates must be built on the teachings of parents rather than of nature.'

Perhaps the most remarkable part of the essay—remarkable especially when one remembers the date when it was written— is that there is in it no discussion whatever of the functions of religion or of religious teaching in the formation of moral attitudes. Spencer's ethics are purely natural: his only concession to religious persons is to say that 'readers may supplement our thoughts in any way they please; we are only concerned that they should be accepted as far as they go'.

But again, let it be remembered that his interest lay elsewhere—in discussing the idea of universal development and not the function of religion, not even really the bringing up of children. His own commentary[1] is significant of this:

'The theory of evolution [he says] furnished guidance [in writing this article] . . . as the ascent through lower forms of life has been effected by the discipline of enjoying the pleasure and suffering the pains which followed this or that kind of conduct; so further ascent above the form of life now reached must be thus effected. Nature attempts no excuses; so, with educational discipline, while there should be no needless restraints, the needful restraints should be unvarying and irresistible . . . moral education is simply a final part of the process by which the emotional nature has been evolved . . .'

About Spencer's third article on Education—Chapter IV of the book—comparatively little need be said. It deals with physical education and appeared in the *British Quarterly Review* for April 1859, having been refused by the *Quarterly Review* possibly, says Spencer, because 'its conceptions, anti-ascetic as they were, did not harmonize with [the editor's] theological system or with the ideas which public school life had fostered in him'. It claimed to be a review of a number of books on physiology, anatomy, and medicine, including Baron Liebig's *Animal Chemistry*. It is chiefly remarkable for two things. First, the good sense and astonishing modernity of many of the views he expounds. He recommends good food and plenty of it, fruit and vegetables—though his praise of meat and his condemnation of milk slops might not be altogether welcome to a Ministry of Food. Secondly, because of the number of idiosyncrasies which he parades. Relaxation and recreation are, of course, warmly recommended: Spencer was their great prophet. And, as regards the education of women, one observes his suspicion of the intellectual type and his preference for the simple and healthy housewife.

But again, the dominant idea was not that ostensibly

---

[1] *Autobiography*, ii, p. 18.

discussed. In fact—using Spencer's own words—'it was congruous with the doctrine of evolution in so far as the method of nature is emphasized . . . it is contended that for bodily welfare the sensations are the most trustworthy guides . . . the truth that among all lower forms of life, uncontrolled by commands, traditions, or creeds, there has been no other prompter to right physical actions than obedience to the sensations: the continual killing off of those in which the two were not rightly adjusted to the needs, having maintained and improved the adjustment. Whence it follows that, inheriting as we do adjustments established during the progress through lower forms of life, our sensations are on the whole trustworthy guides to bodily welfare'.

We come now to the last of the essays on Education, the one printed as Chapter I of the book, the one which has had the greatest *succès de scandale*. It appeared a few months after the article on Physical education, in the *Westminster and Foreign Quarterly Review*, under the title 'What knowledge is of most worth?' The general argument expounded is so well-known that there is scarcely need to repeat it. Briefly, Spencer proposes as a fundamental criterion, which should be applied when considering the worth of any subject taught to young people, the way in which it guides the activities which, together, form the life of man. How to live, how to live completely and happily—that is the essential question for us, he urges. Let us not waste time on trivialities and futilities which in no way help us to realize our aim. 'Our first step [says Spencer] must obviously be to classify, in the order of their importance, the leading kinds of activity which constitute human life. They may be naturally arranged into: 1. those activities which directly minister to self-preservation; 2. those activities which, by securing the necessaries of life, indirectly minister to self-preservation; 3. those activities which have for their end the rearing and discipline of offspring; 4. those activities which are involved in the maintenance of proper social and political relations; 5. those miscellaneous activities which fill up the leisure part of life, devoted to the gratification of the tastes and feelings.'

He then goes to show, at least to his own satisfaction that, for nos. 1 to 4, the revelant knowledge is—Science. Since first things must come first, and since education mirrors life and should be a preparation for life, it would be legitimate to demand that science should play the paramount role in schools. In fact, however, in secondary schools the core of the curriculum consisted of a study of Latin and Greek language and grammar. In Spencer's words[1] . . . 'Knowledge subserving the adjustment which so profoundly concerns men from hour to hour is contemptuously neglected; while the best preparation for complete living is supposed to be familiarity with the words and thoughts, successes and disasters, follies, vices and atrocities, of two peoples whose intelligence was certainly not above ours, whose moral standard was unquestionably lower, and whose acquaintance with the nature of things, internal and external, was relatively small . . .'

The essay, like the three others, was a review, this time of a book in which were printed a series of lectures given at the Royal Institution in 1854,[2] the general theme being the importance of scientific studies in an education intended for all classes of the people. Characteristically, thereby no doubt indicating his support of the idea, the Prince Consort attended the first two which were given by that famous historian of science, Dr. Whewell, Master of Trinity College, Cambridge, and by the great Michael Faraday. Whewell's lecture set the keynote. He took as his theme the influence of the history of science upon intellectual education. It was an eloquent address and the following passages quoted from it will indicate the line of argument:

'Thus two of the great elements of a thorough intellectual culture, Mathematics and Jurisprudence, are an inheritance which we derive from ages long gone by; from two great nations; from the two great nations of antiquity. They are the results of ancient triumphs of man's spirit over the confusion and obscurity of the aspects of the external world; and even over the waywardness and unregulated impulses of his own nature, and the entanglements and conflicts of human society. And being true sciences, they were well fitted to become, as they became, and were fitted to continue, as they have hitherto continued, to be main elements in that discipline by which man is to raise himself above himself; is to raise . . . his intellect into an

---

[1] *Autobiography*, ii, p. 36.   [2] *Lectures on Education* (London, 1855).

habitual condition, superior to the rudeness, dimness, confusion, laxity, insecurity, to which the *undisciplined* impulses of human thought in all ages and nations commonly lead. . . .'

Whewell goes on to show that to use these two sciences only would mean laying too much stress upon *deduction*. But '. . . a modern education [must] convey to the mind an adequate appreciation of and familiarity with the *inductive* process'. This can be achieved by '. . . the exact and solid study of . . . any portion of the circle of natural sciences—Botany, Comparative Anatomy, Geology, Chemistry, for instance. But I say, the *exact* and *solid* knowledge; not a mere verbal knowledge, but a knowledge which is real in character, though it may be elementary and limited in extent . . . a knowledge of things and not merely of the names of things.'

Faraday spoke the following week. For the most part, he defended the thesis that what was needed above all else was an education to strengthen the judgment. He thought that if people learnt more about the laws of nature, their judgment would thereby improve. At the same time he would not wish such an education 'to be altogether repressive of the imagination or confine the exercise of the mind to processes of a mathematical or mechanical character'. Oddly enough, Faraday spent a great deal of his time attacking mesmerism and clairvoyance, and describing simple experiments to disprove the claims of table-turners. 'What [he exclaimed] are the established truths and triumphs of ring-swingers, table-turners, table-speakers?'

After these two giants came Dr. Latham, on the importance of the study of language. This was a highly original talk, for he recommended the teaching of elementary comparative philology —a subject which sixty years earlier had been attempted in the French *Ecoles Centrales* and which, in our own time, has been revived in some American schools under the title of 'General Language'. Latham obviously had in mind a thoroughly scientific approach and summed up as follows: 'To curtail English—to eliminate one of the classical languages—possibly that of Pericles, at any rate either that of Pericles or of Cicero— to substitute for the ordinary elements of a so-called classical education illustrations from the Chinese, the Hungarian, or the Tumali.'

Then came Professor Danberry, of Oxford, on Chemistry,

who spoke wisely and in practical vein. He expressed his gratification that his University had recently (1849) admitted the
physical sciences as proper subjects for examinations. There
was also James Paget, on Physiology, who advanced many of
the arguments which Spencer later used in his essay on physical
education. Dr. W. B. Hodgson spoke warmly about the claims
of economic science, taught with a strong moral aim, and
recommended courses rather similar to those we would nowadays call 'social studies'. He thought such studies bore to the
body politic the same relation as did physiology to the physical
body of individuals. 'Let me (he said) refer you to a most
admirable series of lessons on *The Phenomena of Industrial Life
and the Conditions of Industrial Success* which has recently appeared
under the editorship of that zealous educationist, the Dean of
Hereford. The appearance of this book, and the recognition of
this subject in the last report of the National School Society,
are cheering signs that the omissions of past ages in our school
systems are not destined much longer to continue.' Alas for such
hopes!

And then, perhaps most interesting of all, came that charming
and delightful figure, Professor Tyndall, one of the greatest,
perhaps the greatest, literary stylist among men of science. He
spoke about physics and deplored the fact that . . .

'A few days ago, a Master of Arts, the recipient of a modern
education, stated to me that until he had reached the age of
twenty years he had never been taught anything regarding
Light, Heat, Magnetism, or Electricity: twelve years of his life
previously had been spent among the ancients, all connextion
being thus severed between him and natural phenomena . . .
if new continents of thought reveal themselves to the exploring
human spirits, shall we not possess them? Are we to sacrifice
the hopes and aspirations of the Present out of deference to the
Past?'

The most interesting part of his address was that in which he
criticized Latham and comparative philology.

'When I saw your Lecturer reduced to the necessity of plead-
ing for science, and meekly claiming for it, from the Institution
which we are accustomed to regard as the highest in this land,
a recognition equal to that accorded to philology, I confess that
the effect on me was to excite a certain revolutionary tendency

in a mind which is usually tranquil almost to apathy in these matters. Science behind philology! . . . As the pole of a magnet acting upon soft iron induces in the latter a condition opposed to its own, so the irrationality of those who cast slight upon Science tends, no doubt, to excite an opposite error on the part of their antagonists. . . . But is there no mind in England large enough to see the value of both, and to secure for each of them fair play? . . . Descending . . . to considerations which lie close to us as a nation—as a land of gas and furnaces, of steam, and electricity: as a land which science, practically applied, has made great in peace and mighty in war: I ask you whether this "land of old and just renown", which may God keep unimpaired, has not a right to expect from her institutions a culture more in accordance with her present needs than that supplied by declension and conjugation? And if the tendency should be to lower the estimate of science, by regarding it exclusively as the instrument of material prosperity, let it be their high mission to furnish the proper counterpoise by pointing out its nobler uses, and lifting the national mind to the contemplation of it as the last development of that "increasing purpose" which runs through the ages and widens the thoughts of men.'

My purpose in thus dealing in some detail with the book Spencer was reviewing in the essay on the relative worth of knowledges is two-fold. First, to make plain that when Spencer speaks of 'Science' he uses the word in a very broad sense to indicate any kind of positive and systematic knowledge of a non-dogmatic kind and not simply physics, chemistry and biology. Secondly, that in claiming for science an important place in education Spencer had strong supporters. Indeed he was in much better and more reputable company than he himself probably realized. He stood in the line of a long succession of thinkers and philosophers, a line which stretched back all the way to Bacon and to Rabelais. Let us recall the letter Gargantua wrote to Pantaegruel:

'As to the knowledge of the facts of nature, I would have you devote yourself to them with great care, so that there shall be neither sea, river, nor fountain whose fish you do not know. All the birds of the air, all the trees, shrubs, and fruits of the forests, all the grasses of the earth, all the metals concealed in the depths of the abysses, the precious stones of the entire East and South—none of these should be unknown to you . . . by frequent anatomies, get the perfect knowledge of the microcosm, which is man', etc.

And Spencer, had he known about it, would certainly have approved Comenius's proposals that natural science be taught to all in the people's schools and he would have liked the sentiments expressed in the famous quotation:

'In the place of dead books, why should we not open the living book of nature? There is nothing in the understanding that was not first in the senses. . . . We must offer to the young, not the shadows of things, but the things themselves . . .'

One need not mention Locke, or Ben Franklin, or Bentham —the resemblance between the ideas they urged and those of Spencer is evident and close. But let us be quite clear as to what was being demanded: not merely the addition of a bit of science to a literary curriculum, as one adds a bit of bookbinding or a few minutes of music, but a complete shift of emphasis; the replacement of a linguistic core by a scientific and factual one. This point is often incompletely appreciated. Cavenagh, for instance, says 'While the importance of science in the school curriculum is now recognized, it has not been found necessary to abolish the study of the classics'. And even Spencer himself, when he wrote his *Autobiography*, forgot what it was he had asked thirty-five years earlier . . . 'When the essay was written [he says] its leading thesis, that the teaching of the classics should give place to the teaching of science, was regarded by nine out of ten cultivated people as simply monstrous. Since then the claims of science have received increasing recognition . . . but more space is but reluctantly yielded . . .' Yes, increasing recognition, a little more space, but not the replacement of one core by another, certainly not an educational revolution as thorough as that promoted by the Renaissance and Reformation.

Before considering the effect of Spencer and those who spoke like him on education in England, it will be worth while glancing quickly at the impact of his ideas in France and in the United States.

First, France. Here Spencer found solid allies who were deeply anxious to reform and modernize secondary curricula.

The ground had been well-prepared long before by such men as La Chalotais,[1] Diderot, Condorcet, and many others, especially the group assciated with the *Encyclopédie*. Condorcet, in his dream of progress and of the indefinite improvement of the human species almost anticipated Spencer's own evolutionary doctrine. Diderot, in his scheme for a secondary and higher faculty of arts, placed science right in the centre. Of eight classes proposed, five were devoted to mathematics, mechanics, astronomy, physics, and chemistry. Grammar and the ancient languages were relegated to the last three years. Those glorious institutions of the Revolution, the *Ecoles Centrales*, whose magnificent success and brilliant promise are made evident in the scholarly studies of Vial and Georges Weill, were thoroughly scientific and would have delighted Spencer. Typically and understandably, they were abolished for political reasons by Napoleon in 1802, that is as soon as he had attained absolute power and thus desired an educational system subservient to his will and a system of schools that would train docile administrators.

So there was, in fact, a strong undercurrent in France desirous of reforming the classical and literary curriculum. But the French system is a highly traditional one, always administered by a literary class. And as Gabriel Compayré points out, in such a case 'there is some danger that the instruction may not be that which is best adapted to the needs of other classes'. Furthermore, the claims of scientific curricula had always been urged by radicals, freemasons, men of the left. It was thus even easier than in England to sidetrack and defeat them. As in fact happened and as is happening again to somewhat similar claims advanced since the Second World War.

Let us turn to the United States. Here Spencer met, at first, very genuine success. He found many disciples who admired him enough to provide considerable financial help at a time when he was in difficulties over the publication of the enormous *Synthetic Philosophy*. His doctrine of self-help, his dissenting nonconformity, his rugged individualism, and independence, his suspicion of state action, his faith in automatic and inevitable

[1] 'I wish nothing to be taught children except facts which are attested by the eyes, at the age of seven as at the age of thirty. Nature is the best of teachers.'

186

progress and evolution, evidently made a powerful appeal. Sales of his books were large and he was offered stupendous lecture-fees—which he refused, characteristically enough. But as an educational philosopher he was largely forgotten by the beginning of the present century and now entirely—displaced in general esteem, as I think, by John Dewey. The latter urged practical measures closely in line with those which Spencer recommended, and in a way and within a framework of thought more readily acceptable to Americans, more closely attuned to their circumstances and history.

So, in America, we have the spectacle, perhaps slightly paradoxical, of a partial triumph of the ideas urged by Spencer and his allies, though his own name is forgotten. The enormous industrial progress of the United States and its widespread prosperity is, I have no doubt whatever, connected with the fact that these ideas were, in fact, adopted in the schools of that country. Certainly the knowledge which the Americans acquire helps to secure for them the necessaries of life! The chief reason serving to explain the fact that a reform of the curriculum, giving it a scientific and utilitarian orientation was, in fact, carried through in the U.S.A., is—I am inclined to believe —that over there a middle-class ideology has long been dominant. Such an ideology lays weight on content, on the useful, on the instrumental. In Western Europe, an aristocratic ideology was for long—and perhaps still is—accorded highest respect. As a result our European intellectual class often distrusts the useful, despises the industrial, lays weight on the formal and linguistic graces.

But let us return to the situation in England during the last third of the nineteenth century, and let us attempt to evaluate Spencer's influence.

In the first place, we should note that he numbered among his friends many of the most distinguished scientists of his time. One need but mention the fact that when he found it difficult to continue publication of his *Synthetic Philosophy*, an appeal for money was launched on his behalf and signed by, amongst others, John Stuart Mill, George Grote, Charles Darwin, T. H. Huxley, De Morgan, Babbage, Frankland, Graham, Charles Kingsley, Lyell, Tyndall, H. T. Buckle, G. H. Lewes, Alexander Bain, and Herschel. All these liked Spencer, in part, no doubt because he urged ideas with which they agreed, but in part almost certainly, because they liked him as a man. Though brusque in manner, he was not as tactless as he liked to think. He was generous with money and solicitous for others. He shrank from notoriety and declined all honorary distinctions. And he was full of odd and pleasing eccentricities of manner, taste, and speech.

At the level of educational theory, these friends, however, failed to give Spencer their full support—except, of course, for Alexander Bain who, in his *Education as a Science* works out thoroughly, competently, professionally, the theme enunciated by Spencer—though, alas, much less vigorously and in a much duller way. Perhaps because Spencer had been so extreme, so absolute, so logical to the limit of absurdity, they found it easier to take up a reasonable, conciliatory, middle-of-the-way attitude. Remember Tyndall and the soft iron into which opposed polarity is induced! Listen to the sweet reasonableness of Tyndall himself[1]:

'The circle of human nature is not complete without the arc of the emotions. The lilies of the field have a value for us beyond their botanical ones, a certain lightening of the heart accompanies the declaration that Solomon in all his glory was not arrayed like one of these. The sound of the village bell has a value beyond its acoustical one. The setting sun when it mantles with the bloom of roses the alpine snows, has a value beyond the optical one. . . . I think it very desirable to keep this horizon of the emotions open, and not to permit either priest or philosopher to draw down his shutters between you and it. . . . Here the dead languages, which are sure to be beaten by science in the purely intellectual fight, have an irresistible claim. . . . They supplement the work of science by exalting and refining the aesthetic faculty, and must on this account be cherished by all who desire to see human culture complete . . .'

In similar vein, we have T. H. Huxley's definition of liberal education.[2] We have all heard it many times, but its purple-patch eloquence is an excuse for repetition. Here it is:

[1] Address to students at University College, London, 1869. In *Fragments of Science*, p. 104.
[2] A liberal education, and where to find it. 1868. *In Science and Education*. The whole of that volume is very relevant to the general problems studied in this paper.

'That man, I think, has had a liberal education who has been so trained in his youth that his body is the ready servant of his will, and does with ease and pleasure all the work that, as a mechanism, it is capable of; whose intellect is a clear, cold, logic engine, with all its parts of equal strength, and in smooth working order; ready like a steam-engine, to be turned to any kind of work, and spin the gossamers as well as forge the anchors of the mind; whose mind is stored with a knowledge of the great and fundamental truths of nature and of the laws of her operations; one who, no stunted ascetic, is full of life and fire, but whose passions are trained to come to heel by a vigorous will, the servant of a tender conscience; who has learned to love all beauty, whether of Nature or of art, to hate all vileness, and to respect others as himself.

'Such a one and no other, I conceive, has had a liberal education; for he is, as completely as a man can be, in harmony with Nature. He will make the best of her, and she of him. They will get on together rarely; she as his ever beneficent mother; he as her mouthpiece, her conscious self, her minister, and interpreter.'

Echoes of Bacon and Spencer! Entirely reasonable, balanced, sane—but such persuasive gentleness and mildness had no better fortune than Spencer's own intransigence. Within the field of teaching method, indeed, there were to be found brilliant interpreters of the educational theories propounded— H. E. Armstrong in Chemistry,[1] for instance, and Professor Perry, at a later date, in mathematics. But as regards overall curricula at the secondary level—no. Complete, or almost complete, defeat. In 1864 the Public Schools Commission urged that boys should study at least two scientific subjects. In 1868 the Public Schools Act empowered public schools to alter their statutes to permit the teaching of science. In 1875 a Royal Commission recommended that in all public and endowed schools not less than eight periods a week should be devoted to science teaching. But headmasters were not at all in sympathy

---

[1] With regard to this and the following paragraphs, see H. E. Armstrong, *The Teaching of Scientific Method* (London, 1903). Especially p. 381, where Armstrong advises all teachers to read Spencer's *Education*, 'so that they may have clear ideas on the subject of education.' As further reading he proposes Charles Kingsley; Edgar Allen Poe, especially *Murder in the Rue Morgue* and the *Tales of Mystery and Imagination*; Ruskin's *Sesame and Lilies*.

with this, and went very cautiously and slowly. The defeat of the scientific movement at the secondary level was consecrated and, in a sense, made plain by the defeat of Sadler by Morant. It is not surprising that in 1918 the Prime Minister's Committee moderated the 1875 claim to six periods and in 1936, a Science Masters' Committee modestly asked for four!

On the other hand, the needs of industry had to be met somehow. In 1867, at the International Exhibition in Paris, British exhibitors failed badly—they were awarded only ten per cent of the medals. A few years later, the artificial dyestuffs industry, founded in this country, collapsed for want of trained men—and was taken over by Germany who profited immensely from it, both in financial and in military power. Official investigators were forced to the conclusion that these and similar set-backs were chiefly due to the insufficiency and inferiority of British scientific and technical instruction. The remedy applied, and it has had a measure of success, was to encourage the development of technical education in all its branches. This saved the situation, at least to some degree; but the solution was different from what had originally been asked for. It implied building new institutions by the side of the old, rather than really reforming the old so that these should be better attuned to the conditions of a new age.

So Spencer had failed to get his views accepted in the educational field—or at least had failed in large measure. And he failed, too, in the philosophical field. His great plan, put forward in the *Synthetic Philosophy* in which all human knowledge was to find its proper place and its full interpretation, did not secure acceptance anywhere.[1] Practical men, even close friends, saw nothing in it. When Beatrice Webb tried to interest her father, a close friend of Spencer's, in the 'law of increasing heterogeneity and definitives in structure and function' at work throughout the Universe, her father replied—'Words, my dear, mere words. Spencer's intellect is like a machine racing along without raw material: it is wearing out his body. Poor Spencer, he lacks instinct, my dear, he lacks instinct—you will

---

[1] Nevertheless, Spencer made a genuine contribution to scientific thought. Sir Arthur Thomson said about the *Principles of Biology*: 'Even as a balance-sheet of the facts of life the book is a biological classic; consciously or unconsciously we are all standing on his shoulders.'

discover that instinct is as important as intellect.' Meanwhile, in the professional philosophical field, ideas like his own—and indeed all commonsense and scientific notions—were being displaced by an idealism derived from Hegel. In 1902, towards the end of his life, Spencer writes complainingly to Alexander Bain that too many idealist articles are appearing in the journal *Mind*. 'Oxford and Cambridge too have been captured by this old-world nonsense. What about Scotland? I suppose Hegelianism is rife there also.' And in another letter . . . 'Hegelianism, a German Idealism in England, is really the last refuge of the so-called orthodox. What could be a better defence for incredible dogmas than unthinkable propositions?' Lord Hobhouse tried to console him[1]: 'Though, alas! the generation is froward; and some of your good seed has been devoured by fowls of the air; and some has fallen on barren rock; and some choked by thorns; a great deal has fallen on good ground, and has brought forth fruit manifold, and will assuredly bring forth more in more favourable season.'

Towards the end of his life, Herbert Spencer lived in an abyss of black pessimism—a pessimism towards which he had slowly slipped over the years. What was its cause? A sense of defeat? Yes, perhaps. Recent discoveries had made it clear that the universe was not as simple an affair or as easily explained and mastered as he had thought in his buoyant and assured youth.[2] The consciousness of the meaning of the second law of thermodynamics, the law of increase of entropy, of the apparent running down of the universe towards death and uniformity may—who knows—have gradually percolated into his thought. His faith in science may have got shaken.

Such pessimism was strangely common towards the close of the Victorian age. At the height of his glory, at the time of his jubilee, Lord Kelvin, honoured by the whole world, and in front of the great men of his time, stood up to reply to the paeans of praise.[3] 'One word (he said) characterizes the most strenuous of the efforts for the advancement of science that I have made perseveringly during fifty-five years; that word is

[1] Duncan, *op. cit.*, pp. 457, 458.
[2] *Autobiography*, ii, p. 468 sq.
[3] Silvanus P. Thompson, *The Life of William Thomson, Baron Kelvin of Largs* (London, 1910), p. 984.

FAILURE.' And one is reminded of Tennyson's cry in the night, in *In Memoriam*:

> *Are God and Nature then at strife,*
> *That Nature lends such evil dreams?*
> *So careful of the type she seems,*
> *So careless of the single life;*

Shall man

> *Who loved, who suffered countless ills,*
> *Who battled for the True, the Just,*
> *Be blown about the desert dust,*
> *Or sealed within the iron hills?*

Is this, then, the end of Herbert Spencer? By no means. It is precisely this consciousness of failure that redeems entirely the complacent self-assurance and the brash confidence of his youth. For only an angel could have fulfilled the task he had set himself, just as only gods could have accomplished the hopes of the Victorians, namely to impose their own conception of life upon the whole world and to hold within their grasp the universe of mind and of matter. But it was proper and grand to make the attempt.

And have we now nothing to learn from Spencer? Can we get nothing from his life and thought? Do we fully understand and see the weakness of his arguments? Should only historians of education study his writings?

For my part, I feel convinced that there is still much to be gained from him. In the first place, we may still get from his fervour a deeper realization of the value of the individual, a passion for individual freedom, a suspicion of the state and of the value of state action. To him, liberty was the highest good and we should not lose this vital conviction. Secondly, we get from him a vision of grandeur: his intellectual ambitions were large and generous, they embraced much in their sweep even if his grasp was too weak to hold all he reached for. And it was a synthetic vision, a vision of the whole—not an analytic, a critical one—it had in it something of the old Greek feeling for wholeness and simplicity. This, too, is a precious and invigorating ingredient of one's mental life. Lastly—his faith in science and progress. In these days science has become almost a mantle of Nessus. It clings to us and threatens to destroy us and our civilization. But to be afraid of greater knowledge is to be false to the treasures entrusted to us by our fathers. And then progress. A vulgar and old-fashioned idea? 'Progress is not an accident' said Spencer, that typical Western European of Europe's greatest age, 'progress is a necessity. What we call evil and immorality must disappear. It is certain that man must become perfect.' When we who are Europe's children lose the capacity for responding to such sentiments, then I think our nerve will really have failed and we shall be ready and shall deserve to

> *Be blown about the desert dust,*
> *And sealed within the iron hills.*

8

MATTHEW ARNOLD

*

B. PATTISON

*A lecture delivered at King's College 5 March 1951;
Mr. G. N. Garmonsway in the chair.*

When I was asked to contribute to this series of lectures I said that I was no expert on the history of education during the nineteenth century and that I was interested in Arnold chiefly as a poet and a literary critic. I was assured that a point of view different from that of a historian would give some variety to the series, but I repeat my warning to explain any partial estimate that may result. Nevertheless it is as a poet and a literary critic that Arnold is remembered, and his importance in the history of education is due to his eminence as a man of letters. That gave his writings on education authority in his own time, and we go back to them now because they are an integral part of the permanently valid element in his work.

Much of his writing on education was directed at conditions of his own time, and was the result of his professional duties. Philosophers and students of society have always discussed education for obvious reasons, but until the nineteenth century the only professional writers on education were dons and schoolmasters. The problem of organizing education on a large scale is a comparatively modern one. It is significant that this series includes lectures on a Cabinet Minister and on two civil servants. The administrator had come to play a determining part in education. Arnold himself was a civil servant. For thirty-five years he was an inspector of schools, at first travelling over a great part of the midland and southern counties and Wales, and then concentrating on the metropolitan area, so that he acquired a very complete knowledge of elementary education, which was all the inspectorate was responsible for at that time. But he was never an ordinary inspector. Indeed, he had few qualifications for the post he held. Rugby and Oxford did little to prepare him for the problems of giving the working classes basic instruction, and his only teaching experience was a few months with the Lower Fifth at Rugby. When he was appointed an inspector he was 'a very gentlemanly young man with a slight tinge of the fop'[1] and a reputation for flippancy, who had been for three or four years private secretary to Lord Lansdowne. Arnold wanted to marry, and it was to provide him with a secure livelihood that Lord Lansdowne, the Lord President of the Council, recommended him for an inspectorship. Shortly afterwards his friend, A. H. Clough, also wanted to marry and, in his search for a regular income to allow him to do so, thought of following Arnold's example; but Arnold warned him of the 'hard dull work, low salary, stationariness'[2] that made up the life of a school inspector. He never liked the 'routine work' and never became particularly good at it.

'He was [says a colleague]—to put it mildly—more efficient on the literary side. . . . "Mr Arnold inspects our school in Westminster", a London school manager said to me. "Of course we are much honoured, and the managers make a point of attending to meet him. He arrives in the course of the morning; shakes hands with the managers and teachers; and talks very pleasantly for a few minutes; then walks through the classes between the desks, looking over the children's shoulders at some exercises, and so makes his way to the door, and we see him no more." '[3]

Yet it was also remarked that 'he became the teachers' and children's friend, and . . . none of his colleagues had a shrewder sense of what was wanting in each school he visited

[1] *Correspondence of Henry Crabb Robinson with the Wordsworth Circle*, ed. E. J. Morley, ii, p. 743.
[2] *The Letters of Matthew Arnold to Arthur Hugh Clough*, ed. H. F. Lowry, p. 118.
[3] E. M. Sneyd-Kynnersley, *H.M.I.*, p. 157.

or could reckon it up more readily'.[1] And a very able inspector, whose appointment he himself recommended, gave the considered judgment that 'indirectly, his fine taste, his gracious and kindly manner, his honest and generous recognition of any new form of excellence which he observed, all tended to rise the aims and tone of the teachers with whom he came in contact, and to encourage in them self-respect and respect for their work.[2]

It was fortunate indeed that only twelve years after the first of Her Majesty's Inspectors were appointed the inspectorate should have recruited one of the leading writers of the day, who brought into the elementary schools a breath of refinement and taste. In him the schools also found a powerful advocate of a fuller and deeper education for the working classes. For as a man of letters his influence on public opinion was not negligible, and he was acquainted with people prominent in various fields, including two of the Vice-Presidents of the Council, W. E. Forster, his brother-in-law, and A. J. Mundella. He was consulted on a variety of educational topics. H. A. Bruce asked his advice about the composition of the Taunton Commission, and on three occasions he was sent to report on continental systems of education. It was generally recognized that on the larger issues he spoke with some authority, not only because of his experience but also because of his personal qualities.

If Arnold brought some sweetness and light to the humdrum business of instructing the poorer classes and a sense of values to the discussion of educational adminstration, it is equally true that the drudgery of school visits and reports kept his thinking to some extent within fields he was well-equipped to cultivate. The service of national enlightenment was one for which his temperament and gifts fitted him. In many respects he was a true son of his father; only he preferred schoolmastering on a bigger scale. He regarded himself primarily as a poet and then as a literary critic. As neither of these, however, is he near the first rank, and we cannot entirely share his regret that he was not left more time for purely literary work.

His limitations as a poet are due not so much to a poor ear,

[1] *Cornhill Magazine*, February 1899.
[2] J. G. Fitch, *Thomas and Matthew Arnold*, p. 171.

which produces some very bad lines and often a general flatness, as to a more fundamental inability to embody the really creative forces in him in suitable themes and symbols. He kept on echoing Socrates' and Coleridge's admonition, 'Know thyself', and he realized that the experience from which the true knowledge must come lay deep in the self:

> *Below the surface stream, shallow and light,*
> *Of what we say we feel, below the stream,*
> *As light, of what we think we feel—there flows*
> *With noiseless current strong, obscure and deep,*
> *The central stream of what we feel indeed.*[1]

But it was seldom that he could dive down to the depths of his own personality, and seldomer that he could find fit symbols to convey what he found there. There is an earnestness and an air of struggle in his poetry. He has always 'the old unquiet breast';[2] he is always

> *Weary of myself, and sick of asking what I am,*
> *And what I ought to be.*[3]

But his troubles remain obscure and hardly come into the poetry except by reference. Hence his difficulty in finding suitable subjects. One of his most successful symbols is the Scholar Gipsy, because the figure from Glanvil does not represent what Arnold has chosen him to represent. Arnold warns him to fly from

> *this strange disease of modern life,*
> *With its sick hurry, its divided aims;*

but in fact the Scholar Gipsy was

> *born in days when wits were fresh and clear,*
> *And life ran gaily as the sparkling Thames,*[4]

and he left the world altogether, not merely the world as it had become in Arnold's time. Again, the beautiful simile with which *The Scholar Gipsy* closes has no connexion with the rest of the poem and is most unsuitable for the purpose it is supposed to serve. These inconsistencies suggest that the causes of Arnold's distress, which lends such an attractive melancholy to his poetry,

---

[1] *S. Paul and Protestantism.*   [2] *A Summer Night.*
[3] *Self-Dependence.*   [4] *The Scholar Gipsy.*

were deeper than the dissatisfaction with his own time on which he fathered them; that his real inspiration came from depths he could seldom penetrate in the actual process of composition, and that the medium in which he worked was ill-adapted to his creative powers.

A similar limitation is apparent in his literary criticism. He lacked both Coleridge's psychological insight and philosophical attitude. This he himself admitted, calling himself 'a plain, unsystematic writer, without a philosophy',[1] and warning his readers that 'from a man without a philosophy no one can expect philosophical completeness'.[2] His reactions came from a fine sensibility, but his judgment had few considered principles to guide it in examining particular artistic productions, and many of his swans turn out on closer inspection to be geese. The apparent lucidity of his prose scarcely hides the intuitive nature of his thinking. His thought hardly progresses. He circles round his object, repeating his rather vague terms until his general impression communicates itself to an imagination prepared to be receptive. His difficulty in finding suitable themes for his own poetry gives him an exaggerated notion of the importance of 'great ideas' and 'excellent actions', and a feeling that these should have a significance greater than they ordinarily have outside the artistic construction leads to his unfortunate assertion that 'poetry is a criticism of life'. None of these terms expresses quite what he intended, but they point to interests which distinguish both his poetry and his criticism. To him literature was not an end in itself. It was only a means to a richer and fuller life, and insofar as it represented a tradition it had both individual and social value. 'English civilization', he said, '—the humanizing, the bringing into one harmonious and truly humane life, of the whole body of English society—that is what interests me.'[3]

An awareness of the world around him, both of its conditions and of its ideas, was essential to this central concern. He let a mind trained in the humanist tradition play round the leading questions in contemporary discussion. His work in education supplied material by giving him an extensive knowledge of a wide range of English society, while his speculations on English

[1] *Culture and Anarchy*, ch. iii. [2] *Ibid.*
[3] *Irish Essays*, 'Ecce, Convertimur ad Gentes'.

civilization constantly had implications for education. The weary round of school visits and reports may have helped to keep him in fields where he could operate most profitably.

There is an impressive unity about his works. The main ideas of *Culture and Anarchy* appear in their more practical applications in the educational reports. It is his constant effort to look at education in the full context of contemporary civilization that makes him important as a formative influence on the development of education.

He first became an inspector exactly 100 years ago, in the year of the Great Exhibition. An age of prosperity was just opening. The economic troubles of the hungry 'forties and the political unrest, which had been a danger since Waterloo, passed away after the Chartist fiasco of 1848. The difficult transition from an obsolete Tudor political organization to one more able to cope with a new industrial society had been largely accomplished. The commercial and professional classes had become the centre of political power. With a rising standard of living the working classes turned from political agitation to the organization of trade unions and other agencies of social improvement. A state of equilibrium had been established, but it could only be temporary: by the middle of the 'sixties it was becoming clear that political responsibility would have to be extended to the working classes. Meanwhile, one great social transformation had safely been achieved and there was a breathing space before the next one need be attempted.

Arnold was extremely conscious of the continuity and unity of European civilization, but he knew that the worst way to try and preserve what was valuable in it was to resist change. He neither looked nostalgically back, nor shrank from the future. The Zeitgeist had its contribution to make to the development of the tradition, but 'The fashion of this world passeth away; and I would fain occupy myself with the eternal'.[1] What was needed was to test the present situation by some set of permanent values, and then to call attention to any shortcomings revealed and to suggest correctives for them.

Sweeping away the débris of obsolete social machinery had been the great achievement of the liberalism of the preceding generation. The cramping effects of government regulation and

[1] H. F. Lowry, *op. cit.*, p. 36.

social custom and the consciousness of released energies once they were removed had made freedom appear the most desirable of all conditions. The negative advantage of ensuring that everybody could do what he liked was praised, while the positive corollary of trying to see that what everybody liked was worth doing received less attention. Then again, the attempt to modernize social organization produced an undue concentration on what Arnold called 'machinery', on making things work efficiently, irrespective of the purposes they were to serve. This 'faith in machinery' was encouraged by the materialism accompanying the rapid increase in wealth and by the shift of the centre of power to the commercial middle classes, whose interests had largely been absorbed by the creation of industrialism. These were the Philistines, who had taken over the leadership from an aristocracy no longer able to govern by itself or to impose standards of taste and manners, and whose consequent lack of ideas caused Arnold to name them Barbarians; while, waiting in outer darkness for a chance to join in responsible social activity, was the Populace, an incalculable force to be reckoned with by anybody anxious about the civilized tradition already threatened by the changes of the previous half-century

Arnold *was* anxious about that. 'I see a wave of more than American vulgarity, moral, intellectual, and social, preparing to break over us', he wrote in 1848.[1] To avoid it a new attitude of mind was required. He called it culture. The term is rather vague, but Arnold was not inclined to worry about terminology; he was 'concerned for the thing, not the name'. What he wished to do was to distract attention from 'machinery' and to encourage an inward condition, a critical habit, which would concentrate not on doing but on being, and evaluate whatever was done by some more durable standards than desire or efficiency. There was first a relatively passive quality to be cultivated, 'a desire after the things of the mind simply for their own sakes and for the pleasure of seeing them as they are'.[2] It involved 'getting to know, on all the matters that most concern us, the best that has been thought and said in the world; and through this knowledge, turning a stream of fresh and free thought upon

[1] *The Letters of Matthew Arnold*, 1848-88, G. W. E. Russell, ed. p. 4.
[2] *Culture and Anarchy*, ch. i.

our stock notions and habits'.[1] The rule for its operation is disinterestedness.

'But there is of culture another view, in which not solely the scientific passion, the sheer desire to see things as they are, natural and proper in an intelligent being, appears as the ground of it. There is a view in which all the love of our neighbours, the impulses towards action, help and beneficence, the desire of removing human error, clearing human confusion, and diminishing human misery, the noble aspiration to leave the world better and happier than we found it—motives eminently such as are called social—come in as part of the grounds of culture, and the main and pre-eminent parts. Culture is then properly described not as having its origin in curiosity but as having its object in the love of perfection; it is a study of perfection. It moves by the force not merely or primarily of the scientific passion for pure knowledge but also of the moral and social passion for doing good. As, in the first view of it, we took for its worthy motto Montesquieu's words: "To render an intelligent being yet more intelligent", so in the second view of it there is no better motto which it can have than these words of Bishop Wilson, "To make reason and the will of God prevail".'[2]

Culture, then, has the 'aim of setting ourselves to ascertain what perfection is and to make it prevail'. And 'perfection—as culture from a thorough disinterested study of human nature and human experience learns to conceive it—is a harmonious expansion of all the powers which make the beauty and worth of human nature, and it is not consistent with the over-development of any one power at the expense of the rest.'[3]

The conception of culture is based on a kind of humanism, on the belief that human experience as a whole provides a comprehensive standard of values, and that to be truly human is to try to approximate more and more closely to the whole range of these values. Initially it is an individual matter, but the individual can develop only in society, and his own partial perception of the all-round perfection at which culture aims is supplemented by the collective perception. 'This is the social idea; and the men of culture are the true apostles of equality.'[4] 'It seeks to do away with classes.'[5] 'Civilization is the humaniza-

[1] *Ibid.*   [2] *Ibid.*   [3] *Ibid.*   [4] *Ibid.*   [5] *Ibid.*

tion of man in society. Man is civilized, when the whole body of society comes to life with a life worthy to be called *human*, and corresponding to man's true aspirations and powers.'[1]

In thus adding equality to freedom as a necessary condition for a healthy society Arnold was moving beyond the Liberals of his earlier days, and he claimed to be 'a Liberal of the future rather than the present',[2] a claim substantiated by the later development of liberal thought and action. So, too, with his conception of the State. As more and more of the nation was drawn into responsibility, the State ceased to be the repressive and external force it had been to earlier liberals. Arnold hoped it might become 'the power most representing the right reason of the nation'[3] or 'the nation in its collective and corporate character'.[4] He was therefore one of the first to advocate a national system of education.

'Throughout the country good elementary schools taking the child to the age of thirteen; then good secondary schools, taking him to sixteen, with good classical high schools and commercial high schools, taking him on further to eighteen or nineteen; with good technical and special schools, for those who require them, parallel with the secondary and high schools —this is what is to be aimed at. Without system and concert and thought, it cannot be attained: and these again are impossible without a Minister of Education as a centre in which to fix responsibility, and an Educational Council to advise the Minister and keep him in touch with the tendencies, needs, and school-movement of the time.'[5]

The dangers of over-centralization in such a scheme had been brought home to him on the Continent, and to avoid them he advocated administrative devolution to local authorities. This was not practicable until the reform of local government, already begun in the boroughs, reached the counties in 1888. Since then, however, Arnold's programme has been gradually implemented, and the 1944 Act virtually completed it.

Arnold's official duties were confined to elementary schools, but when he joined the inspectorate 'popular education was

---

[1] *Mixed Essays*, preface.   [2] *Irish Essays*, 'The Future of Liberalism'.
[3] *Culture and Anarchy*, ch. ii.
[4] *Irish Essays*, 'An Unregarded Irish Grievance'.
[5] *The Reign of Queen Victoria*, ed. T. H. Ward, ii, p. 279.

already launched. I was myself continually a witness of the progress it was making; I could see that the cause of popular education was safe'.[1] The greatest danger to it came from the mechanical tests of efficiency imposed by the Revised Code of 1862, against which Arnold conducted a long and determined attack. But the most important educational front seemed to him to be that of middle-class education, and he had the opportunity of giving his views on this in reports on visits to continental countries. He saw that the Philistines were not only the present centre of power but were rapidly assimilating the Barbarians culturally, and that the Populace, 'the children of a future whose day has not yet dawned', 'will have in a cultured, liberalized, ennobled, transformed middle-class, a point towards which it may hopefully work, a goal towards which it may with joy direct its aspirations'.[2] He therefore exerted himself 'to say to the government, "Regard the necessities of a not distant future, and organize your secondary education,"'[3] The exhortation was addressed to the Government. The provision for middle-class education was 'miserably inadequate. It can only become adequate by being treated as a public service, as a service for which the State, the nation in its collective and corporate character, is responsible.'[4] The public schools could be left to carry on for a small fragment of the nation, but otherwise the problem must be treated as a national one and take its place in the general scheme of national education.

The system of national education was only machinery. Arnold's chief concern, however, was not with the machinery by which his 'humanization of man in society' was to be effected but with the process itself. Right through it must go the desire to spread culture, to transform society. He regarded his prime task as an Inspector as being 'to test and quicken the intellectual life of the school'.[5] But he was aware that culture was more than intellectual life.

'And [as Frederick Harrison complained] how do you get it? It is very good to tell me how beautiful this is; but, if a physician tells me only what a beautiful thing good health is,

[1] *Irish Essays*, 'Ecce, Convertimur ad Gentes'.
[2] *A French Eton.*   [3] *Popular Education*, etc.
[4] *Irish Essays*, 'An Unregarded Irish Grievance'.
[5] *Reports on Elementary Schools, 1852–82*, ed. F. S. Marvin.

how happy and strong it makes those who possess it, and omits
to tell me how I can gain health, or say only be healthy, desire,
seek after health, I call him no physician but a quack. So if I
describe in words a very admirable state of the soul, it matters
little what I call it. I might say this beautiful state is such and
such and call it fiddlestick, or sauerkraut, or the like; but
what am I profited, unless I learn how this same fiddelstick, or
sauerkraut, or culture (call it as you please) comes to a man?'[1]
Arnold never gets down to the details of actual education: they
are to him largely machinery. We have already noticed in his
poetry and criticism some uncertainty when he tries to penetrate
below the level of ideas, and 'humanization' must be in part
through human relationships. But on the content of education
as distinct from the process he is fairly specific. For secondary
education he accepted the classics, merely urging that they
should be regarded all the time as literature. The backbone of
the elementary school curriculum was, of course, to be the
teaching of English. Curiously enough he advocated the study
of grammar, because it was 'more effective than arithmetic as a
logical training'.[2] But English literature was the most important
feature in the cultural programme, and particularly poetry.
'Good poetry does indeed tend to form the soul and character;
it tends to beget a love of beauty and of truth in alliance
together; it suggests, however indirectly, high and noble
principles of action, and it inspires the emotion so helpful in
making principles operative.'[3] This is about as near as he gets
to supplying the aesthetic and moral aspects of culture to the
curriculum. He realized that they should be there, but the
limitations already noticed in his poetry and criticism prevent
him from showing very clearly how they might be provided.
On the arts he is strangely silent: even poetry is valued largely
for its content. 'The true aim of schools and instruction', he
tells us, 'is to develop the powers of our mind and to give us
access to vital knowledge.'[4] Among the knowledge most
necessary to people of his time he agreed that the physical
sciences should be included; 'but still it will be *knowledge* only
which they give us; knowledge not put for us into relation with

[1] *The Fortnightly Magazine*, 1867, 'Culture: A Dialogue'.
[2] Marvin, *op. cit.*, p. 213.   [3] *Ibid.*, pp. 186–7.
[4] *Schools and Universities on the Continent.*

our sense for conduct, our sense for beauty, and touched by emotion by being so put.'[1] The core of education to him therefore was a literary discipline. Here the training of the mind and the acquisition of 'vital knowledge' were combined with the development of aesthetic and moral powers. All the rest of the educational process depended on 'having effected in the whole man, by means of letters, a rise in what the political economists call the *standard of life*'.[2] Behind this claim for literary or linguistic training as the centre of the whole educational process is a feeling that complete control of the medium of communication puts the individual in touch with the full range of the community's experience, past and present, and that the extension of such control among members of a society ensures an increase in the continuity, unity, and growth of its civilization. The literary discipline is not exclusive, but it is the most comprehensive means to the end of 'the humanization of man in society'.

It was the end rather than the means on which Arnold continually insisted. To keep the end always in view and to work towards it unceasingly seemed to him an urgent necessity. He had a sense that England was 'on its way either to a great transformation or to a great disaster'.[3] The alternative to Culture was Anarchy, with the collapse of all civilized tradition and 'the beatification of a whole nation through clap-trap'. The masses of the Populace would soon add their weight to that of the Philistines, or they would turn to Jacobinism, with its 'violent indignation with the past, abstract systems of renovation applied wholesale',[4] and its blind following of a Rabbi. Either way the values of civilization would be overwhelmed. The continuity with the best in the past would be broken, and individual caprice or mass regimentation into rigid orthodoxies would destroy all standards and all free play of the mind.

We have had our disasters since Arnold's time, and we have had more than our fill of clap-trap and Jacobinism and Rabbis. Transformation has not kept pace with any of them. *Culture and Anarchy* is still a very topical book. To work out its principles in

[1] *Discoveries in America*, 'Literature and Science'.
[2] Marvin, *op. cit.*, p. 178.   [3] *Friendship's Garland*.
[4] *Culture and Anarchy*, ch. i.

terms of our own circumstances is still the only educational programme capable of effecting 'the humanization of man in society'. No one has indicated more clearly than Arnold all that is involved in saving European civilization in modern conditions. That is the unifying motive of all his work and constitutes his great historical importance. His humanism needs re-statement, but now that his writings on religion are dead that should not be difficult. And a humanism so re-stated is the only sound basis for a theory of education. But the urgency is much greater now than it was in Arnold's day. Those who believe European civilization can still be saved will have to work quickly to interpret Culture in terms of the contemporary situation before Anarchy descends finally and irretrievably.

Arnold was called 'The Prophet of Culture'. He has proved prophetic in more senses than one. Much of what he foresaw has happened, and the essentials of his educational message are as relevant now as they were in his own day. If we regard him as a prophet and do not chop logic with him or expect exact formulations or details about machinery, we can gain more from him than from most writers on education during the past century. Certainly, whether we get it from him or from elsewhere, what he stood for is of supreme importance.

9

W. E. FORSTER
AND THE LIBERAL REFORMERS

*

W. H. G. ARMYTAGE

A lecture delivered at King's College on 26 February 1951;
Professor A. V. Judges in the chair.

'I t is from the West rather than from the East, that the danger to the supremacy of Great Britain is to be apprehended; that is, from the silent and peaceful rivalry of American commerce, the growth of its manufactures, its rapid progress in internal improvements, the superior education of its people, and their economical and pacific government—it is from these, and not from the barbarous policy and impoverishing armaments of Russia, that the grandeur of our commercial and national prosperity is endangered."

These words were written in 1835 by Richard Cobden, then an unknown thirty year old Manchester calico printer. In the thirty years that followed he became a major figure in the Liberal hagiography, and architect of the party programme.

As a prophet, he was both persistent and consistent. In 1851, when the Great Exhibition seemed, if anything, to confirm the majority of Englishmen in their belief that England was the workshop of the world, and that such pre-eminence was due to certain qualities of empiric genius, he raised his voice once more—this time at Manchester on 1 December. He said, just when this feeling was at its height:

'I don't think it is safe for us as a nation to be the most ignorant Protestant people on the face of the earth. This is a period in the world's history when the very security, the trade, and the progress of a nation depend, not so much on the contest of arms, as on the rivalry in the science and the arts which must spring from education. Did any reflecting man walk through the Great Exhibition without feeling that we were apt to be a little under a delusion as the quality of men in other parts of the world and their capacity to create these articles of utility of which we were apt to think sometimes we possess a monopoly of production in this country. I don't think we can wait.'

But still the country waited. The inert mass of educational vested interest, secure in the endowments which it had preserved from the unhallowed scrutiny of the outside world, was slow to respond to the dynamic challenge of the times. Neither the eloquence of William Johnson Fox nor the finesse of Sir John Pakington could counter-act the aversion to state action entertained by many leading nonconformists. Nor could they moderate the jealous (and zealous) control which the Established Church maintained over the schools of the National Society.

By 1867, three years after Cobden's death, and thirty-three years after he had written the warning I quoted at the beginning, it certainly looked as if the country had waited too long. For at another international Exhibition held in Paris, British manufactures were completely outclassed. One observer described their exhibits as 'slovenly intruded heaps of raw material mingled with rusty iron', and a Conservative Government appointed a select committee to dispel the gloom. The evidence of that committee contains the first definite intimations that British industry was but mortal. For those casual observers to whom the Bluebooks were closed, there were more obvious signs: Belgian girders were being used at South Kensington and had even intruded as far as Sheffield, and Glasgow.

As the select committee was told, the silent march of American ingenuity had at last caught up with, and indeed surpassed, the empiric technique of English manufacturers. The sewing-machine, the reaper, and the centrifugal pump, three basic accelerators of the industrial tempo, were all of American origin. So were the machines which made the gimlet headed screws of

Chamberlain and Nettlefold, and the more deadly weapons of the Birmingham Small Arms Factory. Even the very presses of *The Times* and the leading Manchester papers which gave this melancholy news to an English public were American. John Platt, then the largest mechanical engineer in the world, confessed to the committee that it was the established custom amongst his fellows to purchase inventions from the Americans and to use them in England. Similar case histories were outlined to the committee of other trades injured by continental *expertise* in the industrial field.

At Birmingham, centre of the hardware trade, manufacturers were finding that Americans could outsell them even in the colonies. Ploughs, shovels, nails, pumps, locks, and petrol lamps, all the tools that the pioneer communities in Australia and Canada needed so badly, were being increasingly supplied by American competitors. The President of the Birmingham Chamber of Commerce volunteered extensive information in support of this disturbing trend. Not without reason did Birmingham become, in this very year, the active nucleus of a movement to establish some system of universal rate-aided, secular education for the English working-classes.

Nor was this the only argument for immediate state action to educate these classes. For in 1867 they had been given the vote, and though the rhinoceros-hided Robert Lowe (who I regret to say was the first Member of Parliament for this university) had opposed such a concession, he voiced the opinion of everyone when he remarked that it was now imperative to educate the new masters. For masters these industrious classes were surely becoming. The congeries of disreputable friendly societies, pub-centred and narrow-minded, had by 1868 been welded into a national pressure group, presided over by a high command of its own. The mild-mannered Berthier of this artisan general staff was Robert Applegarth, who said in October, 1868:

'Opposition of masters and men does not arise from a desire of either to oppress the other, but rather from ignorance, from misunderstanding of each other's position, and failure to appreciate the other's point of view. I look to education to teach all parties better.'

His colleagues thought likewise, and threw themselves into

the work of the newly-formed Birmingham National Education League, which inherited Cobden's educational programme, his political techniques, and much of his support.

I would like to dilate on the significance of Applegarth for a minute. He had, like countless thousands of his class, emigrated to America in his fifties, but had returned to build his particular utopia in his home town, and among his own countrymen. He represents the gradual closing of that great American escape hatch through which discontented working men had poured for the previous half-century, blessed and encouraged, if the truth be told, by Cobden. As the flow to the prairies dwindled, working men stayed at home to demand the social opportunities of which the previous generation had despaired. Just what the working class vote represented may be seen from the overwhelming triumph of the Liberal party at the polls in 1868. Gladstone was swept into power, and appointed as his Vice-President of the Council a middle-class manufacturer with strong Chartist sentiments—W. E. Forster.

Now W. E. Forster began his working life in a firm which wove imitation oriental fabrics on handlooms. As the handicrafts retreated before the machines, he salvaged his career by entering the most English of all trades—that of wool. Though pre-eminently engaged in trade, the robust tradition of Quaker enlightenment which he inherited from his missonary father and mother persisted long after he had made his fortune. He won further social insights by early friendships with Robert Owen and Thomas Cooper. But none of his friends inspired him so much as Thomas Carlyle. 'His words' said Forster, 'sounded through me like the blast of a trumpet, stirring up all my powers to the battle of life.' Carlyle, you will remember, once called Cobden 'an inspired bagman with a calico millenium', and Forster, though he was substantially a Cobdenite Liberal, referred to Cobden as 'impracticable and un-English'. He was right. Cobden's lack of enthusiasm for trade unions did much to vitiate his educational evangel.

From the moment he married Jane Arnold, and was thereupon ejected from the Quaker faith, Forster became more English every day. The raw secularity of many of the advanced Liberals grew increasingly distasteful to him, especially so as the luminous orbit of his brother-in-law Matthew began to encompass him. In this light the positivism and vulgarity of the middle class became only too clear. So, as the howls of the Liberationist pack for the disestablishment of the church grew in intensity, Forster retreated further to the centre of the Liberal Party, thereby offending a large section of his own constituency of Bradford, who, with singular lack of tact, promptly elected Edward Miall, as his fellow M.P. in 1869. Miall was editor of the *Nonconformist*, a paper which boasted that it represented 'the Dissidence of Dissent and the Protestantism of the Protestant Religion'. He also opposed the notion that the State should initiate a scheme of national education.

Between Miall, the distressed industrialists, the Church, and the urgencies of the times, Forster was placed in a most awkward position when he took office in 1868. Matthew Arnold, described it when he wrote:

'In any matter which, like education, touches many passions and prejudices, we do not get the best our statesmen would naturally devise; and what we do get is given in a manner not to correct popular prejudices, but rather to humour them.'

Forster was soon introduced to these many passions and prejudices of which his brother-in-law had written. In 1869 he presented to the House of Commons his bill for the liberalizing of the endowed schools, drafted along the lines of the Taunton Committee's recommendations, of which he had been a member. But unfortunately for this measure, it suffered the emotional backwash from two other measures—the private Bill for repealing university tests, and Gladstone's Bill for disestablishing the Irish Church. Forster, to save his Bill as it ran the gauntlet both of a select committee and a committee of the whole house, had to jettison three important clauses—one for establishing a state examining body, another allowing local rates to be used for secondary education, and a third which would have resulted in local authorities taking part in the work of reconstruction—a clause which would have meshed with Goschen's plan for reorganizing local government.

Notwithstanding the abrasive treatment it received, the Bill emerged to establish three commissioners, armed with powers to reconstitute all schools whose endowments were more than fifty years old. Contemporary opinion agreed that Forster had done admirably. The *Economist* categorically declared that there were few statesmen who could have steered a Bill full of such contentious material so skilfully and successfully, to receive the Royal Assent. They were inclined to censor him for being a little too biased in favour of the workman's child receiving a liberal rather than a technical education since a child might become a discontented member of his class. These three commissioners became, as Mr. Lowndes has said, the real founders of our secondary-school network. With H. J. Roby as their secretary until 1872, and as their liveliest colleague till 1874, they established schemes for 235 schools—nearly a third of those examined by the Taunton Commission. These schemes included the creation of popular governing bodies, the introduction of science and modern languages as teaching subjects, and some provision for the education of girls, Even more significant however, was a provision in the Act which armed them. For it forbad a teacher from orienting his teaching of non-religious subjects around some sectarian core, and it empowered a parent to withdraw a child from any lessons specifically devoted to religion. As the late Professor Adamson commented, 'The State was preparing to throw religion overboard'.

To Edward Thring, the energetic headmaster of Uppingham, these commissioners were anathema. 'The future looks very dark, and the present feels very cold,' he lamented to a correspondent; 'the bigotry of the Liberals is unspeakable.' He foresaw that they embodied State power which was advancing to crush him and his fellows (the metaphor is his own). 'These powerful and practised red tapists', he growled, 'with nothing at stake, matched against poor me, with only my principles and experience.' He underestimated himself. Rallying such of his colleagues as would listen to him, he organized the Headmasters' Conference in concert with Mitchinson of King's School, Canterbury. He warned them that they were scheduled to be 'boiled down' in a witches' cauldron. His principles and experience won the day. Within two years the Headmasters' Conference was joined by Eton, Winchester, and Shrewsbury to his lively satisfaction. All the endowed schools were now in the boat together, and with Thring to pilot them they sailed gaily into the Liberal winds.

Whereas in 1869 Forster had to take the field against his legitimate parliamentary opponents, in the following year he found himself at odds with a large section of his own party. Though all agreed that it was high time to establish a network of elementary schools throughout the land in view of American and German examples, the control of that network soon became a Nonconformist obsession. Forster at first proposed to supplement the existing voluntary schools by others administered by local boards, supported by a local rate, and with a conscience clause enabling scholars to obtain exemption from religious teaching.

The Nonconformists, however, objected strongly to several things in this first draft Bill. One was the suggestion that existing voluntary schools should also be assisted out of the rates. Another was the non-elective character of the school boards, which in Forster's first Bill were to be appointed by the town council and vestries. A third objection was Forster's intention to afford a year's grace to the voluntary societies in which to fill up such gaps as did exist before school districts were to be assessed for educational deficiencies. The Liberationist pack, which had bayed long and loud for the disestablishment of the Church, claimed that these three proposals would effect a more permanent establishment than ever before, and rivet the Church to the necks of long-suffering Nonconformist ratepayers.

So once more, Forster had to trim and cut his Bill, so much so that when it reached committee Disraeli claimed that it was practically a new one. For Forster had conceded *ad hoc* school boards, the cumulative vote, cut the year's grace to six months, and removed religious instruction from the cognisance of the government inspector. But he refused to accept the full Birmingham programme for secular schools, even though it meant his own ostracism by a large bulk of the Liberal party.

And ostracized he certainly was. Chamberlain now emerged into the political arena to campaign against him. Bright described his Bill as the worst measure passed since 1832. The youthful John Morley drew up a grand indictment against him, roundly trouncing the 'holy army of misologists' subsidized by Forster from the public purse, who, continued Morley, could never have existed had not Forster's permissive compulsion existed. Morley, who later described the struggle as a social one, listed three counts in his indictment which told heavily against Forster. First, the Church had used the six month's grace to increase its schools by 30 per cent. Second, the cumulative vote was working in the Church's favour. Lastly, the 25th clause, which allowed the guardians to pay school fees of necessitous children, was an insult to Nonconformity.

This organized opposition wilfully misinterpreted all Forster's subsequent administrative acts. When in 1871 he introduced a new code in order to leaven the soulless skills of tongue and pen which had formed the basis for government grants for the previous nine years, he was further accused of endeavouring to perpetuate the inefficient voluntary schools. Because standards four to six were now encouraged to study for two specific subjects beyond the three Rs (a pass in which would mean an extra 3s.), and that schedules of heating, lighting, and ventilation were laid down, that attendance grants were increased to 6s., and the grant for a pass in the Procrustean three Rs to 4s., Nonconformists pointed out that all this meant less of a financial load for the voluntary schools. Nor did Forster comfort them by checking the fees of board schools to ensure that there was no unfair competition with voluntary schools.

Forster himself was anxious to repeal the 25th clause, which by 1873 had become, in the words of one caustic onlooker, the small ditch in which two great political armies engaged in civil war. But the Cabinet dropped his Bill, leaving Forster between the two armies just when the working of the Education Act was most difficult, and he was having to force school boards on recalcitrant districts which had previously held out against them on the grounds of expense.

In spite of a series of hostile assessments from Morley to Lynd, Forster's work was a great one. In his five years of office he added 4,982 more schools to the 8,281 which had previously existed. Average attendance increased by over half a million. He himself said 'some education is now secured to all English children. Whether that some is enough to be of real value is now the question; but I do not think the work can stop'. Nor did it, thanks to the school boards. Like active cells they fed life to the system. This he had done by the deliberate sacrifice of his political good name, and the chance of leading his party.

Throughout his term of office, one of Forster's closest friends —indeed, almost his unofficial adjutant—was A. J. Mundella, the brazen-lunged M.P. for Sheffield. Mundella's shrewd supple intelligence and enlightened social conscience had won him, not only a small fortune in the hosiery trade, but also the position of being the mouthpiece of the labour world in the House of Commons. During the vital months which preceded the drafting of the 1870 Act he had done much to encourage Forster to build on foundations already laid, and in the stormy years that followed he laboured long and fruitlessly to unite the Nonconformists with the main body of Liberal opinion, to expand the code, and to make compulsion effective.

For Mundella, like Cobden (whom he called 'the greatest statesman of the century'), saw the educational problem in industrial terms. For him the most vital raw material which the country had to develop was the intelligence of its children. He looked, not only to raising the school leaving age, but also to establishing a hierarchy of local technological colleges in close connection with industry. As a hosiery manufacturer, and as a large employer, he was against half-time employment, which was then legal from before the age of ten. In 1872 he assumed the parliamentary leadership of the Factory Acts Reform Association, which pressed for the raising of the half-time age. For Mundella, increased educational facilities were the only effective means by which social peace could be promoted: and his contemporaries acknowledged by imitating him, that the system of industrial arbitration which he had so successfully pioneered at Nottingham was effective and workable.

When the Liberals fell from power in 1874, Mundella remained to ply the Conservative Government with much advice. His virtue as a parliamentarian was that he would patiently sit for hours until the small hours of the morning, waiting for a chance to speak. It was no small tribute to his patience and perseverance that the Conservative Government passed his Factory Act in 1874, and two years later set up school attendance committees endowed with the same power of enforcing attendance at voluntary schools as that possessed by the school boards. In these six years of Conservative administration, that is from 1874 to 1880, Mundella fought so consistently on behalf of the teachers in elementary schools that he became known as the 'Teacher's Friend'—and their powerful union, the N.U.T. as it became, found in him a ready spokesman. So much indeed did he identify himself with the cause of the schools that Gladstone, on returning to power in 1880, gave him Forster's old office, taking care to assure the Queen (who had expressed misgivings at 'one of the most violent radicals' getting such an office) that Mundella was 'a very religious man, very much for religious education, and never said anything offensive'. The outgoing Conservative Minister of War, Gathorne Hardy, thought otherwise, however, and noted 'he will do mischief'.

The mischief of course, was increased State action to develop the potential of the urban working classes. For, the new generation of Liberals were being armed with a new philosophy by T. H. Green, who had served as a commissioner for the Taunton Commission in 1864–7, and also as a member of the Oxford School Board. Green taught that real political freedom lay in the power of the part of the citizens to make the most and best of themselves, and held, like Arnold, that increased State action could enhance that power.

During Mundella's Vice-Presidency from 1880–5, such state action was immediately forthcoming. Literally his first act was to end the farce of permissive compulsion by ordering all school boards and school attendance committees to frame bye-laws 'forthwith'. Any such authority not complying with the almost peremptory three-clause Mundella Act was obliged to accept a model set of such bye-laws from the Educational Department. Well might the squires groan and the parsons rumble. Within five months no less than 1,200 sets of bye-laws from various authorities came in for approval, and by the beginning of 1881 the entire population of England, with a few minute exceptions, was obliged to send its children to school till they were ten years old. Nor could any child leave for full-time employment until it had attained a certificate at standard v level or had reached the age of thirteen.

Three weeks before this Act became law, Mundella announced his intention to bring in a new code to enrich the barren mental pasture of the children who were now compelled to attend school. Not only were the changes novel, but the ways in which he made them were even more so. For a consultative committee was set up, which, as the Secretary of the Education Department confessed, was something new. Suggestions were received from all interested parties: teachers, inspectors, and industrialists, and hammered into shape. This code blazed new trails in the upper and lower ends of the elementary school. At the lower end, payment by results was moderated and manual employments and play were recognized. As one inspector said after Mundella had left the department 'beyond question, this code has effected an immense improvement in schools and classes for infants'. At the upper end standards VII made their appearance. These, in some cases, crystallized out as 'higher tops' of the elementary schools, and became known as 'higher grade schools'. These higher grade schools in towns like Nottingham, Sheffield, Manchester, and Bradford developed into a new kind of secondary school with a practical bias.

Such schools received added stimulus from the new list of subjects for which grants could now be earned. Heat, light, sound, chemistry, agriculture, and cookery, showed that such schools were regarded as useful vestibules to adulthood. Moreover, for the first time, inspectors were instructed to moderate their severity. Matthew Arnold had actually to plead for one inspector who was threatened with dismissal for being too severe. The inspectorate was reorganized, and teachers of experience were recruited. The Code Committee was retained to modify such articles of the code as were harsh or misunderstood. All were warned to consider the 'health, age, and mental capacity of the children'.

An extensive chain reaction followed upon the introduction of this new code. In the first place, the new subjects made heavy demands on teachers and exposed the inadequacy of existing methods of teacher training. Within four years no less than eleven central pupil teachers' centres had to be created. Mundella was alive to this, and in spite of the bitter opposition of the mining interests, and the parsimony of the Treasury, established a Normal School of Science at South Kensington which opened its doors in October 1881 under T. H. Huxley: a healthy institution which was to develop into the Imperial College of Science and Technology.

But perhaps the most disturbing reaction was upon the voluntary schools, on whose already strained resources the requirements of the new code pressed very heavily. The Archbishop of Canterbury wrote a personal letter to Mundella in which he said that 'the discipline and efficiency' of the voluntary schools 'must inevitably be prejudiced'. Since this letter had no effect, the voluntary schools raised the cry that the provisions of the new code were 'harsh', and caused 'overpressure'. That there was overpressure on the undertrained teachers cannot be doubted, but the voluntaryists paraded a series of cases where deaths of pupils were mysteriously ascribed to its working. Dr. Crichton Browne was commissioned to make a report, and he wrote, 'the infantile lip, that would curl with contempt at any reference to a witch or a ghost, quivers with anxiety at the name of a government inspector, and the examination day has appropriated to itself much of the foreboding that used to belong to the day of judgement'. The *Lancet* however, put its professional finger on the real cause of the trouble when it said 'the educational system is not overworking children, but demonstrating that they are underfed'. This significant fact was not lost upon Mundella, and he urged all local authorities to follow the example of Rousden, a Devonshire village, and provide cheap meals for all the children. He himself became President of a Central Council for Promoting Penny Dinners, which circulated details of the Rousden experiment.

Having swept all the children into schools and widened their horizons, Mundella was anxious to open up further avenues at the top end of the elementary school. In his own constituency, the School Board had built a large composite building, housing at one end a higher grade school, and at the other a local college endowed by the munificence of Mark Firth, a local steelmaster. Mundella had taken part in the promotion of this enterprise, and pointed to its significance for industry. He realized that the neotechnic age had finally killed the concept of apprenticeship, and he looked to a new network of higher grade schools and local colleges to supply industry with its officers. He stressed the Cobdenite theme that this country was engaged in an industrial war for survival against rivals whose educational systems were more in mesh with the driving needs of the age.

Throughout his parliamentary career, he had called attention to the superiority of German practice—so much so that more than once he was accused of lack of patriotism. H. M. Felkin, formerly his business representative in Chemnitz (and incidentally the first English translator of Herbart), published, on Mundella's advice, a small book called *Technical Education in a Saxon Town* as a case history of what could be done by local effort. To obtain a more complete picture of foreign efforts in the field of technical education, Mundella secured the appointment of a Royal Commisson under his great friend Bernhard Samuelson. Samuelson himelf had spent a vast fortune in trying to utilize his Cleveland iron interests for the making of cheap steel, and thought so much of his task on the commission, that he and his fellow colleagues paid their own expenses on tours which took them over the whole of Europe and the U.S.A. Their conclusions were momentous. Lack of good modern secondary schools, they declared, was the greatest defect of our educational system. To remedy it, they indicated that the proposed new county boards and the existing municipal authorities could, with profit, set up more higher grade schools.

But the ghosts of a century's neglect could not be so easily exorcised or reasoned away. Indeed, the cumulative effect of all the administrative activity of these years was to galvanize the vested interests against the government. Teachers, Tories, and Sectarians combined in a new alliance against the code, the higher grade schools, the bureaucratization, and the secularity of outlook inherent in Mundella's policy. The proprietary grammar schools objected to Mundella's description of them as 'the most meretricious element in the whole of our educational system', while Samuel Dill, high master of Manchester Grammar School, complained bitterly of the large new higher grade school for 1,200 which Mundella opened in Manchester, saying 'there are many signs that our place in the educational system is little recognized, and that our capacity of service to the community is quietly ignored'. Lord Norton, an old Conservative Vice-President of the Council, ventured into print in the *Nineteenth Century* with a long blast against Mundella's 'independent educational experiments' and encouragement of the school boards to borrow money for the construction of higher grade schools far outside Mundella's or any other parliamentary authority. He roundly accused Mundella of having 'strongly avowed German preferences' and of 'essaying a flight into continental bureaucracy'.

Other voices joined the chorus of opposition. Canon Gregory, a Cleon of Convocation, lamented that the compromise of 1870 had now been abandoned, and demanded a share in rate aid for Church of England schools. He was joined by Cardinal Manning, who challenged the very basis of the 1870 Act itself, publicly declaring it was unequal and unjust. Manning's words stirred old fires which Mundella had tried to damp down. Since the politicians had interfered so precipitately with education, Manning was determined to lead the church into politics, and he rallied all Catholics to declare that the 1870 Act was 'unequal, unjust and dangerous to the voluntary schools of the country'. He made one stirring public speech on 25 June 1885 urging the middle class to rise up and say that they did not want board schools for their children. He went even further later in the year by publishing advice to Catholics in all the Catholic periodicals as to how they should vote in the general election. They should put, he urged, two questions to their candidates. The first one was 'will you do your utmost to place voluntary schools on an equal footing with board schools?' The second, 'will you do your utmost to obtain a Royal Commission to review the administration of the Act of 1870?'

Manning's intervention was in great measure responsible for an increase in the Conservative vote. Late in 1885 they responded to the second of his queries by appointing a Royal Commission under Lord Cross. Mundella's original place on this commission was taken up by Lyulph Stanley, who led a vigorous minority group in the Liberal interest. This group endorsed the efforts of the school boards in establishing higher grade schools, urged that they should be further empowered to establish technical schools.

The political advocacy of these technical schools devolved upon the third of the trinity of reformers—Arthur Acland.

Socially, intellectually, and physically, Arthur Acland was a complete contrast to both Forster and Mundella. They were robust empirics, he was a wiry intellectual. Their creed stemmed from the social needs of their own class and calling. His was in part a reaction against his own class and calling. For though he belonged to an ancient west country family with roots deep in the soil, and though he began life as an ordained clergyman of the Church of England (he was Mandell Creighton's curate) he soon developed, under the direct stimulus of Carlyle and Arnold, a characteristically Liberal viewpoint that made him one of the leaders of the new generation of his party. When Forster was wrestling with the Nonconformists, Acland was a junior don at Oxford and the centre of a little group which embraced such spirits as R. L. Nettleship, A. C. Bradley, Michael Sadler, Antony Hope, and Cosmo Lang. When Mundella was promoting his Factory Act, Acland was being drawn into university extension, constituting himself as a link between the Co-operative movement and Oxford. He became the first secretary of the Oxford University Extension movement, and was soon in close contact with many of the leaders of Co-operation throughout the north of England. When Mundella became Vice-President of the Council, Acland made the greatest decision of his life, and renounced holy orders. He saw that a great challenge awaited the new lay clerisy of teachers in large industrial towns, and dedicated himself to accept it. The Co-operative Society thought so highly of his lectures that they re-published them. In collaboration with Arthur Ransome, Acland prepared a history of the English social heritage that ran to fourteen editions, and followed this up by organizing the famous Oxford schools for working men.

In the 1885 election—the one in which Manning had so dramatically intervened—Acland was returned for the industrial constituency of Rotherham by a three to one majority. He was then thirty-seven, and much needed by his party, which, in the following year, was stripped of much of its wealth and talent by the great unionist defection. With Sir Henry Roscoe, he undertook the secretaryship of a new educational pressure group —the National Association for the Promotion of Secondary and Technical Education. Not only did he suggest the formation of this body, but he was also its most assiduous and effective propagandist. Both by experience and inclination, he soon established himself as the Liberal spokesman in matters educational during the six years of Conservative rule from 1886 to 1892.

It was in the battle of the schools that he made his name. One of his most typical speeches was made on 28 April 1888, when he moved a resolution calling on the government to undertake the supervision of secondary education. His proposals read like the chapter headings of later educational history which he was himself to make. The appointment of a Royal Commission on Secondary Education, the creation of a real minister of education, the sanitary inspection of schools, a comprehensive register of teachers to eliminate charlatans, and permissive power to local authorities to levy rates for secondary education: these were some of the main proposals of a speech which was supported by both John Morley and A. J. Mundella.

He went on to greater triumphs two years later when, on 21 February 1890, he opened the Liberal attack on the Conservative programme as laid down in the Queen's speech by demanding free education. It was delivered with such earnestness that several times in the course of speaking he thumped the head of Jesse Collings who was seated in front of him. It was a crucial occasion. Joseph Chamberlain, whose biographer has made so much of his earlier educational enthusiasm, made a trimming speech and in the end voted against Acland. But though the motion was lost by sixty votes, the Government gave way a year later, and elementary education was made free. Lord Salisbury told his supporters that remission of fees in board schools was essential, 'for', said he, 'if our opponents should obtain a majority in a future parliament, they would deal with the question in such a manner that the voluntary schools would be swept away'. The *Economist* lamented the frank opportunism of such a move, and censured the Conservatives for 'yielding' to the temptation to pose as benefactors of the working class.

An even more immediate victory than this was scored, four months later, on 10 June 1890, when he challenged the Government's proposal to allot the proceeds of a tax on liquor— some £700,000—to publicans scheduled to lose their licences. Acland argued that it was highly illogical to use the proceeds of a tax on liquor to raise the price of public houses. How much better it would be he declared, to give this money to the newly formed County Councils for the encouragement of technical education. For six weeks the Government wavered, and the fate of the whisky money hung in the balance. Then, as the session drew to a close, the government gave way. Whisky money went to the County Councils. Acland was jubilant. In his diary he wrote 'it was looked on as a triumph for me of a minor kind'.

The Times frowned on what it called the Government's 'surrender' and commented 'it seems as if Ministers have resigned themselves to following the line of least resistance.'

Acland's friends saw where all this was leading. One of them, Edward Grey, told Acland in October of this year that he would be minister for education within six years. Grey was too cautious a prophet—he was four years out. For in the general election of 1892 Acland was returned with the largest Liberal majority in England and made Vice-President of the Council, and, for the first time in a Gladstonian administration, was immediately put in the Cabinet.

Nor was this the only advantage which Acland had over Forster and Mundella when he assumed office. For both of them had been saddled with the onerous and incongruous task of supervising the importation of cattle as well as being responsible for the education of children. Now, thanks to the creation of a separate department to deal with rinderpest and trichinosis, Acland could devote all his energes to education. And these energies, as opposed to those of Forster and Mundella, were allowed free play. For both in the first and second ministries, Gladstone had blocked the way. His hostility to what he called 'construction' (which he defined as 'taking into the hands of the state the business of the individual man') had prevented the creation of a real ministry of education. His rigid control of the Treasury purse strings had made both Forster and Mundella frame their codes around the principle of payment by results, however much they might privately disagree with it. But now, in 1892, Gladstone was an old man 'chained to the oar' of Home Rule, and prepared to let other matters slide. Acland himself wrote in his diary 'each man manages his own department. We have not had a cabinet for weeks. I do not think we have had more than three for the last three months of the parliamentary session'.

Acland's emancipation, very new for a Vice-President, and very real in his case, enabled him to work in close collaboration with Sidney Webb, who, in the same year as Acland became Vice-President, was elected to the chairmanship of the Technical Education Board of the London County Council. Webb borrowed H. Llewellyn Smith, Acland's former assistant in the work of the National Technical Education Association, to sur-

vey the whole field of London's secondary education as a basis
for constructing an elaborate series of scholarship ladders, large
in extent, elaborate in organisation, and diversified in ramifica-
tion, to carry pupils from the lowest elementary school to the
most distinguished university institutions of the time. Poly-
technics rose from eight to twenty-six. Acland further advised
him to appoint a bevy of highly paid officials: forty-two year old
William Garnett became secretary and Dr. Kimmins chief inspector. South Kensington grants were extended to assist the
teaching of modern history, economics, geography, and other
modern subjects till Sidney Webb could boast 'we can now
lawfully teach anything under the sun except ancient Greek and
Theology'.

Acland himself ranged over the whole field of education, initiating important changes. In the elementary school, he raised
the school-leaving age for full-timers to eleven, and issued a
famous circular—321—which laid down minimal requirements
for any school which was anxious to receive a government grant.
These requirements—lobby space for wet garments, play-
grounds, and a sufficiency of windows for light and air, put yet
another heavy strain on the already exhausted resources of the
voluntary schools. Once more the Church rallied to defend its
schools. The two archbishops appointed a committee, which
once more suggested that the only alternative to extinction was a
share in the rates. In the House of Lords, Acland was compared
to Julian the Apostate, and described as a Bengal tiger, thirsting
for the blood of Christians. But the circular was enforced, and
the schools were improved accordingly.

In the sphere of technical education, Acland's changes were
described by Graham Balfour as 'sweeping'. Acland initiated
a minor revolution at South Kensington, where, under the
regimen of Major-General John Donnelly, payment by results
has been conducted with military efficiency and adherence to
the letter of the law. Payment by results in this department was
abolished, and to break the hold which the army officers had
established on the inspectorate, Acland appointed thirteen distinguished and experienced inspectors, who soon became
known as the 'Twelve Apostles' for the almost messianic manner
in which they discharged their task. One of them later became
the chief education officer for the L.C.C., and another head of

the Irish Technical Instruction Board. For evening schools, Acland himself wrote a syllabus on 'The Rights and Duties of a Citizen'—perhaps the first attempt made to teach what we would now call 'Current Affairs'.

Yet he was no doctrinaire. The Consultative Committee which he established to guide him was given an expert intelligence service when he called Michael Sadler from University extension work to organize an Office of Special Inquiries and Reports. Acland was very much aware of the jungle of administrative departments which had, in the previous generation, assumed responsibilities for secondary education. For, in addition to the Charity Commission, there was South Kensington, the Education Department, the Board of Agriculture, and the overlapping school boards and the technical education boards of the country and borough councils. So he appointed a Royal Commission under James Bryce, who had been an assistant commissioner for the Taunton Commission, and had published the most authoritative interpretation of the American Constitution for his generation. This commission drafted the blueprint of the 1902 Act.

Apart from its party flavour, and the cloud of misunderstanding which accompanied its passage, that Act was virtually the same as the one which Forster had prepared in 1869. The intervening years had matured opinion, and endowed the country with a framework of local governmental councils—county and borough, to whom educational functions could be delegated. It was a collectivist Act: indeed, its political sponsor, Arthur Balfour, later groaned 'I did not realize it would mean more expense and more bureaucracy'. Though at the time it was discussed in the House of Commons, there were 2,600,000 children in board schools as compared with 3,000,000 in voluntary schools, the Act itself marked the decline of the voluntary school: so much so that in the year before the last war, State schools educated 8,151,000 children while the voluntary schools mustered only 1,374,000.

So far, all that I have written could be summed up as the Liberals' response to the two fundamental problems of the age: the retreat from handicrafts and the retreat from organized Christianity. I have said much on the first, and yet have not mentioned that the inadequacy of the Liberal response to this was one of the reasons why William Morris became a socialist. I would just like to say a few words on the second, which was a particular difficulty of that time. We have only to look at the universities to see how very real was this retreat from organized Christianity. Acland's own rejection of an Anglican clergyman's career was matched by Leslie Stephen at Cambridge, and with Stephen, we must think of James Ward (who intended to be a Congregationalist minister and ended by becoming a psychologist), and Alfred Marshall (who abandoned his intention to be a clergyman to become one of the most influential economists of his generation). The newer provincial universities, six of which took shape in the 'seventies and 'eighties, reflected this secular trend. At Birmingham theology was at first expressly excluded from the foundation endowed by Sir Josiah Mason. These civic universities were stimulated and encouraged by the three Liberal ministers I have mentioned: Forster suggested the name 'the Victoria University' for Manchester, and actively assisted the new university college at Leeds, Mundella did much to promote the Firth College at Sheffield; and both he and Acland did similar service for the University of Wales.

Yet none of the three Ministers of whom I have spoken can be accused of being arid secularists, like their continental counterparts Ferry and Falk. For at their elbow was Matthew Arnold, illuminating what might have been a barren positivistic road, and moderating the fierce assaults of the individualist nonconformists on one side and the dead weight of vested apathy on the other. Arnold pointed out that educational reform was the first really practicable step towards democracy. He was right. The educational avenues which were being created across class barriers enriched society and toned down the angry impact of class on class.

10

THE TWENTIETH-CENTURY ADMINISTRATOR

*

SIR JOHN MAUD

*A lecture delivered at King's College on 12 March 1951;
Sir Alexander Carr-Saunders in the chair.*

During the first half of the twentieth century, administrators have multiplied in the field of education; but they have existed longer than that. As a boy at a boarding school, in the middle of the half century, I was affected in various ways for better or worse, by administrative action or inaction—for example, in the food I ate, the distance I had to walk to get a can of hot water to bath in, the fancy dress my parents had to buy for me and the contribution they made (according to an income scale) towards paying for my education. When I became a Fellow of an Oxford College I observed more clearly than when I had been an undergraduate that College life involves at least a modest measure of administrative work. When the office of Dean of the College was added to my responsibilities as a Fellow for teaching and research, I began to learn (what in my present capacity at the Ministry of Education I daily find additional reasons for believing) that it is quite impossible to draw a clear line of demarcation between educational administration and education proper.

The duties of a College Dean at Oxford can reasonably be called administrative. In the 'thirties, one gave undergraduates leave to attend their grandmother's funerals outside Oxford,

227

to entertain other of their female acquaintances in College out-side normal hours, and so on. But these and other disciplinary encounters with undergraduates were only the formal part of one's real business as Dean—which was to know the under-graduates personally and be available in case they wanted any kind of personal help. This business was not administrative. It was a fundamental part of University education, and of course the Dean was not the only one of the Fellows to share in it; but the Dean's administrative duties made it a great deal easier for him than for his colleagues.

Sir Michael Sadler was Master of the College when I became Dean, and it was from him that the College learnt for the first time the great advantages of having a College Secretary. The tradition of the College knew nothing of bureaucracy. A great classical scholar was Estates Bursar and administered the Col-lege estates (in Yorkshire and elsewhere) in the intervals of correcting Latin Proses or lecturing on Cicero. An eminent chemist was Domestic Bursar. During rare intervals of absence from the laboratory, he would appoint—or disappoint—College servants and kitchen staff, consider complaints about the food in Hall or demand payment from defaulting undergraduates. True, there was a scatter of clerks in the background, to keep the College books and catch the Bursar for his signature on a letter if they could. But it was from Sadler, and later from Lord Beveridge when he became Master, that the Fellows of the College began reluctantly to learn that education can be posi-tively set forward if educators will deign to use a shorthand typist: if, in fact, they come to believe that administrators can help them, and if they learn the art of delegation.

The College Secretary is my first example of a pioneer of edu-cational thought and practice from among administrators of the twentieth century. Even so, to the end of my time at Oxford no 'official' was ever admitted to the room when the Master and Fellows met to transact College business, and the minutes were written in manuscript by one of the Fellows—and not circulated but read aloud.

You could not find at Oxford (or, I think, at Cambridge) an example of that wholehogging division of labour between edu-cational and administrative staff which is typical of all other Universities known to me, whether in this country or in the

United States of America. I found it for myself, first at Harvard, and then in a College of the University of London.

When I became Master of Birkbeck, I found not a College Secretary such as I had known at Oxford, but something much more like a Permanent Secretary of a Government Department. Indeed, just before I was appointed, the Governors had decided that the title of 'Secretary' was insufficiently dignified to mark the importance of the chief administrative officer of the College —and had changed it to 'Clerk.'

The fact is that when your educational institution consists of more than a thousand souls, as Birkbeck College does, the necessity of administration, and the wisdom of some division of labour, are more obvious than they are in an Oxford College of less than 200 undergraduates and less than twenty Fellows. Size alone tends to breed administrative hacks, even in a quite independent body of educators. But the pace of breeding tends to become hotter in response to two developments: an increasing proportion of students whose fees are paid from public funds, and an increasing proportion of College finances which come from the same source.

We public administrators await with interest the example which universities and colleges will set us, in the second half of the twentieth century, as they try, despite their increasing responsibilities for spending public money, to limit their administrative progeny and at the same time increase the freedom of their educational staff for teaching and research.

Meanwhile, in Mr. Harrod's biography of J. M. Keynes there is evidence that during the first quarter of the twentieth century at least one educational administrator in one university achieved a standard of excellence which we public administrators may set ourselves as an ideal but without much hope. In 1925 Lord Keynes summed up his father's work as chief administrative officer of Cambridge University for 33 years in these words:

'Perfect order and accuracy without a shadow of pedantry and red tape, the machine existing for the University and not the other way round as it sometimes seems to be now. He really helped to create a framework within which learning and science and education could live and flourish without feeling restraint or a hampering hand, and he combined this with himself possessing learning and science and education at the highest level—which no one now seems to be able to do.'[1]

Few schools or colleges, few youth clubs or institutions for adult education, can escape scot-free from the problem of administration. What help is needed from the administrator if the real work of education is to be done as well as it might be? How can that help be given with least expense of man-hours and least danger of interfering with the educator's essential freedom? What sort of person is most likely to do this educational administration well? Those three questions usually need answering even when the school or other educational institution is private. But my main concern is now with schools and colleges which can be said to come within the 'public' sector, because taxpayers and ratepayers are compelled to pay for them and because some at least of those who attend them are compelled to do so. Those three questions raise certain issues in the public sector which do not arise elsewhere. But first I want to suggest that educational administrators have certain features in common whichever side of the public fence they do their work.

Every member of the species is plainly concerned with educational practice. But I believe he ought also to have at least some interest in educational thought. Unless he has, he will sooner or later fall out of sympathy with his colleagues the practitioners and botch his own administrative handiwork, whereas if he interests himself, at least a little, in the ends as well as the means of education, and if he is honest enough to recognize his palpable limitations in this field, he will be much more likely to respect the real educator and understand what he is about—and that respect and understanding are the conditions of his own administrative helpfulness. This is one reason why I think the subject of this lecture is appropriate to a series dealing with pioneers of English educational thought and practice.

The other common characteristic of all educational hacks is that none of them is his own master. By definition, the administrator exists to minister to the needs of someone else—and when the latter is something of an artist, as all teachers and parents should be, it is particularly important that the colleague who ministers to his needs should be, and be known to be, at his service.

[1] R. F. Harrod. *The Life of John Maynard Keynes* (Macmillan, 1951), p. 11.

But let us now consider educational administrators of this century who are also public servants—and first the local administrator. In 1902 education was first brought into the main stream of local government. County Councils and County Borough Councils became the local educational authority for all kinds of education in their respective areas, except that the councils of the larger Boroughs and Urban District were made responsible for elementary education.

That arrangement was not varied until 1944—and even then not fundamentally. Today only the Counties and County Boroughs are education authorities, but certain Boroughs and Urban Districts and certain newly constituted bodies (called Divisional Executives) possess delegated powers of various kinds.

Each local education authority must appoint a Chief Education Officer (the choice of a suitable person is still left to the local authority, but the Minister of Education must first be given a chance to veto anyone in the short list of candidates that he thinks would not be suitable for that particular post). It is of this local administrator, and of his predecessors in office since 1902, that I wish now to speak.

Lord Lugard, the greatest pioneer among colonial administrators this country can boast, coined a famous phrase to describe the task of the British in administering their colonial dependencies in Africa. That task he thought was two-fold: to act as trustee for the native African and serve his interests; and to act as trustee for the wider, world community of which the Africans were a part and which had legitimate interests (for example, in the development of the food and raw material resources of Africa) that the British administrator must also seek to serve. The reconciliation of these two claims was therefore the heart of the matter. The phrase Lord Lugard coined, and made part of the title of his great book, was 'the Dual Mandate.'

I believe those same words aptly describe the heart of the matter for the local administrator whom we are now considering. His first responsibility is to the local education authority: to the Chairman of the Education Committee, to whom he stands in a relation somewhat analogous to that in which a central government administrator such as myself stands to the Minister of Education; to the Committee itself; to the Council of the

County or County Borough—the parent body concerned; and through these representatives to the whole community of the County or County Borough.

Under this head, his task is given him by the local authority, and it is to help the authority to 'provide a varied and comprehensive service' of primary, secondary and further education, suited to the age, ability and aptitude of each member of the local population that wants education, and thus to make the fullest contribution that the local authority thinks possible to the 'spiritual, moral, mental and physical development of the community.'[1]

This task is given the local administrator: he is not his own master. But perhaps the most important part of his task is to help the local authority to define that task and decide how best it can be tackled. For example, the chief education officer may play a crucial part in formulating the development plan for primary and secondary schools; the scheme of further education; the annual programme for educational buildings of all kinds; and the comprehensive estimates of annual expenditure, which of course reflect in terms of money countless policy decisions on such questions as free transport for children attending schools distant from their homes (which may seriously affect the freedom of parents to choose their children's school) or the payment of fees for children attending independent schools or for young people going on to the university.

On none of these questions has the education officer the last word: on some of them he may not have the first word either—for example, the authority may say at the outset that they want the development plan to be based on the principle of the comprehensive secondary school. And however much influence he may be allowed to exercise, certain crucial decisions will be taken by others. First the Chairman, then the Education Committee, then the Finance Committee, then the Council will take a hand before it is decided how much money the local ratepayers will have to spend on education; in what order of priority the building, say, of the new county schools, the new voluntary school, and the new technical college shall (if the Minister agrees) be placed; how many local boys shall be sent at the public expense, say, to Eton or Winchester, or how much help

[1] Education Act, 1944 (7 and 8 Geo. 6. Ch. 31), Section 7.

from the rate-payer shall be given to voluntary organizations such as the boys clubs or the rural music school.

But the mandate given him by the local authority, on the local community's behalf, is not the only one that the chief education officer must respect. In law, it is. But in practice he is more than a trustee for the interests of his legal master, the local authority. He is also a trustee for the interests of the teacher —for the interests of everyone engaged within the County or County Borough in the actual business of education, whether in schools, training colleges, technical colleges, the youth service or the adult education movement—and, through them, for the interests of the children and others who need education.

You may say that this is only part of his first responsibility to the local authority: that if he is to help them provide education, of course he must also help the actual educators and try to secure for them the conditions on which they can do their best work. True enough. Certainly there need be no inconsistency between the interest of the authority and that of the educator. But in practice there may often seem to be, and perhaps the most important educational service the local administrator can render is to help reconcile the claims of the educator and those of the local authority. That is why I suggest he can properly be said to have a dual mandate.

But the local authority and its chief education officer have to provide the local community with a service which shall be an integral part of a national education policy. And so we come to the central administrator, to my colleagues in the Ministry of Education and myself. Ours is a three-fold mandate. We have to help our Minister to 'promote the education of the people of England and Wales', and the progressive development of institutions devoted to that purpose.[1]

He has received a mandate from the nation, expressed from time to time by parliament in statutes; and this he must himself elaborate, squaring his colleagues in the Government wherever necessary—the Chancellor of the Exchequer, for example, wherever money or building resources are involved; and justifying before parliament everything done in his name—in major debates, on the Estimates for example, in minor debates raised on the Adjournment of the House and in answers to parlia-

[1] Education Act, 1944, Section 1.

mentary questions. But a large part of this commission falls to be discharged by us central administrators, though always under the Minister and usually in his name. I say 'usually' because there is at least one important function which since 1861 a civil servant has had to discharge in his own name, that of appearing before the Public Accounts Committee of the House of Commons for cross-examination on any penny of the millions spent by the Department in the preceding year about which a member of the committee may wish to ask a question. This I think is the one occasion on which one of us professional administrators has to answer members of the legislature himself, instead of merely helping his Minister to do so. But for everything else we do the Minister must accept responsibility to parliament. In everything we do, therefore, without exception, we must remember that our mandate is derived from the law and opinion, of the whole nation.

But the Minister is charged, not only to promote education, but to do that in a particular way: namely, to secure the effective execution of the national education policy by local education authorities. We central administrators have therefore a second mandate. Besides meeting the claims of the nation as a whole, we have to help each local authority to meet the claims of its own area. It is a national interest that the local authorities should be strong and should enjoy the full measure of freedom necessary if they are to serve their local community. We servants of the nation must therefore seek to serve also the local authorities, and so to serve them that they are, and feel themselves to be, as free and self-determining as the claims of the nation allow.

But our mandate is more properly described as triple than as dual. No less and no more than our colleagues, the local administrators, we have a real, though not a legal, responsibility to the whole teaching profession—including in that phrase all educators of every kind—and through them to the people they teach. For if you are an educator, the more free you feel and the more free you are in various respects, the better you will educate. The nation, and every local community, has an abiding interest, therefore, in giving its teachers as much as possible of the freedom they think they want—and all the freedom they really need. So the central administrator has much the same responsibility in respect of the teachers as he has in respect of the local authorities. He has to contrive that the national interest in education is so served that both local authority and teacher have as much as possible of the freedom each wants—and all the freedom that each really needs.

Let us now consider certain fields of education in which twentieth-century administrators, both central and local, have pioneered with more or less success these last fifty years. What means of reconciliation between the claims of nation, local community and actual educator have they found?

It is a national interest that there shall aways be enough good teachers. So it falls to us in the Ministry to look ahead and prophesy how many teachers will be needed, year by year, to teach the varying numbers of children of various ages who will need schooling. Such prophecy must of course take account not only of the results of the birth-rate in past years (and any change in the average length of school life) but also of the number of schools and class-rooms which will have become available. For example, whereas from 1910 till 1947 the school population was stationary or falling, between 1947 and 1957 it will have increased by more than one and a half million. But it is only because we believe that the necessary number of new schools will be built in time that we are planning to increase the number of teachers in proportion to the increased number of children.

It is also a national interest that action should be taken to meet the needs revealed by prophecy. My distinguished predecessor Kay-Shuttleworth was anxious, you may remember, to take direct action to this end and to found a State training college. But since 1839 when that effort was made and failed, we central administrators have never tried again. Instead we have followed the second thoughts of Kay-Shuttleworth and contented ourselves with enabling others to run training colleges. We have continued to do as he did and to subsidize voluntary organizations for this purpose—Anglican, Free Church, Roman Catholic, or undenominational. But we have gone on to apply the same principle not only to universities but, since 1904, to local education authorities. So today the actual training of teachers is in the hands of 133 colleges, 76 provided by local authorities and 57 by voluntary bodies, and of 23 university training departments.

Practically speaking the whole running expenditure is met from public funds; but we make these funds available on a principle deliberately related to the number of students in training, not to the ways in which the money is spent, and we also mark our desire to refrain from interference by leaving the colleges and departments free to pick their own students.

When it was decided, in the closing years of the last war, to launch a national emergency movement and offer a special intensive course of teachers training to men and women from the services, the number involved and the need of speed and the difficulty of improvising the new colleges all suggested that now at last the central administrator should take direct action. The temptation was resisted—after a struggle. The whole of the cost (some £20½ million) was met from central funds, on the Ministry of Education vote, and I was cross-examined about it by the Public Accounts Committee. The search for buildings and staff, the interviewing of some 100,000 candidates and much else was done by us. But the 55 emergency training colleges themselves became the responsibility of the local education authorities, not of the Ministry. The success of the whole scheme and the 35,000 men teachers produced, abundantly justified this novel application of a well-tried principle.

Another recent justification of the principle that central government should be the midwife of educational offspring rather than the parent is seen in the Area Training Organizations which now cover the whole field of teacher training in England and Wales. The Board of Education, before the end of the war, persuaded Sir Arnold McNair and a number of other distinguished educationists to form a committee and report on the training of teachers. Out of their report, in 1944, came a suggestion that universities should become centres from which the whole work of training or refreshing teachers in the surrounding area could be fostered. The Minister of Education blessed this idea and wisely agreed that each university concerned should be free to work out its own scheme, in consultation with all other interested parties. With varying speed and other characteristic peculiarities the universities (ancient as well as modern) have now responded to this invitation. Almost every training college in the country is now linked with its neighbours round some University School or Institute. Every student is now recommended for qualified status as a teacher by the appropriate university-centred area organization. And in time every teacher may come to find himself (as teachers in some areas already do), a member of a regional community of learning which takes its quality and draws some inspiration from the university in its midst.

The National Advisory Council on the Training and Supply of Teachers completes the post-war pattern of chosen instruments whereby the central administrator seeks to avoid both the appearance and the character of a dictator, and to bring representative teachers, college principals, professors and local administrators together in the service of the national interest. This council is free to give authoritative advice on every question (except salaries) affecting the qualifications, recruitment, training and distribution of teachers. A tradition has already begun to be established which makes it likely that, within the council's field of competence, a Minister of Education would hesitate before acting in ignorance of its views or contrary to its advice. Already, in fact, it is proving to be an organ of democratic self-determination which the teaching profession in this country has never had before.

Pioneering seems here to have brought some relaxation of control and direction from the centre since the early years of the century, when the syllabus of every training college was prescribed by the old Board and the final examination of all students, except those examined by a university, was conducted by His Majesty's Inspectors (an arrangement which survived till 1926).

Another peculiarly British, and more ingenious, result of pioneering is the Burnham Committee. Lord Burnham was persuaded by Mr. H. A. L. Fisher in 1919 to become the independent chairman of three committees, consisting for the rest of representatives, in equal numbers, of teachers and local authorities, to deal with salaries in elementary, secondary and technical schools respectively. By the time the 1944 Act was passed this method of settling the salaries of teachers on a national scale by collective bargaining had proved such a satisfactory device that it was given statutory recognition. Today there are two committees, one for primary and secondary schools and one for technical colleges, and they have recently, under their new chairman Sir Malcolm Trustram Eve, presented agreed recommendations which the Minister, after squaring the Chancellor of the Exchequer, has accepted and will soon make mandatory upon all local education authorities.

The new scales may not give unqualified satisfaction to teachers. But from 1 April 1951, a man (who more likely than not will have had all the expenses of his training paid from public funds) will receive at least £375 a year from the outset, and (if the local authority chooses) may be earning some £700 when he is teaching sixth-form science and some £1,000 when he is headmaster of a fair-sized school. And though these sums may be less than his real merit deserves, they compare favourably with what he could have expected before the Burnham Committees existed; for then there were no national scales and salaries were settled by local arrangement. Fifty years ago indeed more than half of the certificated men teachers were paid less than £100 a year, and more than half the headmasters less than £150.

Whether the teacher would fare better if he negotiated on salary questions direct with His Majesty's Government it is not for me to guess (though I know what my guess would be). What I can say is that it is wholly to the advantage of the indolent central administrator, and of his relations with the teaching profession, that he can sit back and keep his hands off teachers' salaries until the Burnham Committees have agreed. When they have agreed, the Minister receives from them an incomparably stronger weapon for squaring the Treasury circle than his least indolent official could forge for him, and by simply approving the committees' recommendations he secures for the whole education service all the advantages of national salary scales.

Pensions, on the other hand, are clearly apt for direct central administration. It took eighteen years of this century, however, before the pioneers could persuade the Government that this was so. Again it was Mr. Fisher who made the crucial change and, this time by legislation, established the principle of a national scheme for all teachers in schools aided by the central government.

I have given you some examples of the part the central government has found means of taking, in the course of these last fifty years, in the work of securing enough good teachers for the country as a whole. Pay, pensions, and the training of teachers are subjects in which the administrator has learnt to take constructive action and at the same time to encourage a wide dispersion of decision. But in the appointment of individual teachers, headmasters and headmistresses, we central administrators have declined to take any part at all. Instead we have left responsibility in the hands of the local authorities; they, in turn, have found it wise to disperse decision, within wide discretionary limits, to the governors and managers of individual schools and colleges; and these last, to let headmasters and headmistresses virtually pick their own staff.

We have found it possible to keep our hands off individual appointments but at the same time to intervene at certain points where the national interest has seemed in need of safeguarding. For example, since the war there have not been enough women teachers for the infant and junior schools, and in certain areas the shortage has been far more serious than elsewhere. There could be no question of directing teachers to the places where they were most needed. But we have sought to help the local authorities in such areas by prescribing a maximum number of women teachers for each area: that is to say, by preventing a local authority (like London) from appointing staff who are more urgently needed in, say, Birmingham.

More generally, it used to be normal practice to prescribe for each local authority a total number of teachers which could not be exceeded. This was an economy measure which has been abandoned since the war. But the principle could readily be adapted to serve a quite different purpose. If the Minister thought an authority was failing to appoint enough teachers, he might well prescribe a minimum establishment for that authority.

But perhaps the most essential freedom of the teacher is to decide for himself what to teach and how to teach it. So far as my knowledge goes no country in the world has teachers in its publicly supported schools with as much freedom of this kind as our British teachers have. That, you may feel, does not say much for other countries, and I agree. But I think it says something for the twentieth century administrator that we are considering.

Certainly it says something for Parliament. Until the 1944 Act was passed, *no* subject of the curriculum of any school (unless physical training can be called a subject) was prescribed by law. In 1944 Parliament prescribed one subject—religious instruction, and what can perhaps be described as two educational 'methods'; first, that 'the school-day in every county school and in every voluntary school shall begin with collective worship on the part of all pupils in attendance at the school' (subject, of course, to the right of parents to have their children excused); and secondly that religious instruction in county schools should be in accordance with an 'agreed syllabus' (prepared and adopted by a prescribed and elaborate procedure) and should 'not include any catechism or formulary' distinctive of a particular religious denomination.[1]

In these provisions parliament was not 'pioneering': it was giving the sanction of law to what had come to be common practice in the schools. But what is significant is that these provisions were the only exceptions to the traditional rule. The teachers were still trusted, not commanded, by parliament to teach reading, writing and arithmetic, not to mention citizenship, international understanding, modern languages or any of the other subjects which my Minister is constantly pressed by well-intentioned critics to tell teachers to teach.

Ministers and administrators have been no keener than parliament to teach the teachers their business. Not even on corporal punishment has any Minister yet been beguiled by tempting parliamentary questioners to give a ruling. Sir Philip Morris, in the opening lecture of this series, referred to the significant title of the document in which the old Board of Education ventured to express opinions about educational method: 'the handbook of *suggestions* to teachers.' But in fact the present Ministry has so far proved itself less bold than the old Board in this matter. Hitherto it has issued no further edition of that handbook, but has been content to publish undogmatic pamphlets on particular aspects of teachers' business—on art education, for example. For the rest, it has relied on His Majesty's Inspectors to stimulate and inspire teachers, by formal and informal visits to the schools and by occasional refresher courses—which far more teachers try to attend than space will allow.

[1] Education Act, 1944. Sections 25 to 30.

Freedom is what the teacher needs more than anything, and after freedom the physical materials of his art. Among these, the building in which he teaches is perhaps the most important. Since 1900, much pioneering had been done to secure enough good buildings for education, both by local and by central administrators. I can touch on only a few aspects of that work.

One permanent truth which we have still not taken sufficiently to heart was stated in 1874 by Mr. Robson, the consultant architect to the Committee of Council for Education, 'The plan of a building', he said, 'depends so much upon the method of tuition that an acquaintance with the latter is of the first necessity to the school architect'. He might have added 'and to the administrator who deals with buildings'. Experience has shown that while the *quantity* of educational building at any period is largely determined by events beyond the control of the education service, its *quality* depends chiefly on collaboration between educator, architect and administrator.

Wise local administrators act constantly on this principle. For example, they call together a group of headmasters and headmistresses to discuss the functional aspects of a new school before the architect first puts pen to paper. And the colleague with whom they take as much pains to live on good terms as they take with the treasurer is the chief architect.

As one example of action taken on this principle at the centre, in 1949 we created an 'Architects and Building' Branch in the Ministry, combining for the first time architects and non-technical staff in one unit and recognizing that the contribution we lay administrators ask from our architect colleagues is more than mere advice. Further, though some local authorities have made important advances in the technique of post-war building, their inevitable pre-occupation with current work has made it clear that the central government must accept responsibility for continuous and comprehensive research. In 1949 we therefore created inside the Ministry a small 'development group' to study the related problems of design, cost and technique; and through this device we have brought together, in habitual collaboration round one table, the educator (in the person of His Majesty's Inspector), the architect and quantity surveyor, and the ordinary administrator. We have also found a pioneering local education authority with sufficient boldness to let us act as their architect for the actual construction of a new school. So for the first time in history the Ministry will be faced one of these days with the spectacle of its own handiwork.

Within a year or two of its creation, the old Board issued its first essay in this field of educational building. It was not a very original work and its title was significant: 'Rules to be observed in the Planning and Fitting Up of Public Elementary Schools'. But in 1904 it appointed its first permanent architect, Mr. Felix Clay, and the new era began.

It is sometimes alleged nowadays that His Majesty's Inspectors are distracted from their real work, of helping teachers, by extraneous duties of various administrative kinds. At least they are less distracted now than during the early years of the century when the Board, anxious to review the school accommodation then recognized for grant, set the Inspectors to measure the class-rooms in 20,000 schools (either on the spot or from drawings) and report on the defects they found.

This technique was supplemented by another, that of withholding or threatening to withhold grant, and the progress achieved five years before the outbreak of the 1914 war gave the Board substantial and evident satisfaction. They reported: 'It is not too much to say that, in the areas of the great majority of the local education authorities, five years' steady and consistent administration will put the elementary school buildings into a condition in which they will not, at all events appreciably, prejudice the health of the scholars or handicap the efforts of the teacher.' Today we are perhaps less complacent, though we may be no less inclined to optimistic prophecy. But there are more fundamental changes, and I will mention two of them.

First, the Ministry now feels that it shares with the local authorities a positive responsibility to see that new schools and technical colleges are built, and the local authorities expect and indeed insist that we do our part. Before 1947 this was not so. And, secondly, each year now the Minister has to secure a cut off the joint of national building resources (in terms of manpower and materials as well as money), and see that each of the local authorities gets a fair bite. To decide what is fair he has first of course, to decide which are the most pressing national needs that must be met and the relative pressure of those needs upon the various localities. In practice, therefore, practically no building has been allowed since the war except to provide for the extra million and a half children from the 'bulging birthrate', the shifts of population to new housing estates and the claims of technical education; and the annual building programmes of each local authority have depended on the local incidence of those claims and the actual readiness of the authority to build in response to them.

This new integration of central and local authorities in educational building has meant that the local authorities have been less their own master than ever before. To take one example, the North Riding of Yorkshire County Council have not been able to continue the re-organization of their all-age schools as they would like to have done.

But in practice almost all local authorities have agreed with the Minister's decisions about national priorities, and the Minister has agreed with the proposals of almost all local authorities for applying those priorities to their own areas. Further, the need for central allocation of resources in a period of acute shortage has been so obvious that the new arrangements have been the easier to accept without resentment. In fact, so far as my experience goes, the Ministry's new Regional Priority Officers have come to be regarded, both by local authorities and by the individual schools who have had to apply to them for building licences, as indispensable allies in the struggle for justice against non-educational claimants and not as commissars of a central despotism.

The need for speed, too, has led both central and local administrators to dispense with all but the vestiges of red tape. For many buildings that cost less than £5,000 a local authority now needs no formal approval from the Ministry, and for some of the largest schemes only one formal application need be made once they have been included in an annual programme. The new streamlining works well only for two reasons, first because the Ministry is learning to explain its doctrine in terms of general principle rather than by dictation of details (for example, in the recent *Building Bulletins*), and secondly because both local and central administrators are developing a habit of early, informal consultation. Without these changes in procedure it would be inconceivable that in the five years ending in 1950, despite the competition of housing and industrial development for cruelly limited building capacity, £191 million worth of educational building should be approved. But that has happened, and it represents 1,600 new primary and secondary schools—double the number approved in any previous five-year period—as well as some £16 million worth of building for technical and other kinds of further education.

In the field of finance, pioneering has led to very similar results. In the financial year, 1951-2, we estimate that we shall pay the local authorities £150 million, as what we call main grant, towards £262 million of their total expenditure. In addition we expect to pay them, at special rates of grant, another £28 million which will almost completely cover what they expect to spend on school meals and certain other items. So £178 million of the total £205 million that will have to be justified before parliament as Ministry of Education expenditure will in fact be spent by the local authorities, along with the £14 million that they expect to raise from their own ratepayers. Compared with these figures the net amount of taxpayer's money that we expect to spend ourselves seems almost trivial: less than £30 million—though I should not describe even that sum as chicken-feed, nor the people who will get it (among others, a substantial proportion of the university population of the country and almost everyone in training for the teaching profession) as chicken.

Since the Local Government Act of 1948 was passed, we have paid local authorities their main grant according to an ingenious formula which takes account both of the burden of educational work which an Authority has to shoulder and of its financial ability to carry that burden. The principle implicit in this formula goes back a long way. It was applied in a crude way to some grants made to the old School Boards before they were abolished in 1902. But it was the Kempe Committee on Local Taxation which first produced the modern formula when it reported in 1914, and the formula was first used by the Board of Education in 1917 when Mr. Fisher was President.

It is a fairly complicated one but its effect is quite simple. The less wealthy parts of the country are enabled by the country as a whole to carry out the national policy for education in the ways they think best fitted to meet their local needs. In other words, taxpayers in Bournemouth and other more prosperous parts of the country come to the help of ratepayers in Merthyr Tydfil without depriving the citizens of Merthyr Tydfil of the duty to decide how best their children and adults may be educated.

As with building, so with finance. The close integration of central and local authorities implicit in the present financial arrangements means that there is no part of local educational policy about which we central administrators cannot express the Minister's opinion to some effect. For example, in a famous circular which we issued shortly after the pound sterling was devalued in 1949, we told the local authorities the ways in which the Minister thought that they should not economize and certain other ways in which he thought they should. A financial sanction was well-known to be implicit in everything that this circular said. If, for instance, a local authority declined to make any economy in expenditure on 'distinctive school dress', the Minister could if he liked decline to recognize for grant purposes the relevant part of the authority's expenditure. So the authority would either have to stop spending that money or pay for it wholly out of the rates.

But again in practice this sanction is not used, or even threatened, except on the rarest occasions. In the huge majority of cases, the local authority accepts as reasonable what the Minister suggests to be in the national interest. Freedom, it has been said, is the product of human fellowship and the laws of friendship are its condition. I believe it to be true that in recent years there has been a growing sense of community between central and local administrators, and a growing measure of fellowship and even friendship between the people concerned. And I believe that in consequence the new arrangements for paying main grant are in practice helping to increase rather than decrease the powers and sense of responsibility of most local authorities. But it is also perfectly true that these arrangements could lead to a precisely opposite result.

Whether we consider the relation between central and local administrator, or the relation between the administrator of either kind and the actual educator; and whether we consider the efforts of all concerned to secure enough good teachers, or enough good buildings, or enough money for education—two principles emerge as characteristic of the discoveries made by the pioneers of the last fifty years: the principle of *devolution*, of dispersion of decision and delegation of authority; and the principle of *consultation*. A parallel may perhaps here be observed with the evolution of the British Commonwealth and Empire. Educational 'Dominion Status' has not yet been given to any local authority—but it has been given by the Ministry to institutions, such as the Royal College of Art; and something like it has been given by the wisest local authorities to their individual schools and colleges.

Both these principles are expensive in terms of time. A large outstanding question for the future pioneer is how to economize in the expenditure of time (especially by the educators themselves) without abandoning the habits of devolution and consultation. Sir Philip Morris referred in the first lecture of this series to the astonishing amount of voluntary help which in this country is given traditionally to education. In the next fifty years, will enough men and women be forthcoming to give the unpaid service which we now receive from people like Sir Philip Morris himself, Sir Samuel Gurney Dixon or Sir Alexander Carr Saunders, as chairman of such bodies as the Secondary School Examinations Council, the Central Advisory Council for England or the Committee which recently reported on Education for Commerce? Neither devolution nor consultation, on the scale on which we now use them, can work well unless innumerable men and women are prepared to give up innumerable hours of their time to service on local authorities and on bodies of governors or managers, to the work of associations both of local authorities and of teachers, and of special bodies like the Burnham Committee.

It is an essential part of the administrator's art to contrive that these volunteers can faithfully discharge their duty with the smallest possible expenditure of time, whether on reading papers or travel or actual meetings. No doubt his success or failure here largely depends on the readiness of the volunteers to co-operate —for example, by wide delegation of the Council's functions to the Education Committee and by the willingness of committee members to abstain from the corporate administration of detail. But the skill with which the administrator is allowed to practise this art of time-saving will largely determine whether or not enough good volunteers become available to justify the continued development of our British tradition of educational administration.

There is an even greater contribution that the administrator must make if our democratic tradition is to be developed and enriched, and that is to remain uncorrupted by increasing power. As the sums spent on education from rates and taxes grow and an increasing proportion of it becomes dependent on public funds, the administrator comes under an ever stronger temptation to think he is more important than he is. A writer in the *Cambridge Review* has recently suggested that every civil servant should say to himself in his morning bath; 'I am an evil. Am I a really necessary one?' As an educational administrator I do not personally think I am an evil. Certainly I think my colleagues, both central and local, are necessary (though I think it a proud boast that in the last year or two, while our expenditure and responsibilities have continued to increase, we have reduced our numbers in the Ministry by more than ten per cent). But the more necessary we think ourselves, the more important it becomes to remind ourselves that we are not our own masters. Saint John the Baptist, who constantly assured his hearers that he was of less importance than Another in their midst, should be our patron saint; and though perhaps we should not hope to rival his outspoken style (when he addressed the Sadducees and Pharisees as a generation of vipers) we should make no secret of the fact that the hope of education is in the actual educator and not in us. Our mission is to diminish in stature that education may increase.

INDEX